03,
2014

sham,
McKelvey,
son

piling this book. However,
the publishers or compilers
ormation presented.

a by MacGuru Ltd
acguru.org.uk

nted in Italy by
E.G.O Spa. Lavis

gue record for this book is available
from the British Library

ISBN 978 1 78125 273 4

THE ECONOMIST IN ASSOCIATION WITH
PROFILE BOOKS LTD

Published by Profile Books Ltd,
3A Exmouth House, Pine Street, London EC1R 0JH

This edition published by Profile Books in association with
The Economist, 2014

Material researched and compiled by
Andrea Burgess, Mark Doyle, Ian Emery, James Fra
Andrew Gilbert, Conrad Heine, Carol Howard, Davi
Jane Shaw, Roxana Willis, Christopher W

Typeset in Offic
info@

Pr

A CIP catalo

Contents

Notes

This 2015 edition of *The Economist Pocket World in Figures*
includes new rankings on such diverse topics as teenage
births, skyscrapers, migrants, entrepreneurs, theme parks,
cannabis, and the environment. The world rankings consider
183 countries, all those with a population of at least 1m or a
GDP of at least $3bn; they are listed on pages 250–54. The
country profiles cover 67 major countries. Also included are
profiles of the euro area and the world. The extent and quality
of the statistics available varies from country to country. Every
care has been taken to specify the broad definitions on which
the data are based and to indicate cases where data quality or
technical difficulties are such that interpretation of the
figures is likely to be seriously affected. Nevertheless, figures
from individual countries may differ from standard
international statistical definitions. The term "country" can
also refer to territories or economic entities.

Some country definitions
Macedonia is officially known as the Former Yugoslav Republic
of Macedonia. Data for Cyprus normally refer to Greek Cyprus
only. Data for China do not include Hong Kong or Macau. Data
for Sudan are largely for the country before it became two
countries, Sudan and South Sudan, in July 2011. For countries
such as Morocco they exclude disputed areas. Congo-Kinshasa
refers to the Democratic Republic of Congo, formerly known as
Zaire. Congo-Brazzaville refers to the other Congo. The
Netherlands Antilles was dissolved in 2011 but continues to
appear in some data; Curaçao qualifies for inclusion but there
are few data as yet. Data for the EU refer to the 27 members as
at January 1 2007, unless otherwise noted. (Croatia joined
the EU on July 1 2013.) Euro area data normally refer to the
17 members that had adopted the euro as at December 31
2013: Austria, Belgium, Cyprus, Estonia, France, Finland,
Germany, Greece, Ireland, Italy, Luxembourg, Malta,
Netherlands, Portugal, Slovakia, Slovenia and Spain. (Latvia
joined the euro area on January 1 2014.) For more
information about the EU and the euro area see the glossary
on pages 248–9.

Statistical basis
The all-important factor in a book of this kind is to be able to
make reliable comparisons between countries. Although this
is never quite possible for the reasons stated above, the best
route, which this book takes, is to compare data for the same

year or period and to use actual, not estimated, figures wherever possible. In some cases, only OECD members are considered. Where a country's data is excessively out of date, it is excluded. The research for this edition of *The Economist Pocket World in Figures* was carried out in 2014 using the latest available sources that present data on an internationally comparable basis.

Data in the country profiles, unless otherwise indicated, refer to the year ending December 31 2012. Life expectancy, death and fertility rates are based on 2010–15 projected averages; human development indices for 2012, crude birth rates for 2011, energy and religion data for 2010; marriage and divorce, employment, health and education, consumer goods and services data refer to the latest year for which figures are available; internet hosts are as at January 2014.

Other definitions

Data shown in country profiles may not always be consistent with those shown in the world rankings because the definitions or years covered can differ.

Statistics for principal exports and principal imports are normally based on customs statistics. These are generally compiled on different definitions to the visible exports and imports figures shown in the balance of payments section.

Definitions of the statistics shown are given on the relevant page or in the glossary on pages 248–9. Figures may not add exactly to totals, or percentages to 100, because of rounding or, in the case of GDP, statistical adjustment. Sums of money have generally been converted to US dollars at the official exchange rate ruling at the time to which the figures refer.

Energy consumption data are not always reliable, particularly for the major oil producing countries; consumption per person data may therefore be higher than in reality. Energy exports can exceed production and imports can exceed consumption if transit operations distort trade data or oil is imported for refining and re-exported.

Abbreviations

bn	billion (one thousand million)	ha	hectare
EU	European Union	m	million
kg	kilogram	PPP	Purchasing power parity
km	kilometre	TOE	tonnes of oil equivalent
GDP	Gross domestic product	trn	trillion (one thousand billion)
GNI	Gross national income	...	not available

World rankings

Countries: natural facts

Countries: *the largest[a]*
'000 sq km

1	Russia	17,098		31	Tanzania	947
2	Canada	9,985		32	Nigeria	924
3	United States	9,629		33	Venezuela	912
4	China	9,597		34	Namibia	824
5	Brazil	8,515		35	Mozambique	802
6	Australia	7,692		36	Pakistan	796
7	India	3,287		37	Turkey	784
8	Argentina	2,780		38	Chile	756
9	Kazakhstan	2,725		39	Zambia	753
10	Algeria	2,382		40	Myanmar	677
11	Congo-Kinshasa	2,345		41	Afghanistan	653
12	Saudi Arabia	2,207		42	South Sudan	644
13	Greenland	2,166		43	Somalia	638
14	Mexico	1,964		44	Central African Rep.	623
15	Indonesia	1,911		45	Ukraine	604
16	Sudan	1,879		46	Kenya	592
17	Libya	1,760		47	Madagascar	587
18	Iran	1,629		48	Botswana	582
19	Mongolia	1,564		49	France	552
20	Peru	1,285		50	Yemen	528
21	Chad	1,284		51	Thailand	513
22	Niger	1,267		52	Spain	506
23	Angola	1,247		53	Turkmenistan	488
24	Mali	1,240		54	Cameroon	476
25	South Africa	1,221		55	Papua New Guinea	463
26	Colombia	1,142		56	Sweden	450
27	Ethiopia	1,104		57	Morocco	447
28	Bolivia	1,099			Uzbekistan	447
29	Mauritania	1,031		59	Iraq	435
30	Egypt	1,002		60	Paraguay	407

Mountains: *the highest[b]*

	Name	Location	Height (m)
1	Everest	China-Nepal	8,848
2	K2 (Godwin Austen)	China-Jammu and Kashmir	8,611
3	Kangchenjunga	India-Nepal	8,586
4	Lhotse	China-Nepal	8,516
5	Makalu	China-Nepal	8,463
6	Cho Oyu	China-Nepal	8,201
7	Dhaulagiri	Nepal	8,167
8	Manaslu	Nepal	8,163
9	Nanga Parbat	Jammu and Kashmir	8,126
10	Annapurna I	Nepal	8,091
11	Gasherbrum I	China-Jammu and Kashmir	8,068
12	Broad Peak	China-Jammu and Kashmir	8,047
13	Gasherbrum II	China-Jammu and Kashmir	8,035
14	Xixabangma Feng	China	8,012

a Includes freshwater.
b Includes separate peaks which are part of the same massif.

Rivers: *the longest*

	Name	Location	Length (km)
1	Nile	Africa	6,695
2	Amazon	South America	6,516
3	Yangtze	Asia	6,380
4	Mississippi-Missouri system	North America	5,959
5	Ob'-Irtysh	Asia	5,568
6	Yenisey-Angara-Selanga	Asia	5,550
7	Huang He (Yellow)	Asia	5,464
8	Congo	Africa	4,667
9	Río de la Plata-Paraná	South America	4,500
10	Irtysh	Asia	4,440

Deserts: *the largest non-polar*

	Name	Location	Area ('000 sq km)
1	Sahara	Northern Africa	8,600
2	Arabian	South-western Asia	2,300
3	Gobi	Mongolia/China	1,300
4	Patagonian	Argentina	673
5	Great Victoria	Western and Southern Australia	647
6	Syrian	Middle East	520
7	Great Basin	South-western United States	492
8	Great Sandy	Western Australia	390

Lakes: *the largest*

	Name	Location	Area ('000 sq km)
1	Caspian Sea	Central Asia	371
2	Superior	Canada/United States	82
3	Victoria	East Africa	69
4	Huron	Canada/United States	60
5	Michigan	United States	58
6	Tanganyika	East Africa	33
7	Baikal	Russia	31
	Great Bear	Canada	31

Islands: *the largest*

	Name	Location	Area ('000 sq km)
1	Greenland	North Atlantic Ocean	2,176
2	New Guinea	South-west Pacific Ocean	809
3	Borneo	Western Pacific Ocean	746
4	Madagascar	Indian Ocean	587
5	Baffin	North Atlantic Ocean	507
6	Sumatra	North-east Indian Ocean	474
7	Honshu	Sea of Japan-Pacific Ocean	227
8	Great Britain	Off coast of north-west Europe	218

Notes: Estimates of the lengths of rivers vary widely depending on eg, the path to take through a delta. The definition of a desert is normally a mean annual precipitation value equal to 250ml or less. Australia is defined as a continent rather than an island.

Population: size and growth

Largest populations
Million, 2012

1	China	1,353.6	37	Canada	34.7
2	India	1,258.4	38	Iraq	33.7
3	United States	315.8	39	Afghanistan	33.4
4	Indonesia	244.8	40	Morocco	32.6
5	Brazil	198.4	41	Nepal	31.0
6	Pakistan	180.0	42	Venezuela	29.9
7	Nigeria	166.6	43	Peru	29.7
8	Bangladesh	152.4	44	Malaysia	29.3
9	Russia	142.7	45	Saudi Arabia	28.7
10	Japan	126.4	46	Uzbekistan	28.1
11	Mexico	116.1	47	Yemen	25.6
12	Philippines	96.5	48	Ghana	25.5
13	Vietnam	89.7	49	North Korea	24.6
14	Ethiopia	86.5	50	Mozambique	24.5
15	Egypt	84.0	51	Taiwan	23.2
16	Germany	82.0	52	Australia	22.9
17	Iran	75.6	53	Madagascar	21.9
18	Turkey	74.5	54	Romania	21.4
19	Thailand	69.9	55	Sri Lanka	21.2
20	Congo-Kinshasa	69.6	56	Syria	21.1
21	France	63.5	57	Côte d'Ivoire	20.6
22	United Kingdom	62.8	58	Cameroon	20.5
23	Italy	61.0	59	Angola	20.2
24	South Africa	50.7	60	Burkina Faso	17.5
25	Myanmar	48.7	61	Chile	17.4
26	South Korea	48.6	62	Netherlands	16.7
27	Tanzania	47.7	63	Niger	16.6
28	Colombia	47.6	64	Kazakhstan	16.4
29	Spain	46.8	65	Mali	16.3
30	Ukraine	44.9	66	Malawi	15.9
31	Kenya	42.7	67	Guatemala	15.1
32	Argentina	41.1	68	Ecuador	14.9
33	Poland	38.3	69	Cambodia	14.5
34	Algeria	36.5	70	Zambia	13.9
35	Uganda	35.6	71	Senegal	13.1
36	Sudan	35.0	72	Zimbabwe	13.0

Largest populations
Million, 2025

1	China	1,449.0	11	Ethiopia	124.5
2	India	1,418.7	12	Japan	123.3
3	United States	350.6	13	Philippines	119.2
4	Indonesia	282.0	14	Vietnam	99.8
5	Nigeria	239.9	15	Egypt	97.0
6	Pakistan	218.1	16	Congo-Kinshasa	92.1
7	Brazil	217.5	17	Iran	88.1
8	Bangladesh	177.9	18	Turkey	87.7
9	Mexico	138.2	19	Germany	80.9
10	Russia	137.0	20	Tanzania	69.3

Note: Populations include migrant workers.

Fastest growing populations
Average annual % change, 2010–15

1	Oman	7.9	26	Benin	2.7
2	Qatar	5.9		Congo-Kinshasa	2.7
3	South Sudan	4.0		Kenya	2.7
4	Niger	3.9		Rwanda	2.7
5	Kuwait	3.6	30	Congo-Brazzaville	2.6
6	Jordan	3.5		Ethiopia	2.6
7	Uganda	3.3		Liberia	2.6
8	Burundi	3.2		Togo	2.6
	Eritrea	3.2	34	Cameroon	2.5
	Gambia, The	3.2		French Guiana	2.5
	Zambia	3.2		Guatemala	2.5
12	Angola	3.1		Guinea	2.5
13	Chad	3.0		Mauritania	2.5
	Lebanon	3.0		Mozambique	2.5
	Mali	3.0		United Arab Emirates	2.5
	Tanzania	3.0		West Bank & Gaza	2.5
17	Iraq	2.9	42	Afghanistan	2.4
	Malawi	2.9		Gabon	2.4
	Senegal	2.9		Guinea-Bissau	2.4
	Somalia	2.9		Tajikistan	2.4
21	Burkina Faso	2.8	46	Côte d'Ivoire	2.3
	Equatorial Guinea	2.8		Yemen	2.3
	Madagascar	2.8	48	Ghana	2.1
	Nigeria	2.8		Papua New Guinea	2.1
	Zimbabwe	2.8			

Slowest growing populations
Average annual % change, 2010–15

1	Bulgaria	-0.8		Montenegro	0.1
	Moldova	-0.8		Slovakia	0.1
3	Latvia	-0.6		Virgin Islands (US)	0.1
	Ukraine	-0.6	26	Armenia	0.2
5	Belarus	-0.5		Bermuda	0.2
	Lithuania	-0.5		Italy	0.2
	Serbia	-0.5		Martinique	0.2
8	Croatia	-0.4		Slovenia	0.2
	Georgia	-0.4	31	Albania	0.3
10	Estonia	-0.3		Finland	0.3
	Romania	-0.3		Malta	0.3
12	Hungary	-0.2		Netherlands	0.3
	Puerto Rico	-0.2		Thailand	0.3
	Russia	-0.2		Trinidad & Tobago	0.3
15	Bosnia & Herz.	-0.1		Uruguay	0.3
	Cuba	-0.1	38	Austria	0.4
	Germany	-0.1		Belgium	0.4
	Japan	-0.1		Czech Republic	0.4
19	Greece	0.0		Denmark	0.4
	Poland	0.0		Mauritius	0.4
	Portugal	0.0		Spain	0.4
22	Macedonia	0.1			

Population: matters of breeding and sex

Crude birth rates

Births per 1,000 population, 2010–15

Highest			Lowest		
1	Niger	49.8	1	Japan	8.4
2	Mali	47.3	2	Germany	8.5
3	Chad	46.1	3	Portugal	8.8
4	Burundi	44.8	4	Bosnia & Herz.	8.9
5	Angola	44.3	5	Taiwan	9.0
6	Somalia	43.9	6	Italy	9.2
7	Uganda	43.4		Malta	9.2
8	Zambia	43.0	8	Hong Kong	9.4
9	Congo-Kinshasa	42.9	9	Austria	9.5
	Gambia, The	42.9		Croatia	9.5
11	Nigeria	41.5	11	Bulgaria	9.6
12	Burkina Faso	41.1		Channel Islands	9.6
13	Malawi	39.9		Cuba	9.6
14	Tanzania	39.3		South Korea	9.6
15	Mozambique	39.1	15	Greece	9.8
16	Senegal	38.1		Serbia	9.8
17	Congo-Brazzaville	37.9	17	Hungary	9.9
18	Guinea-Bissau	37.7		Singapore	9.9
19	Cameroon	37.5	19	Slovenia	10.0
20	Guinea	37.1	20	Macau	10.1
21	Eritrea	37.0	21	Romania	10.3
22	Côte d'Ivoire	36.9		Switzerland	10.3
	Sierra Leone	36.9	23	Thailand	10.4

Teenage births

Births per 1,000 women aged 15–19, 2005–10

Highest			Lowest		
1	Niger	209.6	1	North Korea	0.6
2	Angola	192.3	2	South Korea	2.1
3	Chad	181.9	3	Hong Kong	3.1
4	Mali	180.9		Libya	3.1
5	Mozambique	162.5	5	Macau	3.2
6	Malawi	157.2	6	Switzerland	4.5
7	Guinea	154.0	7	Slovenia	4.8
8	Uganda	149.9	8	Japan	5.1
9	Liberia	142.0	9	Netherlands	5.3
10	Zambia	139.7	10	Tunisia	5.7
11	Madagascar	134.3	11	Denmark	5.9
12	Congo-Kinshasa	132.0	12	Singapore	6.0
13	Cameroon	130.7		Sweden	6.0
14	Congo-Brazzaville	130.5	14	Cyprus	6.6
15	Tanzania	130.4	15	Italy	6.8
16	Burkina Faso	129.7	16	China	8.4
17	Somalia	127.2	17	Norway	8.9
18	Côte d'Ivoire	125.6	18	Finland	9.2
19	Nigeria	123.9	19	Luxembourg	9.6
20	Guinea-Bissau	123.5	20	Algeria	9.7
21	Equatorial Guinea	122.9	21	Germany	9.8
22	Sierra Leone	119.0	22	Channel Islands	9.9
23	Afghanistan	117.5	23	France	10.0

Fertility rates, 2015–20
Average number of children per woman

Highest		Lowest	
1 Niger	7.6	1 Hong Kong	1.1
2 Mali	6.9	Macau	1.1
3 Somalia	6.6	Taiwan	1.1
4 Chad	6.3	4 Bosnia & Herz.	1.3
5 Burundi	6.1	Portugal	1.3
6 Congo-Kinshasa	6.0	Singapore	1.3
Nigeria	6.0	South Korea	1.3
8 Angola	5.9	8 Andorra	1.4
Gambia, The	5.9	Germany	1.4
Timor-Leste	5.9	Hungary	1.4
Uganda	5.9	Japan	1.4
12 Burkina Faso	5.7	Macedonia	1.4
Zambia	5.7	Malta	1.4
14 Malawi	5.4	Poland	1.4
15 Mozambique	5.2	Romania	1.4
Tanzania	5.2	Serbia	1.4
17 Afghanistan	5.0	Slovakia	1.4
Congo-Brazzaville	5.0	Thailand	1.4
Guinea	5.0		
Guinea-Bissau	5.0		
Senegal	5.0		
South Sudan	5.0		

Women[a] who use modern methods of contraception

Highest, 2012 or latest, %		Lowest, 2012 or latest, %	
1 China	84.0	1 South Sudan	1.0
United Kingdom	84.0	2 Somalia	1.2
3 Portugal	82.5	3 Chad	1.6
4 Norway	82.2	4 Guinea	3.3
5 Costa Rica	79.9	5 Eritrea	5.1
6 Czech Republic	77.6	6 Congo-Kinshasa	5.5
7 Switzerland	77.5	7 Equatorial Guinea	6.1
Thailand	77.5	8 Mali	6.3
9 Brazil	77.1	9 Benin	7.4
10 Finland	75.4	10 Mauritania	8.0
Hong Kong	75.4	11 Niger	8.3
12 Uruguay	74.8	12 Central African Rep.	8.6
13 France	74.1	Nigeria	8.6
14 Cuba	73.2	14 Sierra Leone	10.0
15 Colombia	72.7	15 Gambia, The	10.1
16 Virgin Islands (US)	72.6	16 Albania	10.2
17 New Zealand	72.3	17 Guinea-Bissau	10.3
18 Puerto Rico	72.2	Liberia	10.3
19 Canada	72.0	19 Mozambique	11.3
Denmark	72.0	20 Côte d'Ivoire	11.9
21 Hungary	71.3	Senegal	11.9
22 United States	70.4	22 Bosnia & Herz.	12.0

a Married women aged 15–49; excludes traditional methods of contraception, such as the rhythm method.

Population: age

Median age[a]

Highest, 2013			Lowest, 2013		
1	Monaco	50.5	1	Niger	15.0
2	Japan	45.9	2	Chad	15.8
3	Germany	45.5		Uganda	15.8
4	Italy	44.3	4	Angola	16.3
5	Bulgaria	43.0		Mali	16.3
6	Greece	42.8		Somalia	16.3
7	Austria	42.7	7	Afghanistan	16.5
8	Croatia	42.6	8	Timor-Leste	16.6
9	Bermuda	42.6		Zambia	16.6
10	Hong Kong	42.4	10	Gambia, The	17.0
	Slovenia	42.4	11	Burkina Faso	17.1
12	Finland	42.3	12	Malawi	17.2
13	Portugal	42.2	13	Mozambique	17.3
14	Liechtenstein	42.1	14	Congo-Kinshasa	17.4
15	Channel Islands	42.0	15	Tanzania	17.5
	Switzerland	42.0	16	Burundi	17.6
17	Netherlands	41.8	17	Nigeria	17.8
	Andorra	41.8	18	Senegal	18.1
19	Martinique	41.7	19	Ethiopia	18.2
20	Belgium	41.6		Rwanda	18.2
21	Latvia	41.5	21	Cameroon	18.3
22	Spain	41.4	22	Benin	18.4
23	Denmark	41.1			

Most old people
% of population aged 60 or over, 2013

Most young people
% of population aged 0–14, 2013

1	Monaco	35.9	1	Niger	50.1
2	Japan	32.3	2	Chad	48.4
3	Italy	27.2		Uganda	48.4
4	Germany	27.1	4	Angola	47.5
5	Bulgaria	26.4	5	Mali	47.4
6	Finland	26.3	6	Somalia	47.2
7	Greece	25.7	7	Afghanistan	46.6
8	Sweden	25.5	8	Gambia, The	45.9
9	Croatia	25.1	9	Timor-Leste	45.8
10	Portugal	24.7	10	Burkina Faso	45.5
11	Latvia	24.3	11	Mozambique	45.4
12	Denmark	24.1	12	Malawi	45.3
	Estonia	24.1	13	Congo-Kinshasa	45.0
	France	24.1	14	Tanzania	44.9
15	Belgium	24.0	15	Burundi	44.6
16	Hungary	23.9	16	Nigeria	44.4
17	Slovenia	23.8	17	Senegal	43.5
18	Austria	23.7	18	Eritrea	43.2
	Czech Republic	23.7	19	Cameroon	43.0
20	Malta	23.5	20	Liberia	42.9
21	Netherlands	23.4		Rwanda	42.9
	Switzerland	23.4	22	Benin	42.8
23	United Kingdom	23.2	23	Ethiopia	42.7

a Age at which there are an equal number of people above and below.

City living

Biggest cities[a]
Population, m, 2020

#	City	Pop.	#	City	Pop.
1	Tokyo, Japan	38.7	21	Chongqing, China	12.5
2	Delhi, India	29.3		Moscow, Russia	12.5
3	Shanghai, China	26.1	23	Kinshasa, Congo-Kins.	12.3
4	Mumbai, India	23.7	24	Osaka, Japan	12.0
5	Mexico City, Mexico	23.2	25	Paris, France	11.7
6	New York, US	22.5	26	Bangalore, India	11.6
7	São Paulo, Brazil	22.2		Jakarta, Indonesia	11.6
8	Beijing, China	20.1		Wuhan, China	11.6
	Dhaka, Bangladesh	20.1	29	Chennai, India	11.3
10	Karachi, Pakistan	17.7	30	Tianjin, China	10.9
11	Kolkata, India	16.7	31	Chicago, US	10.8
12	Lagos, Nigeria	15.8	32	Lima, Peru	10.7
13	Buenos Aires, Argentina	14.9	33	Bogotá, Colombia	10.6
	Los Angeles, US	14.9	34	Bangkok, Thailand	10.3
15	Manila, Philippines	14.4		Hyderabad, India	10.3
16	Guangzhou, China	14.2	36	Lahore, Pakistan	9.8
	Shenzhen, China	14.2		London, UK	9.8
18	Istanbul, Turkey	13.8		Seoul, South Korea	9.8
19	Cairo, Egypt	13.3	39	Chengdu, China	9.1
20	Rio de Janeiro, Brazil	13.0	40	Foshan, China	8.9

Largest urban areas[b]
Sq km

#	City	Area	#	City	Area
1	New York, US	11,642	22	Paris, France	2,845
2	Tokyo, Japan	8,547	23	San Francisco, US	2,797
3	Chicago, US	6,856	24	Dusseldorf, Germany	2,655
4	Atlanta, US	6,851	25	Minneapolis, US	2,647
5	Los Angeles, US	6,299	26	Buenos Aires, Argentina	2,642
6	Boston, US	5,325	27	Seattle, US	2,616
7	Dallas, US	5,175	28	Johannesburg, South Africa	2,590
8	Philadelphia, US	5,131	29	Melbourne, Australia	2,543
9	Moscow, Russia	4,662	30	Tampa, US	2,479
10	Houston, US	4,644	31	Bangkok, Thailand	2,461
11	Nagoya, Japan	3,820	32	St Louis, US	2,393
12	Beijing, China	3,756	33	Pittsburgh, US	2,344
13	Shanghai, China	3,626	34	Toronto, Canada	2,287
14	Detroit, US	3,463	35	Seoul, South Korea	2,266
15	Guangzhou, China	3,432	36	San Juan, Puerto Rico	2,246
16	Washington, DC, US	3,424	37	Delhi, India	2,072
17	Osaka, Japan	3,212	38	Mexico City, Mexico	2,072
18	Miami, US	3,209	39	Cincinnati, Ohio	2,041
19	Phoenix, US	3,196	40	Sydney, Australia	2,037
20	Jakarta, Indonesia	3,108			
21	São Paulo, Brazil	2,849			

a Urban agglomerations. Data may change from year-to-year based on reassessments of agglomeration boundaries.
b A continuously built-up urban development that has no rural land.

EIU city index of culture and environment[a]
100 = Best, 2013

1	Vancouver, Canada	100.0		12	Seattle, United States	95.8
2	Amsterdam, Netherlands	97.2		13	Wellington, New Zealand	95.4
	Berlin, Germany	97.2		14	Lisbon, Portugal	95.1
	Frankfurt, Germany	97.2			Melbourne, Australia	95.1
	London, UK	97.2		16	Barcelona, Spain	94.4
	Munich, Germany	97.2			Los Angeles, US	94.4
	Paris, France	97.2			Madrid, Spain	94.4
	Toronto, Canada	97.2			San Francisco, US	94.4
9	Auckland, New Zealand	97.0			Sydney, Australia	94.4
10	Manchester, UK	96.5			Tokyo, Japan	94.4
11	Copenhagen, Denmark	96.3			Vienna, Austria	94.4
					Washington, DC, US	94.4

Number of skyscrapers[b]
2014

1	New York, US	5,888		13	Los Angeles, US	543
2	Toronto, Canada	1,993		14	São Paulo, Brazil	535
3	Shanghai, China	1,201		15	Moscow, Russia	524
4	Tokyo, Japan	1,174		16	Dubai, UAE	515
5	Chicago, US	1,150		17	Sydney, Australia	464
6	Kiev, Ukraine	1,091		18	Washington, DC, US	454
7	Hong Kong	970		19	Honolulu, US	451
8	Mexico City, Mexico	761		20	Houston, US	438
9	Vancouver, Canada	659		21	Buenos Aires, Argentina	428
10	Montreal, Canada	619		22	San Francisco, US	419
11	Bangkok, Thailand	600		23	Singapore	403
12	London, UK	572		24	Ottawa, Canada	394

Population density
People per sq km, 2012

Highest			Lowest		
1	Macau	20,000.0	1	Mongolia	1.8
2	Monaco	15,500.0	2	French Guiana	2.6
3	Singapore	7,428.6	3	Namibia	2.8
4	Hong Kong	7,100.0	4	Australia	2.9
5	Bahrain	1,625.0		Iceland	2.9
6	Malta	1,333.3	6	Suriname	3.0
7	Bermuda	1,277.8	7	Botswana	3.4
8	Bangladesh	1,045.1		Canada	3.4
9	Channel Islands	820.0		Mauritania	3.4
10	Barbados	750.0	10	Libya	3.6
11	West Bank & Gaza	700.0	11	Gabon	5.6
12	Mauritius	650.0	12	Kazakhstan	5.9
13	Taiwan	644.4	13	Central African Rep.	7.2
14	South Korea	484.0	14	Russia	8.4
15	Lebanon	430.0			

a Based on indicators that include comfortable climate, lack of social restrictions, sport, culture, food and drink.   b Completed high-rise buildings at least 12 stories or 35 metres in height in a metropolitan area.

Percentage of population living in urban areas
2015

Highest			*Lowest*		
1	Bermuda	100.0	1	Burundi	12.1
	Hong Kong	100.0	2	Papua New Guinea	12.8
	Macau	100.0	3	Liechtenstein	14.3
	Monaco	100.0	4	Trinidad & Tobago	14.8
	Singapore	100.0	5	Sri Lanka	15.5
6	Puerto Rico	99.2	6	Malawi	16.3
	Qatar	99.2	7	Uganda	17.3
8	Guadeloupe	98.4	8	Ethiopia	18.1
9	Kuwait	98.3	9	Nepal	18.4
10	Belgium	97.6	10	South Sudan	18.8
11	Virgin Islands (US)	96.0	11	Niger	18.9
12	Malta	95.4	12	Rwanda	20.4
13	Réunion	95.1	13	Cambodia	20.8

Average annual percentage change in urban population
2010–15

Highest			*Lowest*		
1	Burkina Faso	6.0	1	Georgia	-0.4
2	Uganda	5.7		Latvia	-0.4
3	Eritrea	5.0	3	Lithuania	-0.3
4	Niger	4.9		Ukraine	-0.3
5	Mali	4.8	5	Romania	-0.2
	Tanzania	4.8	6	Cuba	-0.1
	Yemen	4.8		Virgin Islands (US)	-0.1
8	Madagascar	4.7	8	Estonia	0.0
9	Rwanda	4.5		Germany	0.0
10	Afghanistan	4.4		Monaco	0.0
	Burundi	4.4		Poland	0.0
	Kenya	4.4			
	Laos	4.4			

Biggest rural populations
m, 2015

1	India	879.7	17	Myanmar	32.5
2	China	608.2	18	Uganda	32.4
3	Pakistan	118.4	19	Brazil	29.1
4	Indonesia	116.5	20	Afghanistan	27.6
5	Bangladesh	110.2	21	Nepal	26.6
6	Nigeria	86.2	22	Mexico	25.0
7	Ethiopia	75.4	23	Sudan	24.8
8	Vietnam	61.4	24	Iran	23.6
9	United States	54.0	25	Germany	20.8
10	Philippines	50.9	26	Turkey	19.2
11	Egypt	49.2	27	Italy	18.9
12	Congo-Kinshasa	47.8	28	South Africa	18.6
13	Thailand	45.6	29	Uzbekistan	18.5
14	Tanzania	37.4	30	Sri Lanka	18.4
15	Russia	36.2	31	Yemen	18.3
16	Kenya	34.5	32	Mozambique	17.7

Migrants

Biggest migrant populations
% of population, 2013

1	United Arab Emirates	83.7	15	Jordan	40.2
2	Qatar	73.8	16	Hong Kong	38.9
3	Monaco	64.2	17	Liechtenstein	33.1
4	Kuwait	60.2	18	Saudi Arabia	31.4
5	Virgin Islands (US)	59.3	19	Oman	30.6
6	Macau	58.8	20	Bermuda	29.2
7	Andorra	56.9	21	Switzerland	28.9
8	Bahrain	54.7	22	Australia	27.7
9	Channel Islands	51.0	23	Israel	26.5
10	Brunei	49.3	24	New Zealand	25.1
11	Guam	48.9	25	New Caledonia	24.6
12	Luxembourg	43.3	26	Gabon	23.6
13	Singapore	42.9	27	Kazakhstan	21.1
14	French Guiana	41.8	28	Guadeloupe	20.8

Biggest migrant populations in rich countries
% of population, 2013

1	Luxembourg	43.3	15	United States	14.3
2	Singapore	42.9	16	Latvia	13.8
3	Hong Kong	38.9		Norway	13.8
4	Switzerland	28.9		Spain	13.8
5	Australia	27.7	19	United Kingdom	12.4
6	Israel	26.5	20	Germany	11.9
7	New Zealand	25.1	21	Netherlands	11.7
8	Canada	20.7	22	France	11.6
9	Cyprus	18.2	23	Slovenia	11.3
10	Croatia	17.6	24	Belgium	10.4
11	Estonia	16.3		Iceland	10.4
12	Ireland	15.9	26	Denmark	9.9
	Sweden	15.9	27	Italy	9.4
14	Austria	15.7	28	Greece	8.9

Fastest growing migrant populations in rich countries
Average annual % increase, 2010–13

1	Luxembourg	11.4	17	Singapore	2.4
2	Cyprus	9.9	18	Netherlands	2.0
3	Ireland	8.8	19	Croatia	1.9
4	South Korea	8.3	20	Austria	1.5
5	Norway	7.9		Portugal	1.5
6	Italy	5.9	22	Japan	1.4
7	Finland	5.6	23	Canada	1.3
8	Malta	5.3	24	Belgium	1.2
9	Romania	4.8		Spain	1.2
10	Switzerland	3.9		United States	1.2
11	United Kingdom	3.7	27	France	1.1
12	New Zealand	3.4		Greece	1.1
13	Sweden	3.1	29	Czech Republic	0.7
14	Denmark	2.9	30	Liechtenstein	0.6
15	Hungary	2.7		Slovenia	0.6
16	Australia	2.5			

Refugees and asylum seekers

Refugees[a], country of origin
'000, 2012

1	Afghanistan	2,586.2	11	China	193.5
2	Somalia	1,136.7	12	Central African Rep.	164.6
3	Iraq	746.2	13	Serbia[b]	157.9
4	Syria	729.0	14	Mali	149.9
5	Sudan	568.9	15	Turkey	135.4
6	Congo-Kinshasa	509.3	16	Sri Lanka	132.7
7	Myanmar	415.4	17	Russia	110.6
8	Colombia	394.1	18	Côte d'Ivoire	100.7
9	Vietnam	336.9	19	Rwanda	97.4
10	Eritrea	285.4	20	West Bank & Gaza	94.9

Countries with largest refugee[a] populations
'000, 2012

1	Pakistan	1,638.5	11	United States	262.0
2	Iran	868.2	12	Yemen	237.2
3	Germany	589.7	13	Bangladesh	230.7
4	Kenya	564.9	14	France	217.9
5	Syria	476.5	15	Venezuela	203.6
6	Ethiopia	376.4	16	South Sudan	202.6
7	Chad	373.7	17	Uganda	197.9
8	Jordan	302.7	18	India	185.7
9	China	301.0	19	Canada	163.8
10	Turkey	267.1	20	Sudan	152.2

Origin of asylum applications to industrialised countries
'000, 2012

1	Afghanistan	36.3	11	Mexico	11.5
2	Syria	24.8	12	Nigeria	11.3
3	Serbia[b]	24.3	13	Georgia	10.7
4	China	24.1	14	Sri Lanka	10.1
5	Pakistan	23.3	15	Congo-Kinshasa	8.6
6	Russia	21.9	16	Albania	7.9
7	Iraq	19.6		Macedonia	7.9
8	Iran	19.1	18	India	7.0
9	Somalia	17.8	19	Turkey	6.8
10	Eritrea	11.9	20	Algeria	6.7

Asylum applications in industrialised countries
'000, 2012

1	United States	83.4	9	Austria	17.4
2	Germany	64.5	10	Turkey	16.7
3	France	54.9	11	Australia	15.8
4	Sweden	43.9	12	Italy	15.7
5	United Kingdom	27.4	13	Norway	9.8
6	Switzerland	26.0	14	Greece	9.6
7	Canada	20.5	15	Poland	9.2
8	Belgium	18.5	16	Netherlands	8.8

a According to UNHCR. Includes people in "refugee-like situations".
b Including Kosovo.

The world economy

Biggest economies

GDP, $bn, 2012

1	United States	16,245		24	Poland	490
2	China	8,227		25	Belgium	483
3	Japan	5,961		26	Argentina	476
4	Germany	3,428		27	Taiwan	475
5	France[a]	2,613		28	Austria	395
6	United Kingdom	2,476		29	South Africa	384
7	Brazil	2,253			United Arab Emirates	384
8	Italy	2,015		31	Venezuela	381
	Russia	2,015		32	Colombia	370
10	India	1,859		33	Thailand	366
11	Canada	1,780		34	Denmark	315
12	Australia	1,532		35	Malaysia	305
13	Spain	1,323		36	Singapore	275
14	Mexico	1,178		37	Chile	270
15	South Korea	1,130		38	Egypt	263
16	Indonesia	878			Hong Kong	263
17	Turkey	789			Nigeria	263
18	Netherlands	771		41	Israel	258
19	Saudi Arabia	711		42	Philippines	250
20	Switzerland	631		43	Greece	249
21	Iran	552		44	Finland	248
22	Sweden	524		45	Pakistan	225
23	Norway	500		46	Iraq	216

Biggest economies by purchasing power

GDP PPP, $bn, 2012

1	United States	16,245		23	Netherlands	726
2	China	12,269		24	Thailand	645
3	India	4,786		25	South Africa	576
4	Japan	4,544		26	Egypt	534
5	Germany	3,434		27	Colombia	498
6	Russia	3,386		28	Malaysia	495
7	France	2,417		29	Pakistan	491
8	Brazil	2,327		30	Belgium	451
9	United Kingdom	2,272		31	Nigeria	442
10	Italy	2,079		32	Switzerland	425
11	Mexico	1,985		33	Philippines	420
12	Spain	1,503		34	Sweden	408
13	South Korea	1,501		35	Venezuela	397
14	Canada	1,435		36	United Arab Emirates	381
15	Turkey	1,373		37	Chile	375
16	Indonesia	1,204		38	Austria	372
17	Australia	996		39	Hong Kong	366
18	Iran	938		40	Romania	363
19	Taiwan	897		41	Vietnam	336
20	Saudi Arabia	883		42	Ukraine	333
21	Poland	878		43	Norway	332
22	Argentina	735		44	Algeria	325

Note: For a list of 183 countries with their GDPs, see pages 250–254.
a Includes overseas departments. b IMF coverage.

Regional GDP

$bn, 2013		*% annual growth 2008–13*	
World	73,982	World	3.0
Advanced economies	45,338	Advanced economies	0.8
G7	34,507	G7	0.7
Euro area (17)	12,716	Euro area (17)	-0.4
Other Asia	13,435	Other Asia	7.7
Latin America & Caribbean	5,775	Latin America & Caribbean	3.0
Other Europe & CIS	4,728	Other Europe & CIS	1.8
Middle East, N. Africa,		Middle East, N. Africa,	
Afghanistan & Pakistan	3,388	Afghanistan & Pakistan	3.7
Sub-Saharan Africa	1,318	Sub-Saharan Africa	4.7

Regional purchasing power

GDP, % of total, 2013		*$ per head, 2013*	
World	100.0	World	12,350
Advanced economies	49.6	Advanced economies	41,650
G7	37.6	G7	43,820
Euro area (17)	13.1	Euro area (17)	34,020
Other Asia	25.9	Other Asia	6,550
Latin America & Caribbean	8.6	Latin America & Caribbean	12,670
Other Europe & CIS	7.5	Other Europe & CIS	14,170
Middle East, N. Africa,		Middle East, N. Africa,	
Afghanistan & Pakistan	5.7	Afghanistan & Pakistan	7,990
Sub-Saharan Africa	2.6	Sub-Saharan Africa	2,570

Regional population

% of total (7.2bn), 2013		*No. of countries[b], 2013*	
World	100.0	World	189
Advanced economies	14.7	Advanced economies	36
G7	10.6	G7	7
Euro area (17)	4.7	Euro area (17)	17
Other Asia	49.0	Other Asia	29
Latin America & Caribbean	8.4	Latin America & Caribbean	32
Other Europe & CIS	6.5	Other Europe & CIS	25
Middle East, N. Africa,		Middle East, N. Africa,	
Afghanistan & Pakistan	8.9	Afghanistan & Pakistan	22
Sub-Saharan Africa	12.5	Sub-Saharan Africa	45

Regional international trade

Exports of goods & services		*Current-account balances*	
% of total, 2013		*$bn, 2013*	
World	100.0	World	403
Advanced economies	61.1	Advanced economies	193
G7	33.4	G7	-243
Euro area (17)	25.3	Euro area (17)	366
Other Asia	17.2	Other Asia	145
Latin America & Caribbean	5.4	Latin America & Caribbean	-153
Other Europe & CIS	7.3	Other Europe & CIS	-55
Middle East, N. Africa,		Middle East, N. Africa,	
Afghanistan & Pakistan	7.1	Afghanistan & Pakistan	321
Sub-Saharan Africa	2.0	Sub-Saharan Africa	-47

Living standards

Highest GDP per head
$, 2012

1	Monaco[a]	163,026	31	New Zealand	38,637
2	Liechtenstein	160,745	32	Hong Kong	36,796
3	Luxembourg	103,925	33	Italy	33,837
4	Norway	99,636	34	Israel	32,567
5	Qatar	93,825	35	Guadeloupe[a]	30,047
6	Bermuda	84,460		Martinique[a]	30,047
7	Channel Islands[bc]	82,658	37	Guam[bc]	28,700
8	Switzerland	78,928	38	Spain	28,292
9	Macau	78,275	39	Puerto Rico	27,678
10	Australia	67,442	40	Réunion[a]	26,848
11	Kuwait	56,374	41	French Polynesia	26,404
12	Denmark	56,364	42	Cyprus	26,070
13	Sweden	55,040	43	Saudi Arabia	25,136
14	United States	51,749	44	Equatorial Guinea	24,036
15	Singapore	51,709	45	Oman	23,570
16	Canada	51,206	46	Bahrain	23,040
17	Austria	46,822	47	South Korea	22,590
18	Japan	46,731	48	Greece	22,456
19	Netherlands	45,990	49	Slovenia	22,011
20	Ireland	45,951	50	Bahamas	21,908
21	Finland	45,723	51	Malta	20,793
22	Belgium	43,427	52	French Guiana[a]	20,588
23	Germany	42,625	53	Taiwan	20,386
24	Iceland	42,339	54	Portugal	20,188
25	United Arab Emirates	41,692	55	Czech Republic	18,690
26	Andorra	41,580	56	Trinidad & Tobago	17,437
27	Brunei	41,127	57	Slovakia	16,856
28	France	39,772	58	Estonia	16,844
29	New Caledonia	39,302	59	Chile	15,452
30	United Kingdom	38,920	60	Barbados	14,917

Lowest GDP per head
$, 2012

1	Somalia	130	17	North Korea	589
2	Burundi	251	18	Tanzania	609
3	Congo-Kinshasa	262	19	Rwanda	620
4	Malawi	268	20	Sierra Leone	635
5	Niger	395	21	Burkina Faso	652
6	Liberia	414	22	Afghanistan	687
7	Madagascar	447	23	Nepal	690
8	Ethiopia	454	24	Mali	699
9	Central African Rep.	483	25	Zimbabwe	714
10	Guinea	492	26	Benin	752
11	Guinea-Bissau	494	27	Bangladesh	752
12	Eritrea	504	28	Haiti	771
13	Gambia, The	507	29	Myanmar[c]	876
14	Uganda	551	30	Kenya	943
15	Mozambique	565		South Sudan	943
16	Togo	574	32	Cambodia	944

a 2011 b Latest available year. c Estimate.

Highest purchasing power
GDP per head in PPP (US = 100), 2012

1	Qatar	176.2		35	Spain	62.1
2	Luxembourg	173.0		36	Israel	60.6
3	Liechtenstein[ab]	172.8		37	Saudi Arabia	60.3
4	Macau	166.8		38	Bahamas	60.1
5	Bermuda[ab]	166.2		39	Cyprus	59.5
6	Norway	127.8		40	South Korea	58.0
7	Monaco[ab]	126.6		41	Equatorial Guinea	57.5
8	Singapore	117.5		42	Malta	56.0
9	Switzerland	102.8		43	Bahrain	55.9
10	Brunei	101.4		44	Guam[ab]	55.5
11	Channel Islands[ab]	100.4		45	Slovenia	55.0
12	United States	100.0		46	Czech Republic	53.2
13	Hong Kong	98.8		47	Guadeloupe[c]	51.6
14	Kuwait	89.6			Martinique[c]	51.6
15	Austria	85.3		49	Trinidad & Tobago	51.3
16	Australia	84.7		50	Barbados	51.2
	Ireland	84.7		51	Oman	50.7
18	Netherlands	83.7		52	Greece	50.3
19	Sweden	82.8		53	Portugal	50.2
20	Denmark	82.7		54	Slovakia	49.9
21	Germany	82.5		55	Estonia	47.2
22	United Arab Emirates	80.0		56	Lithuania	47.1
23	Canada	79.8		57	Réunion[c]	46.2
24	Belgium	78.4		58	Russia	45.6
25	Finland	75.7		59	Poland	44.0
26	Iceland	75.6		60	Hungary	43.7
27	Taiwan	74.3		61	French Polynesia[ab]	42.5
28	New Caledonia[ab]	72.9		62	Latvia	42.1
29	Andorra[ab]	71.9		63	Chile	41.5
30	France	71.1		64	Croatia	40.5
31	United Kingdom	69.0		65	Turkey	35.8
32	Japan	68.8		66	French Guiana[c]	35.5
33	Italy	67.5		67	Romania	34.9
34	New Zealand	63.6		68	Argentina[b]	34.6

Lowest purchasing power
GDP per head in PPP (US = 100), 2012

1	Congo-Kinshasa	0.80		13	Central African Rep.	2.08
2	Burundi	1.07		14	Guinea-Bissau	2.13
3	Eritrea	1.08		15	Ethiopia	2.14
4	Somalia[ab]	1.16		16	South Sudan[b]	2.16
5	Liberia	1.23		17	Haiti	2.33
6	Malawi	1.46			Mali	2.33
7	Zimbabwe[b]	1.47		19	Rwanda	2.57
8	Niger	1.49			Uganda	2.57
9	Madagascar	1.86		21	Sierra Leone	2.58
10	Mozambique	1.95		22	Nepal	2.82
11	Togo	2.00		23	Burkina Faso	2.86
12	Guinea	2.03		24	Benin	3.01

a Latest available year.   b Estimate.   c 2011

The quality of life

Human development index[a]

Highest, 2013

1	Norway	94.4	31	Qatar	85.1
2	Australia	93.3	32	Cyprus	84.5
3	Switzerland	91.7	33	Estonia	84.0
4	Netherlands	91.5	34	Saudi Arabia	83.6
5	United States	91.4	35	Lithuania	83.4
6	Germany	91.1		Poland	83.4
7	New Zealand	91.0	37	Andorra	83.0
8	Canada	90.2		Slovakia	83.0
9	Singapore	90.1	39	Malta	82.9
10	Denmark	90.0	40	United Arab Emirates	82.7
11	Ireland	89.9	41	Chile	82.2
12	Sweden	89.8		Portugal	82.2
13	Iceland	89.5	43	Hungary	81.8
14	United Kingdom	89.2	44	Bahrain	81.5
15	Hong Kong	89.1		Cuba	81.5
	South Korea	89.1	46	Kuwait	81.4
17	Japan	89.0	47	Croatia	81.2
18	Liechtenstein	88.9	48	Latvia	81.0
19	Israel	88.8	49	Argentina	80.8
20	France	88.4	50	Uruguay	79.0
21	Austria	88.1	51	Bahamas	78.9
	Belgium	88.1		Montenegro	78.9
	Luxembourg	88.1	53	Belarus	78.6
24	Finland	87.9	54	Romania	78.5
25	Slovenia	87.4	55	Libya	78.4
26	Italy	87.2	56	Oman	78.3
27	Spain	86.9	57	Russia	77.8
28	Czech Republic	86.1	58	Bulgaria	77.7
29	Greece	85.3	59	Barbados	77.6
30	Brunei	85.2	60	Malaysia	77.3

Human development index[a]

Lowest, 2013

1	Niger	33.7	13	Liberia	41.2
2	Congo-Kinshasa	33.8	14	Malawi	41.4
3	Central African Rep.	34.1	15	Ethiopia	43.5
4	Chad	37.2	16	Gambia, The	44.1
5	Sierra Leone	37.4	17	Côte d'Ivoire	45.2
6	Eritrea	38.1	18	Afghanistan	46.8
7	Burkina Faso	38.8	19	Haiti	47.1
8	Burundi	38.9	20	Sudan	47.3
9	Guinea	39.2		Togo	47.3
10	Mozambique	39.3	22	Benin	47.6
11	Guinea-Bissau	39.6	23	Uganda	48.4
12	Mali	40.7	24	Senegal	48.5

a GDP or GDP per person is often taken as a measure of how developed a country is, but its usefulness is limited as it refers only to economic welfare. The UN Development Programme combines statistics on average and expected years of schooling and life expectancy with income levels (now GNI per person, valued in PPP US$). The HDI is shown here scaled from 0 to 100; countries scoring over 80 are considered to have very high human development, 70–79 high, 55–69 medium and those under 55 low.

Inequality-adjusted human development index[a]
Highest, 2013

1	Norway	89.1	13	Austria	81.8
2	Australia	86.0	14	Luxembourg	81.4
3	Netherlands	85.4	15	Czech Republic	81.3
4	Switzerland	84.7	16	United Kingdom	81.2
5	Germany	84.6	17	Belgium	80.6
6	Iceland	84.3	18	France	80.4
7	Sweden	84.0	19	Israel	79.3
8	Denmark	83.8	20	Japan	77.9
9	Canada	83.3	21	Slovakia	77.8
10	Ireland	83.2	22	Spain	77.5
11	Finland	83.0	23	Italy	76.8
12	Slovenia	82.4	24	Estonia	76.7

Gini coefficient[b]

	Highest 2003–12			*Lowest 2003–12*	
1	Namibia	63.9	1	Sweden	25.0
2	South Africa	63.1	2	Ukraine	25.6
3	Haiti	59.2	3	Norway	25.8
4	Zambia	57.5	4	Slovakia	26.0
5	Honduras	57.0	5	Belarus	26.5
6	Bolivia	56.3	6	Finland	26.9
	Central African Rep.	56.3	7	Romania	27.4
8	Colombia	55.9	8	Afghanistan	27.8
	Guatemala	55.9	9	Bulgaria	28.2
10	Brazil	54.7	10	Germany	28.3
11	Suriname	52.9	11	Montenegro	28.6
12	Lesotho	52.5	12	Kazakhstan	29.0
13	Paraguay	52.4	13	Austria	29.2

Economic freedom index[c]
2014

1	Hong Kong	90.1	14	United Kingdom	74.9
2	Singapore	89.4	15	Luxembourg	74.2
3	Australia	82.0		Netherlands	74.2
4	Switzerland	81.6	17	Taiwan	73.9
5	New Zealand	81.2	18	Finland	73.4
6	Canada	80.2		Germany	73.4
7	Chile	78.7	20	Sweden	73.1
8	Mauritius	76.5	21	Lithuania	73.0
9	Ireland	76.2	22	Georgia	72.6
10	Denmark	76.1	23	Austria	72.4
11	Estonia	75.9		Iceland	72.4
12	United States	75.5		Japan	72.4
13	Bahrain	75.1	26	Czech Republic	72.2

a When there is inequality in the distribution of health, education and income, the IHDI of an average person in society is less than the ordinary HDI.
b The lower its value, the more equally household income is distributed.
c Ranks countries on the basis of indicators of how government intervention can restrict the economic relations between individuals, published by the Heritage Foundation. Scores are from 80–100 (free) to 0–49.9 (repressed) (see Glossary).

Economic growth

Highest economic growth
Average annual % increase in real GDP, 2002–12

#	Country	Value	#	Country	Value
1	Macau	13.8	28	Tanzania	7.0
2	Qatar	13.3	29	Sierra Leone	6.9
3	Azerbaijan	13.0	30	Saudi Arabia	6.7
4	Angola	10.6	31	Georgia	6.5
5	China	10.4		Peru	6.5
6	Turkmenistan	9.8		Vietnam	6.5
7	Armenia	9.6	34	Libya[b]	6.4
8	Chad	9.5		Sri Lanka	6.4
	Myanmar[a]	9.5	36	Burkina Faso	6.2
10	Nigeria	9.4		Congo-Kinshasa	6.2
11	Afghanistan	9.2		Zambia	6.2
12	Ethiopia	9.0	39	Bangladesh	6.1
13	Mongolia	8.7		Timor-Leste	6.1
14	Equatorial Guinea	8.2	41	Singapore	6.0
	Panama	8.2	42	Mauritania	5.9
16	Cambodia	8.0	43	Indonesia	5.7
17	Uzbekistan	7.8		Jordan	5.7
18	India	7.6		Monaco[c]	5.7
	Laos	7.6	46	Cuba[a]	5.6
	Tajikistan	7.6	47	Bahrain	5.5
21	Rwanda	7.4		Kuwait[a]	5.5
22	Ghana	7.3		Papua New Guinea	5.5
23	Kazakhstan	7.2	50	Dominican Rep.	5.4
	Mozambique	7.2	51	Philippines	5.2
25	Argentina	7.1		Uruguay	5.2
	Belarus	7.1	53	Andorra[c]	5.1
	Uganda	7.1		Malaysia	5.1

Lowest economic growth
Average annual % change in real GDP, 2002–12

#	Country	Value	#	Country	Value
1	South Sudan[d]	-12.8		Fiji	1.2
2	Zimbabwe	-2.7		Germany	1.2
3	Puerto Rico	-0.4		Spain	1.2
4	Greece	-0.1	23	Belgium	1.3
	Italy	-0.1		Eritrea	1.3
6	Portugal	0.0		Guinea-Bissau	1.3
7	Bermuda	0.1		United Kingdom	1.3
8	Bahamas	0.5	27	Croatia	1.4
9	Denmark	0.6	28	Finland	1.5
	Jamaica[e]	0.6	29	Austria	1.6
11	Japan	0.8		Norway	1.6
12	North Korea	0.9	31	Côte d'Ivoire	1.7
13	Euro area	1.0		Malta	1.7
	France	1.0	33	Canada	1.8
	Haiti	1.0		Channel Islands[f]	1.8
16	Brunei	1.1		Ireland	1.8
	Hungary	1.1		Slovenia	1.8
	Netherlands	1.1		United States	1.8
19	Barbados	1.2			

a 2002–11   b 2002–09   c 2002–08   d 2008–12   e 2001–12   f 2002–07

Highest economic growth
Average annual % increase in real GDP, 1992–2002

1	Equatorial Guinea	26.7	10	Uganda	7.0
2	Bosnia & Herz.[a]	20.7	11	Albania	6.8
3	Liberia	14.1		Iraq[c]	6.8
4	China	9.8	13	Estonia[d]	6.6
5	Myanmar	8.6	14	Laos	6.4
6	Ireland	7.9	15	Eritrea	6.3
7	Mozambique	7.6	16	Singapore	6.1
8	Cambodia[b]	7.4	17	India	5.8
	Vietnam	7.4		Malaysia	5.8

Lowest economic growth
Average annual % change in real GDP, 1992–2002

1	Ukraine	-4.9	11	Georgia	-0.5
2	Moldova	-3.7	12	Macedonia	0.0
3	Congo-Kinshasa	-3.6		Venezuela	0.0
4	Tajikistan	-3.4	14	Turkmenistan	0.1
5	Burundi	-1.9	15	Montenegro[c]	0.2
6	Kyrgyzstan	-1.2	16	Kazakhstan	0.3
7	North Korea	-1.1	17	Argentina	0.5
8	Russia	-0.9	18	Guinea-Bissau	0.7
9	Serbia	-0.8	19	Japan	0.8
10	Azerbaijan	-0.7			

Highest services growth
Average annual % increase in real terms, 2004–12

1	Liberia	19.0	10	Turkmenistan	10.1
2	Ghana	14.2	11	Mongolia	9.9
3	Macau[e]	13.8	12	Uzbekistan	9.8
4	Afghanistan	13.4	13	Panama	9.6
5	Angola	13.0	14	Ethiopia	9.4
6	Armenia	12.8	15	Rwanda	9.2
7	Azerbaijan	12.7	16	Georgia	8.8
8	China	11.9	17	India	8.5
9	Yemen[f]	11.3			

Lowest services growth
Average annual % change in real terms, 2004–12

1	Puerto Rico[e]	-2.4	10	Hungary[f]	0.7
2	Zimbabwe	-1.2		North Korea	0.7
3	Guinea[e]	-1.0	12	Japan[e]	0.9
4	Brunei	-0.2	13	Norway[f]	1.0
5	Bermuda	0.0	14	Croatia	1.2
6	Congo-Brazzaville[e]	0.1		Denmark[f]	1.2
7	Bahamas	0.2	16	Estonia[f]	1.3
	Niger	0.2		Latvia[f]	1.3
9	Italy[f]	0.5		United Kingdom[f]	1.3

a 1994–2002   b 1993–2002   c 1997–2002   d 1995–2002   e 2004–11
f 2004–10
Note: Rankings of highest and lowest industrial growth 2004–12 can be found on page 46 and highest and lowest agricultural growth 2004–12 on page 49.

Trading places

Biggest exporters

% of total world exports (goods, services and income), 2012

1	Euro area (17)	15.77	22	Australia	1.41
2	United States	11.78	23	Sweden	1.20
3	China	9.16	24	Ireland	1.18
4	Germany	7.79	25	Brazil	1.15
5	Japan	4.51	26	Luxembourg	1.13
6	United Kingdom	4.03	27	Thailand	1.11
7	France	3.75	28	Malaysia	1.10
8	Netherlands	2.96	29	Austria	1.01
9	South Korea	2.69	30	Norway	0.99
10	Italy	2.56	31	Hong Kong	0.97
11	Russia	2.51	32	Poland	0.93
12	Canada	2.44	33	Indonesia	0.84
13	Switzerland	2.05	34	Turkey	0.83
14	Spain	1.87	35	Denmark	0.78
15	Singapore	1.86	36	Czech Republic	0.61
16	Belgium	1.82		Iran	0.61
17	India	1.79	38	Qatar	0.59
18	Saudi Arabia	1.66	39	Kuwait	0.55
19	Mexico	1.58	40	Hungary	0.49
20	United Arab Emirates	1.52		Vietnam	0.49
21	Taiwan	1.48			

Most trade dependent

Trade[a] as % of GDP, 2012

1	Singapore	97.3
2	Slovakia	86.0
3	United Arab Emirates	74.5
4	Belarus	71.6
5	Vietnam	70.4
6	Hungary	70.2
7	Lithuania	69.7
8	Libya	69.4
9	Malaysia	68.0
10	Estonia	67.4
11	Lesotho	65.6
	Netherlands	65.6
13	Belgium	63.9
14	Mauritania	63.1
15	Czech Republic	62.2
16	Slovenia	61.2
17	Panama	61.1
18	Thailand	60.9
19	Equatorial Guinea	60.7
20	Taiwan	59.9
21	Congo-Brazzaville	59.2
22	Puerto Rico	58.1

Least trade dependent

Trade[a] as % of GDP, 2012

1	Bermuda	8.4
2	Sudan	9.8
	Syria	9.8
4	Brazil	10.3
5	United States	11.9
6	Central African Rep.	12.1
7	French Polynesia	12.9
8	Macau	13.3
9	Japan	13.5
10	Cuba	14.5
	Pakistan	14.5
12	Egypt	15.1
13	Argentina	15.4
14	Colombia	16.0
15	Dominican Rep.	16.1
16	Greece	16.4
17	Ethiopia	16.6
18	Burundi	17.1
19	Australia	17.2
20	Rwanda	18.0
21	Myanmar	18.3
	Nepal	18.3

Notes: The figures are drawn wherever possible from balance of payment statistics so have differing definitions from statistics taken from customs or similar sources. For Hong Kong and Singapore, only domestic exports and retained imports are used. Euro area data exclude intra-euro area trade.

a Average of imports plus exports of goods.

Biggest traders of goods[a]
% of world, 2013

Exports			*Imports*	
1 China	11.8		1 United States	12.4
2 United States	8.4		2 China	10.3
3 Germany	7.7		3 Germany	6.3
4 Japan	3.8		4 Japan	4.4
5 Netherlands	3.5		5 France	3.6
6 France	3.1		6 United Kingdom	3.5
7 South Korea	3.0		7 Netherlands	3.1
8 United Kingdom	2.9		8 South Korea	2.7
9 Italy	2.8		9 Canada	2.5
Russia	2.8		Italy	2.5
11 Belgium	2.5		11 India	2.6
12 Canada	2.4		12 Belgium	2.4
13 Mexico	2.0		13 Mexico	2.1
Saudi Arabia[b]	2.0		14 Russia	1.8
15 United Arab Emirates[b]	1.9		Spain	1.8
16 India	1.7		16 Taiwan	1.4
17 Spain	1.7		17 Australia	1.3
18 Taiwan	1.6		Brazil	1.3
19 Australia	1.3		Thailand	1.3
Brazil	1.3		Turkey	1.3
			United Arab Emirates[b]	1.3

Biggest earners from services and income
% of world exports of services and income, 2012

1 Euro area (17)	19.78		24 Denmark	1.20
2 United States	18.38		25 Norway	1.10
3 United Kingdom	7.06		26 Taiwan	0.96
4 Germany	6.70		27 Thailand	0.74
5 France	4.94		28 Malaysia	0.66
6 Japan	4.74		29 Brazil	0.65
7 China	4.57		30 Macau	0.62
8 Luxembourg	3.48		Turkey	0.62
9 Hong Kong	3.06		32 Poland	0.59
10 Netherlands	2.83		33 Finland	0.54
11 Singapore	2.42		34 Greece	0.52
12 Switzerland	2.41		35 Israel	0.49
13 Spain	2.36		36 Hungary	0.46
14 Ireland	2.32		United Arab Emirates	0.46
15 Italy	2.21		38 Saudi Arabia	0.44
16 Belgium	2.08		39 Portugal	0.43
17 Canada	2.01		40 Czech Republic	0.39
18 India	1.99		41 Mexico	0.38
19 South Korea	1.67		42 Ukraine	0.37
20 Sweden	1.54		43 Indonesia	0.34
21 Russia	1.41		Philippines	0.34
22 Australia	1.30		45 Lebanon	0.31
23 Austria	1.24		46 Egypt	0.28

a Individual countries only.   b Estimate.

Balance of payments: current account

Largest surpluses
$m, 2012

1	Germany	255,383		26	Angola	13,851
2	China	193,139		27	Algeria	12,322
3	Euro area (17)	171,381		28	Venezuela	11,016
4	Saudi Arabia	164,764		29	Austria	9,479
5	Kuwait	76,275		30	Ireland	9,245
6	Netherlands	73,596		31	Vietnam	9,062
7	Norway	72,609		32	Oman	8,312
8	Russia	71,282		33	Philippines	6,949
9	United Arab Emirates	66,553		34	Brunei	5,684
10	Qatar	62,031		35	Hong Kong	4,147
11	Japan	60,859		36	South Sudan	3,317
12	Switzerland	53,914		37	Luxembourg	3,163
13	Taiwan	50,672		38	Bahrain	2,938
14	Singapore	49,385		39	Trinidad & Tobago[b]	2,898
15	South Korea	43,335		40	Timor-Leste	2,740
16	Sweden	31,358		41	Bangladesh	2,576
17	Iraq	29,541		42	Gabon[c]	2,504
18	Iran	26,272		43	Côte d'Ivoire[b]	2,276
19	Libya	23,836		44	Bolivia	2,138
20	Réunion[a]	23,797		45	Slovakia	2,039
21	Nigeria	20,353		46	Cuba[a]	1,490
22	Denmark	18,750		47	Slovenia	1,486
23	Macau	18,710		48	Hungary	909
24	Malaysia	18,638		49	Israel	850
25	Azerbaijan	14,976		50	Bermuda	771

Largest deficits
$m, 2012

1	United States	-440,423		22	New Zealand	-6,963
2	United Kingdom	-94,270		23	Peru	-6,842
3	India	-91,471		24	Mozambique	-6,297
4	Australia	-64,341		25	Sudan	-6,242
5	Canada	-62,256		26	Greece	-6,172
6	France	-57,246		27	Jordan	-5,694
7	Brazil	-54,246		28	Italy	-5,529
8	Turkey	-48,497		29	Ghana	-4,778
9	Indonesia	-24,074		30	Portugal	-4,359
10	South Africa	-20,016		31	Kenya	-4,253
11	Poland	-18,263		32	Serbia	-4,229
12	Spain	-16,295		33	Tanzania	-4,195
13	Mexico	-14,767		34	Sri Lanka	-4,045
14	Ukraine	-14,335		35	Dominican Rep.	-4,037
15	Colombia	-11,834		36	Panama	-3,816
16	Morocco	-9,843		37	Tunisia	-3,721
17	Belgium	-9,353		38	Mongolia	-3,362
18	Chile	-9,083		39	Finland	-3,124
19	Afghanistan	-7,570		40	Ethiopia	-2,985
20	Romania	-7,487		41	Papua New Guinea	-2,834
21	Egypt	-6,972		42	Uzbekistan	-2,708

Note: Euro area data exclude intra-euro area trade. a 2010 b 2011 c Estimate.

Largest surpluses as % of GDP
2012

1	Timor-Leste	211.9	26	Germany	7.4
2	Macau	42.9	27	Malaysia	6.1
3	Kuwait	41.6	28	Algeria	6.0
4	Libya	38.2		Sweden	6.0
5	Brunei	33.5	30	Denmark	5.9
6	South Sudan	32.5	31	Vietnam	5.8
7	Qatar	32.2	32	Luxembourg	5.7
8	Saudi Arabia	23.2	33	Iran	4.8
9	Azerbaijan	22.5	34	Ireland	4.4
10	Singapore	18.0	35	South Korea	3.8
11	United Arab Emirates	17.3	36	Russia	3.5
12	Norway	14.5	37	Slovenia	3.3
13	Bermuda	14.1		Suriname	3.3
14	Iraq	13.7	39	Venezuela	2.9
15	Gabon[a]	13.6	40	Philippines	2.8
16	Trinidad & Tobago[b]	12.4	41	Swaziland	2.6
17	Angola	12.1	42	Austria	2.4
18	Taiwan	10.7	43	China	2.3
19	Oman	10.6		Eritrea[a]	2.3
20	Bahrain	9.7	45	Bangladesh	2.2
21	Netherlands	9.6		Cuba[c]	2.2
22	Côte d'Ivoire[b]	9.2		Slovakia	2.2
23	Switzerland	8.5	48	Malta	1.9
24	Bolivia	7.9	49	Hong Kong	1.6
25	Nigeria	7.8	50	Nepal	1.5

Largest deficits as % of GDP
2012

1	Mozambique	-44.2	22	Kosovo[b]	-14.2
2	Afghanistan	-36.9	23	Jamaica	-12.9
3	Mongolia	-32.7	24	Nicaragua	-12.7
4	Liberia	-32.0	25	Georgia	-12.1
5	Sierra Leone	-31.0	26	Armenia	-12.0
6	Mauritania[a]	-30.6	27	Ghana	-11.7
7	West Bank & Gaza	-28.6	28	Rwanda	-11.6
8	Zimbabwe	-25.6	29	Serbia	-11.3
9	Lesotho	-24.0	30	Sudan	-10.6
10	Burundi	-23.4	31	Panama	-10.5
11	Kyrgyzstan	-23.1	32	Kenya	-10.4
12	Guinea	-19.6		Senegal	-10.4
13	Malawi	-18.8	34	Morocco	-10.3
14	Bahamas	-18.4	35	Barbados	-10.1
	Jordan	-18.4	36	Albania	-9.9
16	Papua New Guinea	-18.1		Congo-Kinshasa	-9.9
17	Montenegro	-17.6	38	Bosnia & Herz.	-9.0
18	Haiti	-17.3		Chad[c]	-9.0
19	New Caledonia[b]	-16.8	40	Uganda	-8.7
	Niger	-16.8	41	Cambodia	-8.6
21	Tanzania	-14.9		Honduras	-8.6

a Estimate.   b 2011   c 2010

Official reserves[a]
$m, end-2013

1	China	3,880,368		16	Mexico	180,200
2	Japan	1,266,851		17	Thailand	167,230
3	Euro area (17)	748,678		18	Italy	145,742
4	Saudi Arabia	737,797		19	France	145,161
5	Switzerland	536,235		20	Malaysia	134,854
6	Russia	509,692		21	Turkey	131,054
7	United States	448,509		22	Libya[b]	123,195
8	Taiwan	433,214		23	Poland	106,221
9	Brazil	358,816		24	United Kingdom	104,419
10	South Korea	345,694		25	Indonesia	99,387
11	Hong Kong	311,186		26	Denmark	88,677
12	India	298,092		27	Philippines	83,182
13	Singapore	277,798		28	Israel	81,786
14	Algeria	201,437		29	Iraq	77,747
15	Germany	198,535		30	Canada	71,937

Official gold reserves
Market prices, $m, end-2013

1	Euro area (17)	417,439		14	Portugal	14,812
2	United States	314,975		15	Venezuela	14,237
3	Germany	131,170		16	Saudi Arabia	12,505
4	Italy	94,950		17	United Kingdom	12,015
5	France	94,312		18	Lebanon	11,108
6	China	40,821		19	Spain	10,906
7	Switzerland	40,277		20	Austria	10,843
8	Russia	40,089		21	Belgium	8,807
9	Japan	29,634		22	Philippines	7,494
10	Netherlands	23,718		23	Algeria	6,724
11	India	21,599		24	Thailand	5,902
12	Turkey	20,127		25	Kazakhstan	5,565
13	Taiwan	16,404		26	Singapore	4,934

Workers' remittances
Inflows, $m, 2012

1	India	68,821		16	Italy	7,326
2	China	57,987		17	Indonesia	7,212
3	Philippines	24,641		18	Poland	6,935
4	Mexico	23,366		19	Lebanon	6,918
5	France	21,676		20	Morocco	6,508
6	Nigeria	20,633		21	United States	6,285
7	Egypt	19,236		22	Sri Lanka	6,000
8	Bangladesh	14,120		23	Russia	5,788
9	Pakistan	14,006		24	Guatemala	5,031
10	Germany	13,964		25	Nepal	4,793
11	Belgium	10,123		26	Thailand	4,713
12	Vietnam	10,000		27	Colombia	4,019
13	Spain	9,633		28	El Salvador	3,927
14	South Korea	8,474		29	Portugal	3,904
15	Ukraine	8,449		30	Romania	3,674

a Foreign exchange, SDRs, IMF position and gold at market prices.   b November 2013.

Exchange rates

The Economist's Big Mac index

		Big Mac prices in local currency	in $	Implied PPP[a] of the $	Actual $ exchange rate	Under (−)/ over (+) valuation against $, %
Countries with the most under-valued currencies, January 2014						
1	India[b]	95.00	1.54	20.54	61.85	−67
2	South Africa	23.50	2.16	5.08	10.88	−53
3	Malaysia	7.40	2.23	1.60	3.32	−52
4	Ukraine	19.00	2.27	4.11	8.38	−51
5	Hong Kong	18.00	2.32	3.89	7.76	−50
	Indonesia	27,939.00	2.30	6,041.95	12,140.00	−50
7	Egypt	16.93	2.43	3.66	6.96	−47
8	Russia	89.00	2.62	19.25	33.94	−43
	Taiwan	79.00	2.62	17.08	30.16	−43
10	Sri Lanka	350.00	2.68	75.69	130.80	−42
11	China[c]	16.60	2.74	3.59	6.05	−41
12	Mexico	37.00	2.78	8.00	13.33	−40
13	Vietnam	60,000.00	2.84	12,975.31	21,090.00	−38
14	Saudi Arabia	11.00	2.93	2.38	3.75	−37
	Thailand	96.00	2.92	20.76	32.88	−37
16	Japan	310.00	2.97	67.04	104.25	−36
17	Philippines	135.00	2.98	29.19	45.23	−35
	Poland	9.20	3.00	1.99	3.07	−35
19	Argentina	21.00	3.03	4.54	6.92	−34
	Pakistan	320.00	3.04	69.20	105.42	−34
21	UAE	12.00	3.27	2.60	3.67	−29
22	Czech Republic	70.45	3.47	15.24	20.28	−25
	Lithuania	8.80	3.46	1.90	2.55	−25
	South Korea	3,700.00	3.47	800.14	1,067.30	−25
25	Peru	10.00	3.56	2.16	2.81	−23
26	Singapore	4.60	3.60	0.99	1.28	−22
27	Chile	2,000.00	3.69	432.51	541.95	−20
28	Turkey	8.50	3.76	1.84	2.26	−19
29	Hungary	860.00	3.85	185.98	223.10	−17
30	Costa Rica	2,150.00	4.28	464.95	501.92	−7
Countries with the most over-valued currencies, January 2014						
1	Norway	48.00	7.80	10.38	6.16	69
2	Venezuela	45.00	7.15	9.73	6.29	55
3	Switzerland	6.50	7.14	1.41	0.91	54
4	Sweden	40.70	6.29	8.80	6.47	36
5	Brazil	12.40	5.25	2.68	2.36	13
6	Denmark	28.50	5.18	6.16	5.50	12
7	Canada	5.54	5.01	1.20	1.11	8
	Israel	17.50	5.02	3.78	3.49	8
9	Euro area[d]	3.66	4.96	1.26[e]	1.36[e]	7
10	Uruguay	105.00	4.91	22.71	21.38	6
11	United Kingdom	2.79	4.63	1.66[f]	1.66[f]	0

a Purchasing-power parity: local price in the 41 countries listed divided by United States price ($4.62, average of four cities).
b Maharaja Mac. c Average of five cities. d Weighted average of prices in euro area.
e Dollars per euro. f Dollars per pound.

Public finance

Government debt
As % of GDP, 2013

1	Japan	227.2		16	Netherlands	86.9
2	Greece	186.9		17	Germany	86.1
3	Italy	145.7		18	Slovenia	70.3
4	Portugal	135.4		19	Israel	68.4
5	Ireland	132.3		20	Finland	66.7
6	Iceland	129.5		21	Poland	66.0
7	France	113.0		22	Slovakia	59.0
8	United Kingdom	107.0		23	Denmark	58.8
9	Euro area (15)	106.4		24	Czech Republic	58.6
10	Belgium	104.5		25	Sweden	52.0
11	United States	104.1		26	Switzerland	42.3
12	Spain	99.6		27	New Zealand	41.8
13	Canada	97.0		28	South Korea	35.6
14	Hungary	88.8		29	Australia	34.4
15	Austria	87.3		30	Norway	34.2

Government spending
As % of GDP, 2013

1	Finland	58.4		16	Norway	44.8
2	Denmark	57.7		17	Germany	44.5
3	France	57.0		18	Czech Republic	43.9
4	Belgium	54.2			Luxembourg	43.9
5	Sweden	53.0		20	New Zealand	43.5
6	Austria	51.8			Spain	43.5
7	Italy	51.4		22	Japan	42.9
8	Slovenia	50.8		23	Ireland	42.7
9	Euro area (15)	49.5		24	Poland	42.5
10	Netherlands	49.2		25	Israel	42.0
11	Hungary	48.7		26	Canada	41.4
12	Greece	47.9		27	United States	38.7
13	Iceland	47.2		28	Estonia	38.6
	United Kingdom	47.2		29	Slovakia	36.1
15	Portugal	46.3		30	Australia	35.4

Tax revenue
As % of GDP, 2012

1	Denmark	48.0		14	Iceland	37.2
2	Belgium	45.3		15	Czech Republic	35.5
	France	45.3		16	United Kingdom	35.2
4	Italy	44.4		17	Greece	33.8
5	Sweden	44.3		18	New Zealand	32.9
6	Finland	44.1			Spain	32.9
7	Austria	43.2		20	Estonia	32.5
8	Norway	42.2			Portugal	32.5
9	Hungary	38.9		22	Poland[a]	32.3
10	Netherlands[a]	38.6		23	Israel	31.6
11	Luxembourg	37.8		24	Canada	30.7
12	Germany	37.6		25	Japan[a]	28.6
13	Slovenia	37.4		26	Slovakia	28.5

Note: Includes only OECD countries.   a 2011

Democracy

Democracy index
Most democratic = 100, 2013

Most			Least		
1	Norway	88.3	1	Yemen	26.5
2	Sweden	87.0	2	Syria	29.2
3	Finland	86.7	3	Central African Rep.	31.0
4	Switzerland	85.9	4	Togo	35.8
5	Denmark	84.4	5	Guinea	36.2
6	Netherlands	83.5	6	Pakistan	38.2
7	Germany	82.2	7	Nigeria	38.7
8	New Zealand	81.5	8	Libya	38.9
9	Austria	81.2	9	China	39.1
10	Belgium	81.1	10	Bahrain	39.4
11	Ireland	80.9	11	Burundi	39.5
12	Australia	80.8	12	Haiti	40.2
13	Canada	80.6	13	Egypt	41.2
14	United Kingdom	79.9	14	Madagascar	42.8
15	United States	78.8	15	Burkina Faso	43.1
16	France	78.2	16	Mozambique	43.2
17	Spain	76.9	17	Niger	43.8
18	Portugal	75.7	18	Zambia	44.4
19	Slovenia	75.4	19	Morocco	44.6
20	Japan	74.8	20	Kenya	44.8

Parliamentary seats
Lower or single house, seats per 100,000 population, February 2014

Most			Least		
1	Liechtenstein	67.6	1	India	0.04
2	Monaco	63.2	2	United States	0.13
3	Andorra	35.4	3	Pakistan	0.18
4	Iceland	19.1	4	Bangladesh	0.19
5	Malta	16.3	5	Nigeria	0.21
6	Equatorial Guinea	13.2	6	China	0.22
7	Montenegro	13.0		Indonesia	0.22
8	Luxembourg	11.3	8	Brazil	0.26
9	Barbados	10.5	9	Philippines	0.29
10	Bahamas	10.1	10	Russia	0.32

Women in parliament
Lower or single house, women as % of total seats, February 2014

1	Rwanda	63.8		Spain	39.7
2	Andorra	50.0	13	Norway	39.6
3	Cuba	48.9	14	Mozambique	39.2
4	Sweden	45.0	15	Denmark	39.1
5	South Africa	44.8	16	Netherlands	38.7
6	Senegal	43.3	17	Costa Rica	38.6
7	Finland	42.5	18	Timor-Leste	38.5
8	Ecuador	41.6	19	Mexico	37.4
9	Belgium	41.3	20	Angola	36.8
10	Nicaragua	40.2	21	Argentina	36.6
11	Iceland	39.7	22	Germany	36.5

Inflation

Consumer price inflation

Highest, 2013, %			Lowest, 2013, %	
1	Venezuela[a]	40.7	1 Greece	-0.9
2	Sudan[a]	36.5	2 Mali[a]	-0.6
3	Iran	35.2	3 Georgia	-0.5
4	Malawi	27.7	4 Ukraine	-0.3
5	Belarus	18.3	5 Switzerland	-0.2
6	Eritrea[a]	12.3	6 Bosnia & Herz.	-0.1
7	Guinea[a]	12.0	7 Latvia	0.0
8	Ghana[a]	11.7	South Sudan	0.0
9	Uzbekistan[a]	11.2	Sweden	0.0
10	Yemen[a]	11.1	10 Chad	0.2
11	Argentina[a]	10.6	11 Bahamas[a]	0.3
	Timor-Leste[a]	10.6	12 Brunei	0.4
13	Nepal[a]	9.9	Bulgaria	0.4
14	Sierra Leone[a]	9.8	Cyprus	0.4
15	Mongolia[a]	9.6	Japan	0.4
16	India	9.5	Portugal[a]	0.4
17	Jamaica	9.4	17 Gabon	0.5
18	Angola[a]	8.8	Ireland[a]	0.5
	Burundi[a]	8.8	19 Guinea-Bissau[a]	0.6
20	Bhutan[a]	8.7	20 Congo-Kinshasa	0.8
21	Uruguay	8.6		
22	Nigeria	8.5		

Highest average annual consumer price inflation, 2008–13, %			Lowest average annual consumer price inflation, 2008–13, %	
1	Belarus	28.6	1 Japan	-0.4
2	Venezuela[a]	28.5	2 Qatar	-0.1
3	Sudan[a]	22.4	Switzerland	-0.1
4	Iran	21.7	4 Ireland[a]	0.1
5	South Sudan[b]	20.4	5 Brunei	0.4
6	Congo-Kinshasa	16.5	6 Taiwan	0.8
7	Eritrea[a]	16.4	7 Sweden	0.9
8	Ethiopia[a]	15.9	8 Senegal	1.0
9	Malawi	14.2	United Arab Emirates	1.0
10	Sierra Leone[a]	13.8	10 Morocco	1.2
11	Guinea[a]	13.6	11 Guinea-Bissau[a]	1.4
12	Ghana[a]	12.3	Nigera	1.4
13	Angola[a]	12.1	Portugal[a]	1.4
14	Pakistan	11.9	14 Bosnia & Herz.	1.5
	Uzbekistan[a]	11.9	Canada	1.5
16	Nigeria	11.5	France	1.5
17	Tanzania	11.1	Gabon	1.5
18	Yemen[a]	11.0	Germany	1.5
19	Egypt	10.9	19 United States	1.6
	Uganda	10.9	20 Bahamas[a]	1.7
21	India	10.6	Latvia	1.7
22	Nepal[a]	10.0	Norway	1.7
	Vietnam	10.0	Slovenia	1.7

a Estimate.   b 2011–13

Commodity prices

End 2013, % change on a year earlier		2005–13, % change	
1 Coconut oil	58.3	1 Gold	217.5
2 Wool (NZ)	28.1	2 Tin	202.9
3 Hides	23.6	3 Corn	177.1
4 Cocoa	21.4	4 Soya meal	131.6
5 Palm oil	11.7	5 Soyabeans	130.8
6 Lamb	9.1	6 Lead	118.7
7 Cotton	8.1	7 Wheat	114.9
8 Oil[a]	7.3	8 Palm oil	103.0
9 Wool (Aus)	5.8	9 Soya oil	103.0
10 Soya meal	4.1	10 Copper	99.2
11 Beef (US)	3.8	11 Sugar	79.2
12 Zinc	2.5	12 Oil[a]	73.0
13 Timber	-3.7	13 Rice	67.8
14 Beef (Aus)	-4.0	14 Cotton	66.3
15 Tin	-4.1	15 Rubber	65.1
16 Lead	-5.7	16 Cocoa	59.0
17 Copper	-6.6	17 Coconut oil	54.0
18 Soyabeans	-7.5	18 Tea	52.5
19 Aluminium	-13.5	19 Beef (Aus)	52.3
20 Sugar	-15.5	20 Wool (Aus)	52.2
21 Nickel	-18.2	21 Hides	45.1
22 Coffee	-19.0	22 Lamb	40.0
23 Soya oil	-21.0	23 Zinc	38.5
24 Wheat	-22.2	24 Beef (US)	35.7
25 Rubber	-26.7	25 Coffee	33.5
26 Gold	-27.3	26 Wool (NZ)	32.1

The Economist's house-price indicators

Q4 2013[b], % change on a year earlier		Q1 2008–Q4 2013[b], % change	
1 United States	13.6	1 Hong Kong	96.3
2 Brazil	12.8	2 Austria	37.1
3 Hong Kong	9.7	3 Switzerland	27.8
4 China	8.7	4 Germany	25.2
New Zealand	8.7	5 South Africa	23.4
6 Germany	8.1	6 Canada	23.0
South Africa	8.1	China	23.0
8 Australia	7.6	8 Singapore	22.1
9 India	7.0	9 Australia	17.6
10 Ireland	5.6	10 Belgium	15.5
11 United Kingdom	5.5	11 Sweden	11.8
12 Austria	5.0	12 New Zealand	9.1
Switzerland	5.0	13 United Kingdom	1.7
14 Singapore	3.9	14 France	-0.4
15 Canada	3.4	15 United States	-5.9
16 Sweden	3.1	16 Italy	-12.2
17 Denmark	2.7	17 Japan	-15.4
18 Belgium	2.4	18 Denmark	-16.0
19 France	-1.5	19 Netherlands	-19.2
20 Japan	-1.6	20 Spain	-30.0

a West Texas Intermediate.   b Or latest.

Debt

Highest foreign debt[a]
$bn, 2012

1	China	754.0	24	Czech Republic	101.8
2	Russia	539.5	25	Israel	97.0
3	Brazil	440.5	26	Colombia	79.1
4	South Korea	425.1	27	Venezuela	72.1
5	India	379.1	28	Pakistan	61.9
6	Poland	365.1	29	Philippines	61.4
7	Mexico	354.9	30	Iraq	60.2
8	Turkey	337.5	31	Vietnam	59.1
9	Indonesia	254.9	32	Croatia	59.0
10	Hungary	203.8	33	Peru	54.1
11	United Arab Emirates	162.3	34	Bulgaria	50.8
12	Hong Kong	146.9	35	Egypt	40.0
13	Qatar	139.1	36	Latvia	37.1
14	South Africa	137.5	37	Kuwait	35.3
15	Kazakhstan	137.1	38	Belarus	34.4
16	Saudi Arabia	136.2	39	Serbia	34.2
17	Ukraine	135.1	40	Morocco	33.8
18	Thailand	134.2	41	Lebanon	29.0
19	Romania	131.9	42	Lithuania	27.9
20	Taiwan	130.8	43	Bangladesh	26.1
21	Argentina	121.0	44	Estonia	25.8
22	Chile	116.9	45	Tunisia	25.5
23	Malaysia	104.0	46	Sri Lanka	25.4

Highest foreign debt burden[a]
Total foreign debt as % of GDP, 2012

1	Hungary	173.4	22	Macedonia	70.0
2	Papua New Guinea	153.9	23	Lebanon	68.4
3	Latvia	130.9	24	Montenegro	68.3
4	Estonia	115.0	25	Lithuania	65.9
5	Croatia	105.0	26	Bosnia & Herz.	61.1
6	Bulgaria	102.9	27	Jordan	59.8
7	Jamaica	99.5	28	Gambia, The	58.7
8	Kyrgyzstan	99.1	29	Tunisia	58.4
9	Serbia	94.8	30	El Salvador	58.1
10	Nicaragua	86.7	31	Hong Kong	55.9
11	Georgia	85.4	32	Belarus	55.3
12	Mauritania	82.3	33	Bahrain	53.8
13	Kazakhstan	79.0	34	Albania	53.1
14	Romania	78.9	35	Mongolia	53.0
15	Moldova	78.5	36	Tajikistan	52.7
16	Ukraine	77.9	37	Czech Republic	51.8
17	Zimbabwe	75.5	38	Vietnam	44.1
18	Poland	74.6	39	Chile	43.6
19	Laos	73.4		Sri Lanka	43.6
20	Armenia	72.9	41	Turkey	43.1
21	Qatar	72.3	42	Cambodia	42.9

a Foreign debt is debt owed to non-residents and repayable in foreign currency; the figures shown include liabilities of government, public and private sectors. Longer-established developed countries have been excluded.

Highest foreign debt[a]

As % of exports of goods and services, 2012

1	Sudan	863.3	14	Madagascar	151.5
2	Papua New Guinea	372.2	15	Georgia	151.4
3	Burundi	234.4	16	Poland	150.2
4	Croatia	217.4	17	Nicaragua	149.1
5	Laos	214.1	18	Brazil	148.9
6	Jamaica	212.6	19	Kazakhstan	145.7
7	Central African Rep.	206.0	20	Albania	143.7
8	Zimbabwe	202.9	21	Bulgaria	139.2
9	Latvia	185.4	22	Bosnia & Herz.	138.6
10	Serbia	184.7	23	Gambia, The	137.7
11	Romania	182.5	24	Hungary	136.0
12	Turkey	158.6	25	Pakistan	134.6
13	Ethiopia	157.9	26	Tanzania	132.5

Highest debt service ratio[b]

Average, %, 2012

1	Sudan	65.1	15	Chile	20.1
2	Hungary	37.1	16	Armenia	19.4
3	Ukraine	35.4	17	Cyprus	18.9
4	Serbia	33.5	18	Israel	17.8
5	Latvia	31.9	19	Mexico	16.8
6	Croatia	31.6		Zimbabwe	16.8
7	Romania	30.6	21	Indonesia	16.6
8	Lithuania	27.6	22	Brazil	15.4
9	Turkey	26.0	23	Cuba	14.6
10	Jamaica	25.9	24	Bosnia & Herz.	13.8
11	Kazakhstan	24.7	25	Argentina	13.3
12	Georgia	22.4		Costa Rica	13.3
13	Poland	21.7	27	Moldova	13.1
14	Colombia	21.3			

Household debt[c]

As % of gross disposable income, 2012

1	Denmark	321.1	14	Japan	128.8
2	Netherlands	311.5	15	Finland	123.2
3	Ireland	230.4	16	United States	114.9
4	Norway	213.7	17	Greece	109.7
5	Switzerland	186.4	18	France	104.5
6	Australia	180.0	19	Belgium	98.4
7	Sweden	172.0	20	Estonia	97.0
8	South Korea	163.8	21	Italy	94.4
9	Luxembourg	153.4	22	Germany	93.2
10	United Kingdom	150.3	23	Austria	92.8
11	Portugal	147.6	24	Czech Republic	66.7
12	Canada[d]	146.5	25	Hungary	62.6
13	Spain	140.9	26	Poland	58.9

b Debt service is the sum of interest and principal repayments (amortisation) due on outstanding foreign debt. The debt service ratio is debt service as a percentage of exports of goods, non-factor services, primary income and workers' remittances.
c OECD countries. d 2010

Aid

Largest recipients of bilateral and multilateral aid
$m, 2012

1	Afghanistan	6,725	24	Haiti	1,275
2	Vietnam	4,116	25	Malawi	1,175
3	Ethiopia	3,261	26	Burkina Faso	1,159
4	Turkey	3,033	27	Serbia	1,090
5	Congo-Kinshasa	2,859	28	Senegal	1,080
6	Tanzania	2,832	29	South Africa	1,067
7	Kenya	2,654	30	Tunisia	1,017
8	Côte d'Ivoire	2,636	31	Mali	1,001
9	Bangladesh	2,152		Zimbabwe	1,001
10	Mozambique	2,097	33	Somalia	999
11	Pakistan	2,019	34	Sudan	983
12	West Bank & Gaza	2,001	35	Zambia	958
13	Nigeria	1,916	36	Niger	902
14	Ghana	1,808	37	Rwanda	879
15	Egypt	1,807	38	Cambodia	807
16	Syria	1,672	39	Nepal	770
17	India	1,668	40	Ukraine	769
18	Uganda	1,655	41	Colombia	764
19	South Sudan	1,578	42	Lebanon	710
20	Morocco	1,480	43	Yemen	709
21	Jordan	1,417	44	Papua New Guinea	665
22	Iraq	1,301	45	Georgia	662
23	Brazil	1,288	46	Bolivia	659

Largest recipients of bilateral and multilateral aid
$ per head, 2012

1	West Bank & Gaza	494.5	25	Papua New Guinea	92.8
2	Kosovo	314.3	26	Armenia	91.9
3	Timor-Leste	233.9	27	Nicaragua	88.9
4	Afghanistan	225.5	28	Kyrgyzstan	84.7
5	Jordan	224.3	29	Mozambique	83.2
6	Montenegro	166.2	30	Senegal	78.7
7	Lebanon	160.5	31	Gambia, The	77.5
	Mongolia	160.5	32	Rwanda	76.7
9	Serbia	150.9	33	Syria	74.6
10	Bosnia & Herz.	149.0	34	Sierra Leone	74.1
11	Georgia	146.8		Suriname	74.1
12	South Sudan	145.6	36	Malawi	73.8
13	Lesotho	137.8	37	Zimbabwe	73.0
14	Mauritius	137.7	38	Honduras	72.0
15	Liberia	136.3	39	Swaziland	71.6
16	Moldova	132.9	40	Ghana	71.3
17	Côte d'Ivoire	132.8	41	Macedonia	70.7
18	Haiti	125.3	42	Burkina Faso	70.4
19	Fiji	122.7	43	Zambia	68.0
20	Namibia	117.2	44	Mali	67.4
21	Albania	108.0	45	Bolivia	62.7
22	Mauritania	107.6	46	Kenya	61.5
23	Somalia	98.0		Laos	61.5
24	Tunisia	94.4	48	Tanzania	59.3

Largest bilateral and multilateral donors[a]
$m, 2012

1	United States	30,687	15	Belgium	2,315
2	United Kingdom	13,892	16	Spain	2,037
3	Germany	12,939	17	South Korea	1,597
4	France	12,028	18	Finland	1,320
5	Japan	10,605	19	Saudi Arabia	1,299
6	Canada	5,650	20	Austria	1,106
7	Netherlands	5,523	21	United Arab Emirates	1,070
8	Australia	5,403	22	Ireland	808
9	Sweden	5,240	23	Portugal	581
10	Norway	4,753	24	Russia	465
11	Switzerland	3,045	25	New Zealand	449
12	Italy	2,737	26	Poland	421
13	Denmark	2,693	27	Luxembourg	399
14	Turkey	2,533	28	Greece	327

Largest bilateral and multilateral donors[a]
% of GDP, 2012

1	Sweden	1.00	15	Canada	0.31
2	Norway	0.95	16	Austria	0.28
3	Denmark	0.86		United Arab Emirates	0.28
4	Netherlands	0.72	18	Portugal	0.27
5	Luxembourg	0.70	19	New Zealand	0.26
6	United Kingdom	0.56	20	Malta	0.21
7	Finland	0.53	21	Iceland	0.19
8	Belgium	0.48		United States	0.19
	Switzerland	0.48	23	Japan	0.18
10	France	0.46		Saudi Arabia	0.18
11	Germany	0.38	24	Spain	0.15
	Ireland	0.38	25	Italy	0.14
13	Australia	0.35		South Korea	0.14
14	Turkey	0.32	28	Greece	0.13

Largest financial resource donors[b]
% of GNI, 2012

1	Sweden	2.63	14	Japan	0.80
2	United Kingdom	2.57	15	Denmark	0.74
3	Netherlands	2.56	16	Finland	0.61
4	Switzerland	2.33	17	Ireland	0.56
5	Australia	1.46		Italy	0.56
6	Austria	1.15	19	Belgium	0.55
7	France	1.11	20	New Zealand	0.39
8	South Korea	1.09	21	Greece	0.36
9	Canada	1.04	22	Portugal	0.23
10	Germany	1.00	23	Iceland	0.22
11	Luxembourg	0.99	24	Spain	0.15
12	United States	0.98	25	Czech Republic	0.12
13	Norway	0.88			

a China also provides aid, but does not disclose amounts.
b Including other financial resources to developing countries and multinational organisations.

Industry and services

Largest industrial output
$bn, 2012

1	China	3,728	23	Netherlands	168
2	United States[a]	2,812	24	Switzerland	160
3	Japan[a]	1,534	25	Thailand	159
4	Germany	936	26	Iraq	133
5	Russia	617	27	Argentina	131
6	Canada	512		Poland[b]	131
7	Brazil	503	29	Colombia	127
8	India	452	30	Malaysia	125
	United Kingdom	452	31	Nigeria	121
10	Saudi Arabia	445	32	Sweden	116
11	France	440	33	Austria	102
12	Italy	437	34	Egypt	99
13	Indonesia	412	35	South Africa	98
14	Mexico	408	36	Algeria	96
15	Australia	404	37	Belgium	94
16	South Korea	398	38	Chile	89
17	Taiwan[a]	364	39	Philippines	78
18	Spain	314	40	Kazakhstan	76
19	United Arab Emirates	232	41	Singapore	69
20	Venezuela[b]	191	42	Angola	68
21	Norway	188	43	Czech Republic	66
22	Turkey	187	44	Peru	65

Highest growth in industrial output
Average annual % increase in real terms, 2004–12

1	Liberia	22.7	11	Chad[e]	9.6
2	Timor-Leste[c]	21.7	12	Panama	9.3
3	Azerbaijan	18.9	13	Afghanistan	8.7
4	Laos	14.3	14	Belarus	8.6
5	Ghana[d]	12.9		Cambodia	8.6
6	Togo[c]	12.0	16	Uganda	8.4
7	Ethiopia	11.5	17	Tanzania	8.3
8	China	11.4	18	Congo-Kinshasa	8.1
9	Angola	10.2	19	Bangladesh	7.9
10	Rwanda	9.8	20	Sri Lanka	7.8

Lowest growth in industrial output
Average annual % change in real terms, 2004–12

1	Palau	-8.1	11	Brunei	-1.5
2	Greece[e]	-5.4		Denmark	-1.5
3	Bermuda	-3.8		Portugal	-1.5
4	Eritrea[f]	-2.4	14	Croatia	-1.3
5	Barbados	-2.3		Italy	-1.3
	Jamaica	-2.3	16	Norway	-1.1
7	Luxembourg	-2.2	17	Botswana	-1.0
8	Spain	-1.7	18	Canada[g]	-0.8
	United Kingdom	-1.7		Moldova	-0.8
10	New Zealand[f]	-1.7	20	Latvia[g]	-0.7

a 2011 b 2010 c 2004–11 d 2006–12 e 2005–12 f 2004–09 g 2004–10

Largest manufacturing output
$bn, 2012

1	China[a]	1,925	21	Argentina	84
2	United States[b]	1,801	22	Poland[a]	76
3	Japan[b]	1,091	23	Malaysia	74
4	Germany	687	24	Saudi Arabia	72
5	South Korea	316		Sweden	72
6	Italy	282	26	Austria	65
7	Russia	260	27	Belgium	55
8	Brazil	254	28	Singapore	54
9	India	243	29	Philippines	51
10	France	233		Venezuela[a]	51
11	United Kingdom	220	31	Puerto Rico	48
12	Indonesia	210	32	Colombia	44
13	Mexico	198		Czech Republic	44
14	Canada	164		Ireland	44
15	Spain	162	35	South Africa	43
16	Thailand	124	36	Egypt	37
17	Turkey	123	37	United Arab Emirates	34
18	Switzerland	113	38	Finland	33
19	Australia	108	39	Norway	32
20	Netherlands	87	40	Pakistan	31

Largest services output
$bn, 2012

1	United States[b]	10,969	27	Austria	249
2	Japan[b]	4,257	28	South Africa	238
3	China	3,669	29	Hong Kong	237
4	Germany	2,105	30	Nigeria	231
5	France	1,854	31	Denmark	208
6	United Kingdom	1,726	32	Singapore	190
7	Italy	1,329	33	Colombia	189
8	Brazil	1,311	34	Greece	176
9	Canada	1,216	35	Thailand	162
10	Russia	1,031	36	Venezuela[a]	154
11	Australia	997	37	Chile	152
12	India	971		Finland	152
13	Spain	869	39	Malaysia	150
14	Mexico	692	40	United Arab Emirates	149
15	South Korea	592	41	Philippines	143
16	Netherlands	512	42	Portugal	137
17	Turkey	442	43	Ireland	135
18	Switzerland	433	44	Egypt	117
19	Indonesia	339	45	Pakistan	116
20	Sweden	337	46	Peru	109
21	Belgium	334	47	Kazakhstan	107
	Taiwan	334	48	Czech Republic	106
23	Poland[a]	268	49	Ukraine	92
24	Argentina	259	50	Algeria	84
25	Norway	254	51	Romania	77
26	Saudi Arabia	250	52	Iraq	73

a 2010   b 2011

Agriculture

Largest agricultural output
$bn, 2012

1	China	830		Italy	36
2	India	302	17	Australia	35
3	United States[a]	174	18	Malaysia	31
4	Indonesia	127		Vietnam	31
5	Nigeria	102	20	Philippines	30
6	Brazil	100		Spain	30
7	Japan[a]	68	22	Canada	27
8	Russia	66		South Korea	27
9	Turkey	63	24	Germany	26
10	Pakistan	53	25	Colombia	22
11	France	46	26	Venezuela[b]	21
12	Thailand	45	27	Bangladesh	20
13	Mexico	41	28	Ethiopia	19
14	Argentina	39	29	Algeria	18
15	Egypt	36	30	Saudi Arabia	16

Most economically dependent on agriculture
% of GDP from agriculture, 2012

1	Sierra Leone[a]	56.7	14	Benin[b]	32.4
2	Chad	55.8	15	Togo[a]	31.3
3	Central African Rep.	54.3	16	Mozambique	30.3
4	Ethiopia	48.8	17	Malawi[a]	30.2
5	Congo-Kinshasa	44.9	18	Kenya	29.9
6	Guinea-Bissau	43.7	19	Laos	28.0
7	Burundi	40.6	20	Sudan	27.7
8	Liberia	38.8	21	Tanzania	27.6
9	Niger	38.2	22	Tajikistan	26.5
10	Nepal	37.0	23	Afghanistan	24.6
11	Cambodia	35.6	24	Pakistan	24.4
12	Nigeria	33.1	25	North Korea	23.4
13	Rwanda	33.0		Uganda[a]	23.4

Least economically dependent on agriculture
% of GDP from agriculture, 2012

1	Macau[a]	0.0		Japan[a]	1.2
	Singapore	0.0		United States[a]	1.2
3	Hong Kong	0.1	16	Taiwan	1.4
4	Luxembourg[a]	0.3	17	Austria[b]	1.5
5	Trinidad & Tobago	0.6		Barbados	1.5
6	Belgium[b]	0.7	19	Canada	1.6
	Brunei	0.7		Norway[b]	1.6
	Puerto Rico[a]	0.7	21	France[c]	1.8
	United Kingdom[b]	0.7		Sweden[b]	1.8
10	Bermuda	0.8	23	Italy[b]	1.9
11	Germany[b]	0.9		Malta[b]	1.9
	United Arab Emirates[b]	0.9	25	Netherlands[b]	2.0
13	Denmark[b]	1.2	26	Bahamas	2.1

a 2011   b 2010   c 2009

Highest growth in agriculture
Average annual % increase in real terms, 2004–12

1	Angola	12.8	10	Afghanistan	6.1
2	Equatorial Guineaa	9.5		Uzbekistan	6.1
3	Liberia	8.8	12	Cambodia	6.0
4	Ethiopia	8.3	13	Nigeria	5.7
5	Mozambique	7.6		Sudan	5.7
6	Tajikistan	7.1	15	Burkina Faso	5.5
7	Sierra Leonea	6.4	16	Central African Rep.	5.4
8	Algeriaa	6.2		Mauritania	5.4
	Mali	6.2			

Lowest growth in agriculture
Average annual % change in real terms, 2004–12

1	Luxembourg	-5.6	9	Zimbabwe	-3.7
2	United Arab Emiratesa	-5.3	10	Bulgaria	-3.4
3	Denmark	-4.4	11	Hong Kong	-3.3
4	Bahamas	-4.3	12	Maltab	-3.1
	Moldova	-4.3	13	Greecec	-3.0
6	Romania	-4.2	14	Seychelles	-2.2
7	Hungaryb	-4.1	15	Samoa	-1.9
8	Czech Republic	-4.0	16	Germany	-1.8

Biggest producers
'000 tonnes, 2012

Cereals

1	China	540,830	6	France	70,982
2	United States	356,962	7	Russia	68,767
3	India	286,500	8	Canada	50,067
4	Brazil	89,908	9	Vietnam	48,467
5	Indonesia	88,422	10	Ukraine	45,740

Meat

1	China	79,429	6	India	6,292
2	United States	42,548	7	Mexico	6,079
3	Brazil	24,961	8	France	5,690
4	Germany	8,194	9	Spain	5,439
5	Russia	8,137	10	Argentina	4,662

Fruit

1	China	137,067	6	Philippines	16,371
2	India	71,073	7	Mexico	15,918
3	Brazil	38,369	8	Turkey	14,975
4	United States	26,549	9	Spain	13,996
5	Indonesia	17,744	10	Italy	13,889

Vegetables

1	China	573,935	5	Iran	23,486
2	India	109,141	6	Egypt	19,825
3	United States	35,948	7	Russia	16,084
4	Turkey	27,819	8	Mexico	13,599

a 2004–11 b 2004–10 c 2005–12 d 2004–09

Commodities

Wheat

Top 10 producers, 2012–13 '000 tonnes		Top 10 consumers, 2012–13 '000 tonnes	
1 EU27	131,571	1 China	122,040
2 China	120,580	2 EU27	115,700
3 India	94,880	3 India	84,190
4 United States	61,755	4 United States	38,319
5 Russia	37,717	5 Russia	33,410
6 Canada	27,205	6 Pakistan	23,420
7 Pakistan	23,300	7 Egypt	18,840
8 Australia	22,461	8 Turkey	18,550
9 Turkey	17,500	9 Iran	16,260
10 Ukraine	15,761	10 Ukraine	11,850

Rice[a]

Top 10 producers, 2012–13 '000 tonnes		Top 10 consumers, 2012–13 '000 tonnes	
1 China	143,000	1 China	144,000
2 India	105,240	2 India	94,000
3 Indonesia	36,550	3 Indonesia	38,127
4 Bangladesh	33,820	4 Bangladesh	34,474
5 Vietnam	27,700	5 Vietnam	20,500
6 Thailand	20,200	6 Philippines	12,850
7 Myanmar	11,715	7 Thailand	10,600
8 Philippines	11,428	8 Myanmar	10,400
9 Brazil	7,990	9 Japan	8,250
10 Japan	7,756	10 Brazil	7,850

Sugar[b]

Top 10 producers, 2012 '000 tonnes		Top 10 consumers, 2012 '000 tonnes	
1 Brazil	39,740	1 India	24,880
2 India	29,190	2 EU27	19,540
3 EU27	18,310	3 China	15,340
4 China	12,990	4 Brazil	12,910
5 Thailand	10,370	5 United States	10,340
6 United States	8,170	6 Russia	5,650
7 Mexico	5,800	7 Indonesia	5,570
8 Russia	5,260	8 Pakistan	4,880
9 Pakistan	5,150	9 Mexico	4,510
10 Australia	3,870	10 Egypt	3,190

Coarse grains[c]

Top 5 producers, 2012–13 '000 tonnes		Top 5 consumers, 2012–13 '000 tonnes	
1 United States	286,075	1 United States	276,310
2 China	213,136	2 China	214,879
3 EU27	141,899	3 EU27	147,470
4 Brazil	84,761	4 Brazil	58,069
5 India	41,550	5 India	36,400

Tea

Top 10 producers, 2012
'000 tonnes

1	China	1,700
2	India	1,000
3	Kenya	369
4	Sri Lanka	330
5	Turkey	225
6	Vietnam	217
7	Iran	158
8	Indonesia	150
9	Argentina	100
10	Japan	86

Top 10 consumers, 2012
'000 tonnes

1	China	1,482
2	India	939
3	Turkey	231
4	Russia	173
5	Pakistan	127
6	United Kingdom	125
7	United States	123
8	Japan	121
9	Egypt	95
10	Iran	80

Coffee

Top 10 producers, 2012–13
'000 tonnes

1	Brazil	3,050
2	Vietnam	1,320
3	Indonesia	764
4	Colombia	570
5	Ethiopia	486
6	India	315
7	Honduras	294
8	Peru	248
9	Mexico	234
10	Uganda	192

Top 10 consumers, 2012–13
'000 tonnes

1	United States	1,361
2	Brazil	1,220
3	Germany	554
4	Japan	417
5	France	349
6	Italy	345
7	Russia	226
8	Indonesia	220
9	Canada	210
10	Spain	206

Cocoa

Top 10 producers, 2012–13
'000 tonnes

1	Côte d'Ivoire	1,449
2	Ghana	835
3	Indonesia	420
4	Cameroon	225
	Nigeria	225
6	Ecuador	192
7	Brazil	185
8	Peru	69
9	Dominican Rep.	68
10	Colombia	48

Top 10 consumers, 2011–12
'000 tonnes

1	United States	770
2	Germany	330
3	United Kingdom	223
4	France	218
5	Russia	205
6	Brazil	200
7	Japan	160
8	Spain	107
9	Canada	89
10	Italy	85

a Milled.
b Raw.
c Includes: maize (corn), barley, sorghum, oats, rye, millet, triticale and other.

Copper

Top 10 producers[a], 2012		*Top 10 consumers[b], 2012*	
'000 tonnes		*'000 tonnes*	
1 Chile	5,434	1 China	8,840
2 China	1,642	2 United States	1,758
3 Peru	1,299	3 Germany	1,107
4 United States	1,196	4 Japan	985
5 Australia	914	5 South Korea	717
6 Zambia	782	6 Italy	570
7 Russia	720	7 Russia	494
8 Congo-Kinshasa	608	8 India	456
9 Canada	579	9 Brazil	432
10 Mexico	500	Taiwan	432

Lead

Top 10 producers[a], 2012		*Top 10 consumers[b], 2012*	
'000 tonnes		*'000 tonnes*	
1 China	2,838	1 China	4,673
2 Australia	622	2 United States	1,500
3 United States	345	3 India	524
4 Peru	249	4 South Korea	429
5 Mexico	238	5 Germany	381
6 Russia	138	6 Japan	273
7 India	115	7 Spain	244
8 Bolivia	81	8 Brazil	238
9 Sweden	64	9 United Kingdom	229
10 Canada	61	10 Italy	195

Zinc

Top 10 producers[a], 2012		*Top 10 consumers[c], 2012*	
'000 tonnes		*'000 tonnes*	
1 China	4,930	1 China	5,396
2 Australia	1,542	2 United States	904
3 Peru	1,281	3 India	561
4 United States	738	4 South Korea	557
5 India	725	5 Japan	479
6 Mexico	660	6 Germany	474
7 Canada	612	7 Italy	247
8 Bolivia	390	8 Belgium	239
9 Kazakhstan	371	Brazil	239
10 Ireland	340	10 Russia	231

Tin

Top 5 producers[a], 2012		*Top 5 consumers[b], 2012*	
'000 tonnes		*'000 tonnes*	
1 China	115.9	1 China	176.4
2 Indonesia	90.0	2 United States	30.7
3 Peru	26.1	3 Japan	27.7
4 Bolivia	19.7	4 Germany	17.6
5 Brazil	13.7	5 South Korea	16.2

Nickel

Top 10 producers[a], 2012
'000 tonnes

1	Indonesia	622.2
2	Philippines	322.4
3	Russia	268.7
4	Australia	244.0
5	Canada	204.5
6	New Caledonia	131.7
7	China	93.3
8	Brazil	89.6
9	Cuba	68.3
10	Colombia	51.6

Top 10 consumers[b], 2012
'000 tonnes

1	China	837.3
2	Japan	159.3
3	United States	125.6
4	South Korea	107.8
5	Germany	88.8
6	Italy	64.7
7	Taiwan	56.8
8	India	33.0
9	Spain	32.5
10	South Africa	32.0

Aluminium

Top 10 producers[d], 2012
'000 tonnes

1	China	20,267
2	Russia	4,024
3	Canada	2,781
4	United States	2,070
5	Australia	1,864
6	United Arab Emirates	1,861
7	India	1,714
8	Brazil	1,436
9	Norway	1,202
10	Bahrain	890

Top 10 consumers[e], 2012
'000 tonnes

1	China	20,274
2	United States	4,845
3	Germany	2,086
4	Japan	1,982
5	India	1,690
6	South Korea	1,278
7	Brazil	1,021
8	Turkey	925
9	Italy	754
10	Russia	685

Precious metals

Gold [a]
Top 10 producers, 2012
tonnes

1	China	403.1
2	Australia	253.0
3	United States	234.9
4	Russia	182.6
5	Peru	161.8
6	South Africa	154.2
7	Canada	105.3
8	Mexico	102.8
9	Ghana	98.6
10	Uzbekistan	73.2

Silver [a]
Top 10 producers, 2012
tonnes

1	Mexico	5,358
2	China	3,639
3	Peru	3,481
4	Australia	1,728
5	Russia	1,400
6	Poland	1,280
7	Bolivia	1,207
8	Chile	1,151
9	United States	1,060
10	Kazakhstan	963

Platinum
Top 3 producers, 2012
tonnes

1	South Africa	127.2
2	Russia	24.9
3	United States/Canada	9.6

Palladium
Top 3 producers, 2012
tonnes

1	Russia	89.9
2	South Africa	72.2
3	United States/Canada	27.8

a Mine production.   b Refined consumption.   c Slab consumption.
d Primary refined production.   e Primary refined consumption.

Rubber (natural and synthetic)

Top 10 producers, 2012		*Top 10 consumers, 2012*	
'000 tonnes		*'000 tonnes*	
1 China	4,592	1 China	8,899
2 Thailand	3,879	2 EU28	3,430
3 Indonesia	3,063	3 United States	2,716
4 EU28	2,597	4 Japan	1,676
5 United States	2,311	5 India	1,427
6 Japan	1,627	6 Thailand	896
7 Russia	1,476	7 Brazil	846
8 South Korea	1,436	8 Russia	818
9 India	1,029	9 Indonesia	794
10 Malaysia	1,028	10 Germany	793

Raw wool

Top 12 producers[a], 2012, '000 tonnes

1 China	400	7 Argentina	55
2 Australia	362	Russia	55
3 New Zealand	165	9 Turkey	51
4 United Kingdom	68	10 India	46
5 Iran	62	11 Pakistan	43
6 Morocco	56	12 South Africa	40

Cotton

Top 10 producers, 2012–13		*Top 10 consumers, 2012–13*	
'000 tonnes		*'000 tonnes*	
1 China	7,300	1 China	8,290
2 India	6,095	2 India	4,845
3 United States	3,770	3 Pakistan	2,416
4 Pakistan	2,204	4 Turkey	1,350
5 Brazil	1,261	5 Brazil	887
6 Australia	1,002	6 Bangladesh	800
7 Uzbekistan	1,000	7 United States	751
8 Turkey	858	8 Indonesia	493
9 Turkmenistan	335	9 Vietnam	412
10 Burkina Faso	260	10 Thailand	360

Major oil seeds[b]

Top 5 producers, 2012–13		*Top 5 consumers, 2012–13*	
'000 tonnes		*'000 tonnes*	
1 United States	92,370	1 China	116,365
2 Brazil	84,055	2 United States	57,237
3 Argentina	52,360	3 EU25	46,745
4 China	50,390	4 Brazil	40,090
5 India	33,270	5 Argentina	39,220

Oil[c]

Top 10 producers, 2013		*Top 10 consumers, 2013*	
'000 barrels per day		*'000 barrels per day*	
1 Saudi Arabia[d]	11,525	1 United States	18,887
2 Russia	10,788	2 China	10,756
3 United States	10,003	3 Japan	4,551
4 China	4,180	4 India	3,727
5 Canada	3,948	5 Russia	3,313
6 United Arab Emirates[d]	3,646	6 Saudi Arabia[d]	3,075
7 Iran[d]	3,558	7 Brazil	2,973
8 Iraq[d]	3,141	8 South Korea	2,460
9 Kuwait[d]	3,126	9 Canada	2,385
10 Mexico	2,875	10 Germany	2,382

Natural gas

Top 10 producers, 2013		*Top 10 consumers, 2013*	
Billion cubic metres		*Billion cubic metres*	
1 United States	687.6	1 United States	737.2
2 Russia	604.8	2 Russia	413.5
3 Iran[d]	166.6	3 Iran[d]	162.2
4 Qatar[d]	158.5	4 China	161.6
5 Canada	154.8	5 Japan	116.9
6 China	117.1	6 Canada	103.5
7 Norway	108.7	7 Saudi Arabia[d]	103.0
8 Saudi Arabia[d]	103.0	8 Germany	83.6
9 Algeria[d]	78.6	9 Mexico	82.7
10 Indonesia	70.4	10 United Kingdom	73.1

Coal

Top 10 producers, 2013		*Top 10 consumers, 2013*	
Million tonnes oil equivalent		*Million tonnes oil equivalent*	
1 China	1,840.0	1 China	1,925.3
2 United States	500.5	2 United States	455.7
3 Australia	269.1	3 India	324.3
4 Indonesia	258.9	4 Japan	128.6
5 India	228.8	5 Russia	93.5
6 Russia	165.1	6 South Africa	88.2
7 South Africa	144.7	7 South Korea	81.9
8 Kazakhstan	58.4	8 Germany	81.3
9 Poland	57.6	9 Poland	56.1
10 Colombia	55.6	10 Indonesia	54.4

Oil reserves[c]

Top proved reserves, end 2013			
% of world total			
1 Venezuela[d]	17.7	5 Iraq[d]	8.9
2 Saudi Arabia[d]	15.8	6 Kuwait[d]	6.0
3 Canada	10.3	7 United Arab Emirates[d]	5.8
4 Iran[d]	9.3	8 Russia	5.5

a Greasy basis. b Soybeans, sunflower seed, cottonseed, groundnuts and rapeseed.
c Includes crude oil, shale oil, oil sands and natural gas liquids. d Opec member.

Energy

Largest producers
Million tonnes of oil equivalent, 2011

1	China	2,433	16	United Arab Emirates	190
2	United States	1,785	17	South Africa	163
3	Russia	1,315	18	Kazakhstan	160
4	Saudi Arabia	602	19	Kuwait	154
5	India	541	20	Algeria	146
6	Canada	409	21	Iraq	142
7	Indonesia	395	22	France	136
8	Iran	354	23	United Kingdom	130
9	Australia	297	24	Germany	124
10	Nigeria	257	25	Colombia	121
11	Brazil	249	26	Angola	92
12	Mexico	228	27	Egypt	88
13	Qatar	211	28	Ukraine	85
14	Venezuela	201	29	Malaysia	84
15	Norway	195	30	Argentina	77

Largest consumers
Million tonnes of oil equivalent, 2011

1	China	2,728	16	Italy	167
2	United States	2,191	17	South Africa	141
3	India	749	18	Spain	126
4	Russia	731		Ukraine	126
5	Japan	461	20	Australia	123
6	Germany	312	21	Thailand	119
7	Brazil	270	22	Nigeria	118
8	South Korea	260	23	Turkey	112
9	France	253	24	Poland	101
10	Canada	252	25	Pakistan	85
11	Iran	212	26	Argentina	80
12	Indonesia	209	27	Egypt	78
13	United Kingdom	188		Kazakhstan	78
14	Saudi Arabia	187	29	Netherlands	77
15	Mexico	186	30	Malaysia	76

Energy efficiency[a]
GDP per unit of energy use, 2011

Most efficient

1	Hong Kong	21.2
2	Colombia	13.2
3	Peru	12.9
4	Ireland	12.6
5	Botswana	12.3
	Switzerland	12.3
7	Panama	12.1
8	Dominican Rep.	11.8
9	Albania	11.6
10	Malta	11.2

Least efficient

1	Congo-Kinshasa	0.9
2	Trinidad & Tobago	1.5
3	Turkmenistan	1.7
4	Uzbekistan	1.8
5	Iceland	1.9
6	Mozambique	2.0
7	Togo	2.1
8	Ukraine	2.3
	Zambia	2.3
10	Ethiopia	2.4
11	Kazakhstan	2.5

a 2005 PPP $ per kg of oil equivalent.

Net energy importers
% of commercial energy use, 2011

Highest			Lowest		
1	Hong Kong	100	1	Congo-Brazzaville	-905
2	Lebanon	97	2	Gabon	-615
	Luxembourg	97	3	Norway	-594
	Singapore	97	4	Angola	-579
5	Cyprus	96	5	Qatar	-535
	Jordan	96	6	Mongolia	-435
	Moldova	96	7	Brunei	-388
	Morocco	96	8	Azerbaijan	-377
9	Malta	94	9	Kuwait	-375
10	Dominican Rep.	89	10	Colombia	-281
	Japan	89	11	Iraq	-253
12	Ireland	86	12	Algeria	-248

Largest consumption per head
Kg of oil equivalent, 2011

1	Iceland	17,964	12	Saudi Arabia	6,738
2	Qatar	17,419	13	Singapore	6,452
3	Trinidad & Tobago	15,691	14	Finland	6,449
4	Kuwait	10,408	15	Norway	5,681
5	Brunei	9,427	16	Australia	5,505
6	Oman	8,356	17	Belgium	5,349
7	Luxembourg	8,046	18	South Korea	5,232
8	United Arab Emirates	7,407	19	Sweden	5,190
9	Bahrain	7,353	20	Russia	5,113
10	Canada	7,303	21	Turkmenistan	4,839
11	United States	7,032	22	Kazakhstan	4,717

Sources of electricity
% of total, 2011

Oil			Gas		
1	Benin	99.4	1	Bahrain	100.0
	Eritrea	99.4		Qatar	100.0
	Malta	99.4		Turkmenistan	100.0
4	Cyprus	96.4	4	Trinidad & Tobago	99.7
5	Lebanon	95.1	5	Brunei	99.0

Hydropower			Nuclear power		
1	Albania	100.0	1	France	79.4
	Paraguay	100.0	2	Slovakia	54.5
3	Mozambique	99.9	3	Belgium	54.2
	Nepal	99.9	4	Ukraine	46.3
5	Zambia	99.7	5	Hungary	43.6

Coal		
1	Botswana	100.0
2	Kosovo	97.8
3	Mongolia	95.1
4	South Africa	93.8
5	Estonia	87.9

Workers of the world

Labour-force participation

% of working-age population[a] working or looking for work, 2013 or latest

Highest			Lowest		
1	Tanzania	89.2	1	Timor-Leste	38.1
2	Madagascar	88.7	2	Moldova	40.0
3	Qatar	86.7	3	Jordan	41.3
4	Equatorial Guinea	86.6	4	Iraq	42.2
5	Zimbabwe	86.4	5	Puerto Rico	42.4
6	Rwanda	86.0	6	Algeria	43.2
7	Eritrea	84.7	7	Syria	43.6
8	Mozambique	84.4	8	Iran	44.8
9	Ethiopia	83.8	9	Bosnia & Herz.	45.3
10	Burkina Faso	83.5	10	Lebanon	47.2
11	Nepal	83.4	11	Tunisia	47.5
12	Malawi	83.0	12	Afghanistan	47.9
13	Burundi	82.5	13	Morocco	48.5
	Cambodia	82.5		Yemen	48.5
15	Togo	80.9	15	Egypt	49.0
16	Zambia	79.4		Italy	49.0
17	United Arab Emirates	79.3	17	Turkey	49.4
18	Chad	78.7	18	Montenegro	50.0
19	Myanmar	78.6	19	Croatia	51.3
20	North Korea	78.1	20	Hungary	51.8
21	Laos	77.6		South Africa	51.8
	Uganda	77.6	22	Malta	52.2
23	Gambia, The	77.5	23	Serbia	52.3
24	Vietnam	77.2	24	Martinique	52.6
25	Botswana	76.7	25	Belgium	53.0
26	Senegal	76.5	26	Bulgaria	53.1
27	Peru	76.1		Libya	53.1
28	Bahamas	74.1	28	Greece	53.2

Most male workforce

Highest % men in workforce
2012

1	Qatar	88.4
2	Saudi Arabia	85.8
3	Syria	84.9
4	Oman	84.5
	United Arab Emirates	84.5
6	Afghanistan	83.7
7	Algeria	82.9
8	Iraq	82.5
9	Iran	81.8
	Jordan	81.8
11	Bahamas	80.5
12	Pakistan	78.0
13	Lebanon	76.4
14	Kuwait	76.2
15	Egypt	75.8
16	India	74.8

Most female workforce

Highest % women in workforce
2012

1	Mozambique	53.1
2	Rwanda	52.4
3	Martinique	52.1
4	Burundi	51.4
5	Malawi	51.3
6	Timor-Leste	51.1
7	Nepal	50.8
8	Guadeloupe	50.6
9	Lithuania	50.5
10	Laos	50.1
	Latvia	50.1
12	Cambodia	50.0
	Ghana	50.0
14	Congo-Kinshasa	49.8
	Myanmar	49.8
16	Tajikistan	49.7

a Aged 15 and over.

Highest rate of unemployment
% of labour force[a], 2012 or latest

1	Macedonia	31.0	25	Sudan	14.8
	Mauritania	31.0	26	Albania	14.7
3	Réunion	28.5		Ireland	14.7
4	Bosnia & Herz.	28.2	28	Slovakia	13.9
5	Lesotho	26.5	29	Jamaica	13.7
6	Spain	25.2	30	Bahamas	13.6
7	South Africa	25.0	31	Lithuania	13.2
8	Greece	24.2	32	Iran	13.1
9	Guadeloupe	22.9		Zambia	13.1
10	Swaziland	22.5	34	Dominican Rep.	13.0
11	Martinique	21.0	35	Tunisia	12.8
12	Gabon	20.3	36	Suriname	12.7
13	Montenegro	19.6	37	Bulgaria	12.3
	Serbia	19.6	38	Jordan	12.2
15	Argentina	18.5	39	Egypt	11.9
16	Botswana	17.7	40	Cyprus	11.8
17	Yemen	17.6	41	Barbados	11.6
18	Namibia	16.7	42	Tajikistan	11.5
19	Puerto Rico	15.9	43	Turkmenistan	11.3
20	Croatia	15.8		Uzbekistan	11.3
21	Portugal	15.6	45	Hungary	10.9
22	Iraq	15.1	46	Italy	10.7
23	Georgia	15.0	47	Colombia	10.4
24	Latvia	14.9			

Highest rate of youth unemployment
% of labour force aged 15–24[a], 2012 or latest

1	Bosnia & Herz.	57.5	23	Namibia	34.2
2	Martinique	56.2	24	Slovakia	34.0
3	Greece	54.8	25	Suriname	33.4
4	Spain	54.3	26	Jamaica	32.9
5	Réunion	54.2	27	Iraq	32.1
6	Macedonia	53.8	28	Botswana	31.7
7	Guadeloupe	52.0	29	Jordan	31.3
	South Africa	52.0	30	Puerto Rico	30.4
9	Serbia	45.9	31	Ireland	30.3
10	Mauritania	45.3	32	Bahamas	29.3
11	Croatia	44.2		Tunisia	29.3
12	Guinea-Bissau	42.0	34	Iran	28.9
13	Swaziland	41.9	35	Latvia	28.4
14	Montenegro	41.3	36	Bulgaria	28.2
15	Armenia	38.3	37	Hungary	28.1
16	Portugal	37.7	38	Saudi Arabia	27.8
17	Gabon	36.8	39	Bahrain	27.5
18	Lesotho	35.9	40	Cyprus	26.8
19	Egypt	35.7	41	Barbados	26.4
20	Georgia	35.5		Poland	26.4
21	Italy	35.3	43	Albania	26.3
22	Yemen	34.8		Lithuania	26.3

a ILO definition.

The business world

Global competitiveness
2014

Overall	Government	Business
1 United States	United Arab Emirates	United States
2 Switzerland	Hong Kong	Switzerland
3 Singapore	Switzerland	Hong Kong
4 Hong Kong	Singapore	Ireland
5 Sweden	Qatar	Malaysia
6 Germany	Norway	Norway
7 Canada	New Zealand	Singapore
8 United Arab Emirates	Canada	Sweden
9 Denmark	Australia	Germany
10 Norway	Sweden	Canada
11 Luxembourg	Denmark	Denmark
12 Malaysia	Taiwan	Netherlands
13 Taiwan	Finland	Finland
14 Netherlands	Ireland	Luxembourg
15 Ireland	Malaysia	United Arab Emirates
16 United Kingdom	Germany	Australia
17 Australia	United Kingdom	Taiwan
18 Finland	Netherlands	United Kingdom
19 Qatar	Luxembourg	Japan
20 New Zealand	Kazakhstan	Austria
21 Japan	Chile	Israel
22 Austria	United States	Indonesia
23 China	Estonia	New Zealand
24 Israel	Israel	Qatar
25 Iceland	Indonesia	Thailand
26 South Korea	South Korea	Belgium
27 France	Iceland	Philippines
28 Belgium	Thailand	China
29 Thailand	Latvia	Turkey
30 Estonia	Poland	Chile
31 Chile	Jordan	Iceland
32 Kazakhstan	Lithuania	Estonia
33 Czech Republic	Peru	Kazakhstan
34 Lithuania	China	India
35 Latvia	South Africa	Lithuania
36 Poland	Austria	Poland
37 Indonesia	Russia	France
38 Russia	Czech Republic	Latvia
39 Spain	Turkey	South Korea
40 Turkey	Philippines	Czech Republic
41 Mexico	Mexico	Mexico
42 Philippines	Japan	Spain
43 Portugal	Belgium	Peru
44 India	Bulgaria	Slovakia

Notes: Overall competitiveness of 60 economies is calculated by combining four factors: economic performance, government efficiency, business efficiency and infrastructure. Column 1 is based on more than 300 criteria, using hard data and survey data. Column 2 looks at public finance, fiscal policy, institutional and societal frameworks and business legislation. Column 3 includes productivity, labour market, finance, management practices and attitudes and values.

The business environment

		2014–18 score	2009–13 score	2009–13 ranking
1	Singapore	8.65	8.56	1
2	Switzerland	8.52	8.41	2
3	Hong Kong	8.39	8.34	3
4	Canada	8.30	8.15	7
5	Australia	8.29	8.18	5
6	Sweden	8.26	8.20	4
7	United States	8.25	8.02	8
8	Finland	8.18	7.99	11
	New Zealand	8.18	8.16	6
10	Denmark	8.16	8.01	9
11	Norway	8.01	7.89	13
12	Germany	7.98	7.99	10
13	Chile	7.89	7.81	14
14	Taiwan	7.85	7.68	16
15	Ireland	7.79	7.30	20
16	Netherlands	7.78	7.94	12
17	Belgium	7.69	7.69	15
18	Austria	7.62	7.61	17
19	Malaysia	7.56	7.15	24
20	Israel	7.50	7.17	23
21	Qatar	7.46	7.29	21
22	United Kingdom	7.44	7.41	19
23	Estonia	7.38	7.19	22
	France	7.38	7.47	18
25	Spain	7.36	7.01	26
26	South Korea	7.35	7.04	25
27	Japan	7.33	6.98	27
28	Czech Republic	7.31	6.96	28
29	Poland	7.29	6.87	31
30	United Arab Emirates	7.22	6.95	29
31	Slovakia	7.20	6.94	30
32	Mexico	6.91	6.83	32
33	Slovenia	6.84	6.62	36
34	Thailand	6.78	6.43	38
35	Bahrain	6.76	6.80	33
36	Cyprus	6.73	6.65	34
37	Hungary	6.63	6.63	35
38	Portugal	6.62	6.61	37
39	Costa Rica	6.59	6.17	44
	Latvia	6.59	6.26	43
41	Lithuania	6.58	6.14	45
	Saudi Arabia	6.58	6.33	40
43	Brazil	6.57	6.33	41
44	Kuwait	6.55	6.05	48
	Turkey	6.55	6.35	39

Note: Scores reflect the opportunities for, and hindrances to, the conduct of business, measured by countries' rankings in ten categories including market potential, tax and labour-market policies, infrastructure, skills and the political environment. Scores reflect average and forecast average over given date range.

Business creativity and research

Entrepreneurial activity

Percentage of population aged 18–64 who are either a nascent entrepreneur[a]
or owner-manager of a new business

Highest, 2013		Lowest, 2013	
1 Nigeria	39.9	1 Italy	3.4
Zambia	39.9	2 Hong Kong[c]	3.6
3 Bolivia[b]	38.6	3 Japan	3.7
4 Ecuador	36.0	4 France	4.6
5 Malawi	28.1	5 Tunisia[d]	4.8
6 Ghana	25.8	6 Algeria	4.9
7 Indonesia	25.5	Belgium	4.9
8 Uganda	25.2	Serbia[c]	4.9
9 Chile	24.3	9 Germany	5.0
10 Yemen[c]	24.0	10 Suriname	5.1
11 Colombia	23.7	11 Spain	5.2
12 Peru	23.4	12 Finland	5.3
13 Angola	22.2	13 Denmark[d]	5.4
14 Botswana	20.9	14 Greece	5.5
15 Panama	20.6	15 Russia	5.8
16 Trinidad & Tobago	19.5	16 United Arab Emirates[f]	6.2
17 Philippines	18.5	17 Norway	6.3
18 Namibia[d]	18.2	18 Slovenia	6.5
19 Thailand	17.7	19 Macedonia	6.6
20 New Zealand[e]	17.6	Malaysia	6.6
21 Dominican Rep.[c]	17.5	21 South Korea	6.9
22 Brazil	17.3	22 United Kingdom	7.1
23 Barbados[d]	17.1	23 Czech Republic	7.3
24 Argentina	15.9	24 Egypt[d]	7.8
25 Morocco[c]	15.7	25 Switzerland	8.2
		Taiwan	8.2

Brain drain[g]

Highest, 2013		Lowest, 2013	
1 Myanmar	1.7	1 Qatar	6.0
2 Serbia	1.8	2 Finland	5.8
Venezuela	1.8	Switzerland	5.8
4 Bosnia & Herz.	1.9	4 United States	5.7
Bulgaria	1.9	5 Norway	5.6
Burundi	1.9	6 United Arab Emirates	5.5
Kyrgyzstan	1.9	7 Hong Kong	5.4
Moldova	1.9	8 Germany	5.1
9 Ukraine	2.0	Luxembourg	5.1
10 Algeria	2.1	Singapore	5.1
Mauritania	2.1	Sweden	5.1
Romania	2.1	12 Chile	5.0
Yemen	2.1	United Kingdom	5.0
14 Chad	2.2		

a An individual who has started a new firm which has not paid wages for over three
  months.   b 2010   c 2009   d 2012   e 2005   f 2011
g Scores: 1=talented people leave for other countries; 7=they stay and pursue
  opportunities in the country.

Total expenditure on R&D

% of GDP, 2012 or latest			*$bn, 2012 or latest*	
1	South Korea	4.03	1	United States	453.5
2	Israel	3.93	2	Japan	199.2
3	Finland	3.55	3	China	163.1
4	Sweden	3.41	4	Germany	100.0
5	Japan	3.35	5	France	59.1
6	Taiwan	3.06	6	South Korea	49.2
7	Switzerland	2.99	7	United Kingdom	42.6
8	Denmark	2.98	8	Canada	30.8
9	Germany	2.92	9	Australia	28.3
10	Austria	2.84	10	Italy	25.5
11	Slovenia	2.80	11	Brazil	24.9
12	United States	2.79	12	Russia	22.7
13	Iceland	2.40	13	Sweden	17.8
14	Venezuela	2.37	14	Spain	17.2
15	Australia	2.27	15	India	17.0
	France	2.27	16	Netherlands	16.6
17	Belgium	2.24	17	Switzerland	15.0
18	Estonia	2.19	18	Taiwan	14.6
19	Netherlands	2.16	19	Austria	11.2
20	Singapore	2.04	20	Belgium	10.8
21	China	1.98	21	Israel	10.1
22	Czech Republic	1.88	22	Denmark	9.4
23	United Kingdom	1.73	23	Finland	8.8
24	Ireland	1.72	24	Norway	8.3
25	Canada	1.69	25	Venezuela	7.8
26	Norway	1.65	26	Turkey	6.7

Patents

No. of patents granted by applicant's country of origin, average 2010–12			*No. of patents in force by applicant's country of origin, per 100,000 people, 2012*	
1	Japan	311,726	1	Japan	1,861
2	United States	207,335	2	Switzerland	1,380
3	China	118,360	3	Taiwan	1,372
4	South Korea	95,283	4	South Korea	1,360
5	Germany	73,551	5	Luxembourg	938
6	Taiwan	68,199	6	Finland	759
7	France	36,250	7	Sweden	660
8	Russia	23,454	8	United States	536
9	Italy	18,981	9	Germany	486
10	United Kingdom	18,425	10	Netherlands	474
11	Switzerland	17,946	11	France	436
12	Netherlands	15,145	12	Denmark	431
13	Sweden	11,257	13	Austria	392
14	Canada	10,869	14	Israel	312
15	Finland	6,224	15	Norway	296
16	Australia	5,864	16	Belgium	256
17	Belgium	5,520	17	Canada	249
18	Spain	5,043	18	Iceland	186
19	Austria	4,987	19	Australia	175
20	Denmark	4,244	20	United Kingdom	171

Business costs and foreign direct investment

Office rents

Rent, taxes and operating expenses, $ per sq. ft., Q3 2013

1	London (West End), UK	259.36
2	Hong Kong (Central)	234.30
3	Beijing (Finance Street), China	197.05
4	Beijing (CBD), China	189.67
5	Hong Kong (West Kowloon)	170.42
6	Moscow, Russia	165.05
7	New Delhi (Connaught Place, CBD), India	156.65
8	Tokyo (Marunouchi Otemachi), Japan	154.67
9	London (City), UK	142.71
10	Paris, France	122.10
11	New York (Midtown Manhattan), US	120.65
12	Shanghai (Pudong), China	119.50
13	Rio de Janeiro, Brazil	112.22
14	Shanghai (Puxi), China	111.69
15	Mumbai (Bandra Kurla Complex), India	109.24
16	São Paulo, Brazil	105.11
17	Sydney, Australia	104.39
18	San Francisco (Downtown), US	102.00

Minimum wage

Minimum wage as a ratio of the median wage of full-time workers, 2012

1	Turkey	0.73
2	Chile[a]	0.67
3	France	0.62
4	New Zealand	0.60
	Slovenia	0.60
6	Portugal	0.58
7	Israel	0.57
8	Hungary	0.54
9	Australia	0.53
10	Belgium	0.51
	Latvia	0.51
12	Ireland	0.48
	Lithuania	0.48
14	Netherlands	0.47
	Poland	0.47
	Slovakia	0.47
	United Kingdom	0.47
18	Canada	0.45
	Romania	0.45
20	Spain	0.44

Foreign direct investment[b]

Inflows, $m, 2012			Outflows, $m, 2012		
1	United States	167,620	1	United States	328,869
2	China	121,080	2	Japan	122,551
3	Hong Kong	74,584	3	China	84,220
4	Brazil	65,272	4	Hong Kong	83,985
5	United Kingdom	62,351	5	United Kingdom	71,415
6	Australia	56,959	6	Germany	66,926
7	Singapore	56,651	7	Canada	53,939
8	Russia	51,416	8	Russia	51,058
9	Canada	45,375	9	Switzerland	44,313
10	Chile	30,323	10	France	37,197
11	Ireland	29,318	11	Sweden	33,428
12	Luxembourg	27,878	12	South Korea	32,978
13	Spain	27,750	13	Italy	30,397
14	India	25,543	14	Mexico	25,597
15	France	25,093	15	Singapore	23,080
16	Indonesia	19,853	16	Chile	21,090
17	Colombia	15,823	17	Norway	20,847
18	Kazakhstan	14,022	18	Ireland	18,966
19	Sweden	13,711	19	Luxembourg	17,273

Note: CBD is Central Business District.

a 2011   b Investment in companies in a foreign country.

Business red tape, corruption and piracy

Number of days taken to register a new company

Lowest, 2013		Highest, 2013	
1 New Zealand	0.5	1 Suriname	208
2 Georgia	2.0	2 Venezuela	144
Macedonia	2.0	3 Equatorial Guinea	135
Rwanda	2.0	4 Brazil	108
5 Australia	2.5	5 Cambodia	104
Hong Kong	2.5	6 Brunei	101
Portugal	2.5	Congo-Brazzaville	101
Singapore	2.5	8 Haiti	97
9 Armenia	4.0	9 Timor-Leste	94
Belgium	4.0	10 Laos	92
Netherlands	4.0	11 Zimbabwe	90
12 Albania	4.5	12 Eritrea	84
Iceland	4.5	13 Myanmar	72
Liberia	4.5	14 Angola	66
		Namibia	66
		16 Chad	62

Corruption perceptions index[a]

2013, 100 = least corrupt

Lowest		Highest	
1 Denmark	91	1 Afghanistan	8
New Zealand	91	North Korea	8
3 Finland	89	Somalia	8
Sweden	89	4 Sudan	11
5 Norway	86	5 South Sudan	14
Singapore	86	6 Libya	15
7 Switzerland	85	7 Iraq	16
8 Netherlands	83	8 Syria	17
9 Australia	81	Turkmenistan	17
Canada	81	Uzbekistan	17
11 Luxembourg	80	11 Yemen	18
12 Germany	78	12 Chad	19
Iceland	78	Equatorial Guinea	19
14 United Kingdom	76	Guinea-Bissau	19
		Haiti	19

Business software piracy

% of software that is pirated, 2011

1 Zimbabwe	92	Belarus	87
2 Georgia	91	11 Indonesia	86
3 Bangladesh	90	Iraq	86
Libya	90	Pakistan	86
Moldova	90	14 Algeria	84
6 Yemen	89	Sri Lanka	84
7 Armenia	88	Ukraine	84
Venezuela	88	17 Cameroon	83
9 Azerbaijan	87		

a This index ranks countries based on how much corruption is perceived by business
  people, academics and risk analysts to exist among politicians and public officials.

Businesses and banks

Largest non-financial companies
By market capitalisation, $bn, end December 2013

1	Exxon Mobil	United States	438.7
2	Apple	United States	434.1
3	Google	United States	376.4
4	Berkshire Hathaway	United States	292.5
5	Microsoft	United States	287.7
6	General Electric	United States	282.0
7	Johnson & Johnson	United States	260.5
8	Chevron	United States	239.0
9	Roche Holdings	Switzerland	238.1
10	Nestlé	Switzerland	234.4
11	Wal-Mart Stores	United States	231.8
12	PetroChina	Hong Kong	229.4
13	Royal Dutch Shell	United Kingdom	226.4
14	Procter & Gamble	United States	211.1
15	China Mobile	Hong Kong	208.4
16	IBM	United States	197.8
17	Pfizer	United States	196.0
18	Novartis	Switzerland	194.6
19	AT&T	United States	183.8
20	Amazon.com	United States	183.0
21	The Coca-Cola Company	United States	181.8
22	Anheuser-Busch	Belgium	171.3
23	Samsung Electronics	South Korea	170.6
24	Toyota Motor	Japan	163.4

By net profit, $bn, end December 2013

1	Apple	United States	37.0
2	Gazprom	Russia	35.8
3	Exxon Mobil	United States	32.6
4	Samsung Electronics	South Korea	27.3
5	BP	United Kingdom	23.5
6	Pfizer	United States	22.0
7	Microsoft	United States	21.9
8	Chevron	United States	21.4
9	PetroChina	Hong Kong	21.1
10	China Mobile	Hong Kong	19.8
11	Berkshire Hathaway	United States	19.5
12	AT&T	United States	18.2
13	Rosneft	Russia	17.1
14	Wal-Mart Stores	United States	17.0
15	IBM	United States	16.5
16	Royal Dutch Shell	United Kingdom	16.4
17	Anheuser-Busch	Belgium	14.4
18	Johnson & Johnson	United States	13.8
19	General Electric	United States	13.1
20	Google	United States	12.9
21	Roche Holdings	Switzerland	12.1
22	Volkswagen	Germany	12.0
23	Toyota Motor	Japan	11.6
24	Verizon Communications	United States	11.5

Largest banks
By market capitalisation, $bn, end December 2013

1	Wells Fargo	United States	238.7
2	JPMorgan Chase	United States	219.7
3	Industrial & Commercial Bank of China	China	207.8
4	HSBC	United Kingdom	206.6
5	China Construction Bank	Hong Kong	188.6
6	Bank of America	United States	164.9
7	Agricultural Bank of China	China	159.6
8	Citigroup	United States	157.9
9	Bank of China	Hong Kong	128.6
10	Banco Santander	Spain	101.7
11	Commonwealth Bank of Australia	Australia	101.3
12	BNP Paribas	France	97.0
13	Royal Bank of Canada	Canada	96.7
14	Westpac Banking Group	Australia	94.6
15	Lloyds Banking Group	United Kingdom	93.4

By assets, $bn, end December 2013

1	Industrial & Commercial Bank of China	China	3,126
2	HSBC	United Kingdom	2,671
3	China Construction Bank	Hong Kong	2,538
4	Mitsubishi UFJ	Japan	2,489
5	BNP Paribas	France	2,482
6	JPMorgan Chase	United States	2,416
7	Agricultural Bank of China	China	2,406
8	Bank of China	Hong Kong	2,292
9	Deutsche Bank	Germany	2,222
10	Barclays	United Kingdom	2,174
11	Crédit Agricole	France	2,119
12	Bank of America	United States	2,102
13	Mizuho Financial	Japan	1,883
14	Citigroup	United States	1,880
15	Société Générale	France	1,703

Largest sovereign-wealth funds
By assets, $bn, April 2014

1	Government Pension Fund, Norway	838	
2	Abu Dhabi Investment Authority, UAE	773	
3	SAMA Foreign Holdings, Saudi Arabia	676	
4	China Investment Corporation	575	
5	SAFE Investment Company, China	568	
6	Kuwait Investment Authority	410	
7	Hong Kong Monetary Authority Investment Portfolio	327	
8	Government of Singapore Investment Corporation	320	
9	Temasek Holdings, Singapore	173	
10	Qatar Investment Authority	170	

Note: Countries listed refer to the company's domicile.

Stockmarkets

Largest market capitalisation

$bn, end 2013

1	NYSE Euronext (US)	17,950	21	Moscow Exchange	771
2	NASDAQ OMX	6,085	22	Singapore Exchange[d]	744
3	Japan Exchange		23	Mexican Exchange	526
	Group – Tokyo	4,543	24	Bursa Malaysia	500
4	London SE Group	4,429	25	Saudi Stock Exchange –	
5	NYSE Euronext (Europe)	3,584		Tadawul	467
6	Hong Kong Exchanges	3,101	26	Stock Exchange of	
7	Shanghai SE	2,497		Thailand	354
8	TMX Group	2,114	27	Indonesia SE	347
9	Deutsche Börse	1,936	28	Tehran SE	346
10	SIX Swiss Exchange	1,541	29	Oslo Bors	265
11	Shenzhen SE	1,452		Santiago SE	265
12	Australian SE[a]	1,366	31	Japan Exchange	
13	NASDAQ OMX Nordic			Group – Osaka	238
	Exchange[b]	1,269	32	Philippine SE	217
14	Korea Exchange[c]	1,235	33	Warsaw SE	205
15	BSE India	1,139	34	Colombia SE	203
16	BME Spanish Exchanges	1,117		Tel Aviv SE	203
17	National Stock		36	Borsa Istanbul	196
	Exchange India	1,113	37	Irish SE	170
18	BM&F BOVESPA	1,020	38	Qatar Exchange	153
19	Johannesburg SE	943	39	Wiener Börse	118
20	Taiwan SE Corp.	823	40	Abu Dhabi SE	110

Stockmarket gains and losses

$ terms, % change December 31st 2012 to December 31st 2013

Largest gains

1	Argentina (MERV)	42.5
2	US (NAScomp)	38.3
3	Pakistan (KSE)	38.1
4	Greece (Athex Comp)	33.8
5	Germany (DAX)	31.1
6	Denmark (OMXCB)	30.7
7	US (S&P 500)	29.6
8	Japan (Nikkei 225)	28.9
9	Spain (Madrid SE)	28.3
10	Saudi Arabia (Tadawul)	26.5
	US (DJIA)	26.5
12	Japan (Topix)	24.6
13	Euro area (FTSE Euro 100)	24.4
14	Switzerland (SMI)	23.8
15	Israel (TA-100)	23.7
16	Belgium (BEL 20)	23.4
17	Euro area (EURO STOXX 50)	23.3
	France (CAC 40)	23.3
19	Netherlands (AEX)	22.5
20	Sweden (OMXS30)	22.2

Largest losses

1	Turkey (BIST)	-28.0
2	Brazil (BVSP)	-26.7
3	Indonesia (JSX)	-21.6
4	Chile (IGPA)	-21.2
5	Colombia (IGBC)	-18.8
6	Thailand (SET)	-13.1
7	Czech Republic (PX)	-8.8
8	Russia (RTS)	-5.5
9	South Africa (JSE AS)	-4.5
10	China (SSEA)	-4.1
11	India (BSE)	-3.5
12	Singapore (STI)	-3.2
13	Mexico (IPC)	-3.1
14	Australia (All Ord)	-1.6
15	South Korea (KOSPI)	2.2
16	Canada (S&P TSX)	2.7
17	Hong Kong (Hang Seng)	2.8
18	Malaysia (KLSE)	3.2
19	China (SSEB)	3.6
20	Hungary (BUX)	4.7

a Includes investment funds. b Copenhagen, Helsinki, Iceland, Stockholm, Tallinn, Riga and Vilnius Stock Exchanges. c Includes Kosdaq. d Includes domestic listings and many foreign listings.

Value traded[a]

$bn, 2013

1	NASDAQ OMX	26,644
2	NYSE Euronext (US)	15,309
3	Japan Exchange Group – Tokyo	6,496
4	Shenzhen SE	3,939
5	Shanghai SE	3,800
6	London SE Group	3,732
7	NYSE Euronext (Europe)	3,123
8	Deutsche Börse	1,500
9	Hong Kong Exchanges	1,447
10	Korea Exchange[b]	1,361
11	TMX Group	1,333
12	BME Spanish Exchanges	1,202
13	Australian SE[c]	976
14	SIX Swiss Exchange	794
15	BM&F BOVESPA	744
16	NASDAQ OMX Nordic Exchange[d]	738
17	Taiwan SE Corp.	632
18	Moscow Exchange	505
19	National Stock Exchange India	454
20	Johannesburg SE	380
21	Borsa Istanbul	375
22	Saudi Stock Exchange – Tadawul	365
23	Stock Exchange of Thailand	361
24	Singapore Exchange[e]	279
25	Japan Exchange Group – Osaka	201
26	Mexican Exchange	174
27	Bursa Malaysia	160
28	Oslo Bors	137
29	GreTai Securities Market	135
30	Indonesia SE	125
31	Warsaw SE	86
32	BSE India	82
33	Tehran SE	66
34	Tel Aviv SE	63

Number of listed domestic companies[f]

End 2013

1	BSE India	5,294
2	TMX Group	3,886
3	Japan Exchange Group – Tokyo	3,419
4	BME Spanish Exchanges	3,245
5	London SE Group	2,736
6	NASDAQ OMX	2,637
7	NYSE Euronext (US)	2,371
8	Australian SE[c]	2,055
9	Korea Exchange	1,813
10	National Stock Exchange India	1,679
11	Hong Kong Exchanges	1,643
12	Shenzhen SE	1,536
13	Japan Exchange Group – Osaka	1,163
14	NYSE Euronext (Europe)	1,062
15	Shanghai SE	953
16	Bursa Malaysia	910
17	Warsaw SE	895
18	Taiwan SE Corp.	866
19	Singapore Exchange[g]	776
20	NASDAQ OMX Nordic Exchange[d]	755
21	Deutsche Börse	720
22	GreTai Securities Market	658
23	Stock Exchange of Thailand	584
24	Tel Aviv SE	508
25	Indonesia SE	483
26	Johannesburg SE	375
27	BM&F BOVESPA	363
28	Tehran SE[h]	314
29	Santiago SE	306
30	HoChiMinh SE	301
31	Colombo SE	289
32	Luxembourg SE	274
33	SIX Swiss Exchange	272
34	Lima SE	271
35	Moscow Exchange	262
36	Philippine SE	257
37	Athens Exchange	251
38	Amman SE	239

Note: Figures are not entirely comparable due to different reporting rules and calculations. a Includes electronic and negotiated deals. b Includes Kosdaq. c Includes investment funds. d Copenhagen, Helsinki, Iceland, Stockholm, Tallinn, Riga and Vilnius Stock Exchanges. e Main board, Sesdaq and Clob International. f Domestic and foreign. g Main board and Sesdaq. h Some 90 companies have been relegated to the "Unofficial Board".

Transport: roads and cars

Longest road networks
Km, 2012 or latest

1	United States	6,584,594	26	Hungary	206,113
2	India	4,442,762	27	Iran	202,189
3	China	4,265,355	28	Philippines	197,186
4	Brazil	1,577,506	29	Nigeria	196,808
5	Canada	1,409,027	30	Thailand	193,018
6	Japan	1,218,718	31	Ukraine	169,613
7	Russia	1,117,357	32	Malaysia	156,497
8	France	1,059,562	33	Belgium	154,593
9	South Africa	828,237	34	Egypt	146,982
10	Australia	824,008	35	Netherlands	138,429
11	Spain	664,832	36	Peru	133,621
12	Germany	643,603	37	Czech Republic	130,591
13	Sweden	579,564	38	Greece	118,260
14	Italy	508,071	39	Algeria	116,301
15	Indonesia	501,929	40	Austria	116,200
16	United Kingdom	419,826	41	Sri Lanka	114,093
17	Poland	415,886	42	Ghana	109,515
18	Mexico	387,032	43	South Korea	106,802
19	Turkey	374,502	44	Belarus	98,671
20	Pakistan	270,083	45	Kazakhstan	98,433
21	Saudi Arabia	251,319	46	Ireland	97,180
22	Argentina	230,970	47	Venezuela	96,156
23	Romania	227,320	48	New Zealand	94,715
24	Colombia	226,558	49	Norway	94,324
25	Vietnam	211,204	50	Tanzania	86,472

Densest road networks
Km of road per km² land area, 2012 or latest

1	Monaco	38.1		Sri Lanka	1.7
2	Macau	24.3		Switzerland	1.7
3	Malta	9.8		United Kingdom	1.7
4	Bermuda	8.3	27	Austria	1.4
5	Bahrain	6.0		Cyprus	1.4
6	Singapore	5.4		India	1.4
7	Belgium	5.1		Ireland	1.4
8	Barbados	3.7	31	Estonia	1.3
9	Netherlands	3.3		Lithuania	1.3
10	Japan	3.2		Poland	1.3
11	Puerto Rico	3.0		Spain	1.3
12	Liechtenstein	2.5		Sweden	1.3
13	Hungary	2.2	36	Latvia	1.1
14	Hong Kong	2.0		Mauritius	1.1
	Jamaica	2.0		South Korea	1.1
	Luxembourg	2.0		Taiwan	1.1
17	France	1.9	40	Portugal	1.0
	Guam	1.9		Romania	1.0
	Slovenia	1.9	42	Greece	0.9
20	Germany	1.8		Israel	0.9
21	Czech Republic	1.7		Qatar	0.9
	Denmark	1.7		Slovakia	0.9
	Italy	1.7			

Most crowded road networks
Number of vehicles per km of road network, 2012 or latest

1	Monaco	427.3		26	Malaysia	73.6
2	Hong Kong	312.2		27	Armenia	73.3
3	Singapore	246.3		28	Germany	72.2
4	Macau	238.0		29	Honduras	71.0
5	Kuwait	223.4		30	Portugal	69.4
6	South Korea	180.6		31	Switzerland	65.5
7	Taiwan	172.6		32	Netherlands	65.1
8	Jordan	161.2		33	Iran	64.5
9	Guatemala	141.7		34	Saudi Arabia	61.4
10	Israel	141.5		35	Thailand	60.6
11	El Salvador	130.2		36	Brunei	60.1
12	Bahrain	115.6		37	Bermuda	59.3
13	Mauritius	111.8		38	Croatia	55.8
14	Guam	102.9		39	Greece	55.0
15	Malta	97.0		40	Poland	54.7
16	Puerto Rico	93.5		41	Morocco	54.2
17	Mexico	91.3		42	Venezuela	51.4
18	United Kingdom	85.4		43	Slovakia	49.7
19	Qatar	84.3		44	Moldova	49.2
20	Barbados	83.9		45	Ukraine	48.5
21	Italy	83.6		46	Fiji	47.7
22	Bulgaria	80.3		47	Bahamas	47.3
23	Liechtenstein	77.3		48	Chile	46.4
24	Tunisia	75.6			Finland	46.4
25	Luxembourg	75.3		50	Kazakhstan	45.2

Longest distance travelled
Average distance travelled per car per year, km, 2012

1	Chile	28,908		21	Finland	15,178
2	India	23,927		22	Kazakhstan	15,148
3	Peru	22,381		23	Morocco	14,986
4	Ecuador	21,925		24	Portugal	14,973
5	Azerbaijan	21,058		25	Indonesia	14,557
6	United States	19,885		26	Iceland	14,243
7	Singapore	18,647		27	China	14,170
8	Pakistan	18,412		28	Norway	13,829
9	Belgium	18,251		29	Switzerland	13,799
10	Ireland	17,798		30	Germany	13,794
11	Iran	17,792		31	Moldova	13,761
12	Russia	17,276		32	Latvia	13,691
13	Estonia	17,029		33	Czech Republic	13,397
14	Slovenia	17,019		34	France	13,391
15	Tunisia	16,320		35	Australia	13,117
16	Austria	16,276		36	New Zealand	13,095
17	Israel	16,125		37	Netherlands	13,053
18	Sweden	15,808		38	Japan	12,849
19	Canada	15,621		39	Croatia	12,824
20	Denmark	15,370		40	Hong Kong	12,798

Highest car ownership
Number of cars per 1,000 population, 2012

1	Monaco	782		Estonia	461
2	Liechtenstein	768	27	Greece	454
3	Luxembourg	680	28	Czech Republic	440
4	New Zealand	641	29	Portugal	428
5	Iceland	639	30	Barbados	422
6	Puerto Rico	629	31	Cyprus	420
7	Italy	617	32	United States	410
8	Malta	596	33	Ireland	406
9	Lithuania	576	34	Brunei	405
10	Finland	572	35	Denmark	397
11	Australia	560	36	Bulgaria	383
12	Austria	543	37	Trinidad & Tobago	370
13	Switzerland	536	38	Malaysia	360
14	Germany	530	39	Saudi Arabia	353
15	Slovenia	521	40	Croatia	340
16	Poland	507		Lebanon	340
17	Belgium	500	42	Bermuda	337
	France	500		Slovakia	337
	United Kingdom	500	44	Kuwait	332
20	Norway	492	45	Bahrain	328
21	Spain	483	46	Japan	305
22	Netherlands	475	47	Belarus	303
23	Sweden	469	48	Hungary	299
24	Guam	462	49	South Korea	296
25	Canada	461	50	Latvia	289

Lowest car ownership
Number of cars per 1,000 population, 2012

1	Ethiopia	1	21	Mali	10
	Somalia	1		Pakistan	10
3	Bangladesh	2		Tanzania	10
	Burundi	2	24	Mozambique	11
	Chad	2	25	Cameroon	14
	Laos	2		Malawi	14
	Liberia	2	27	Kenya	16
8	Rwanda	3		Senegal	16
	Uganda	3	29	Côte d'Ivoire	17
10	Congo-Kinshasa	4		India	17
11	Gambia, The	5		Nicaragua	17
	Nepal	5		Nigeria	17
	Sierra Leone	5		Yemen	17
14	Guinea	6	34	Ghana	19
	Myanmar	6		Zambia	19
	Papua New Guinea	6	36	Cuba	21
17	Eritrea	7		Vietnam	21
	Niger	7	38	Benin	22
19	Burkina Faso	9		Congo-Brazzaville	22
	Philippines	9	40	Sri Lanka	23

Car production
Number of cars produced, '000, 2012

1	China	15,524		21	Malaysia	510
2	Japan	8,554		22	Belgium	507
3	Germany	5,389		23	Argentina	497
4	South Korea	4,167		24	Italy	397
5	United States	4,106		25	Romania	327
6	India	3,286		26	Taiwan	278
7	Brazil	2,624		27	South Africa	275
8	Russia	1,969		28	Hungary	215
9	Mexico	1,810		29	Pakistan	180
10	France	1,683		30	Australia	179
11	Spain	1,540		31	Sweden	163
12	United Kingdom	1,465		32	Slovenia	127
13	Iran	1,389		33	Austria	124
14	Czech Republic	1,172		34	Portugal	116
15	Canada	1,040		35	Vietnam	103
16	Thailand	958		36	Ukraine	70
17	Slovakia	900		37	Morocco	58
18	Indonesia	744			Venezuela	58
19	Turkey	577		39	Philippines	49
20	Poland	540		40	Egypt	37

Cars sold
New car registrations, '000, 2012

1	China	15,495		26	Austria	336
2	United States	7,186		27	Switzerland	328
3	Japan	4,572		28	Sweden	280
4	Germany	3,083		29	Poland	274
5	Russia	2,935		30	Taiwan	268
6	Brazil	2,852		31	Colombia	262
7	India	2,063		32	Ukraine	243
8	United Kingdom	2,045		33	Chile	240
9	France	1,899		34	Israel	191
10	Italy	1,402		35	Algeria	183
11	South Korea	1,324		36	Czech Republic	174
12	Iran	1,012		37	Denmark	171
13	Australia	883		38	Norway	138
14	Indonesia	781		39	Pakistan	134
15	Thailand	769		40	Peru	129
16	Canada	759		41	Finland	111
17	Spain	700		42	Singapore	97
18	Mexico	612		43	Portugal	95
19	Argentina	596		44	Ireland	80
20	Turkey	556		45	New Zealand	77
21	Malaysia	552		46	Kenya	75
22	United Arab Emirates	537		47	Egypt	73
23	Netherlands	503		48	Jordan	72
24	Belgium	487		49	Slovakia	69
25	South Africa	438		50	Azerbaijan	68

Transport: planes and trains

Most air travel
Million passenger-km[a] per year, 2012

1	United States	1,379,093	16	Australia	93,660
2	China	478,218	17	Spain	85,173
3	United Kingdom	259,321	18	Turkey	83,705
4	Germany	217,780	19	Indonesia	82,927
5	United Arab Emirates	217,057	20	Netherlands	80,475
6	France	163,188	21	Qatar	66,167
7	Singapore	136,054	22	Thailand	59,724
8	Russia	133,032	23	Mexico	55,356
9	Canada	120,050	24	Italy	52,328
10	India	112,227	25	Malaysia	38,600
11	Brazil	111,774	26	Saudi Arabia	37,439
12	Hong Kong	110,943	27	Norway	35,868
13	Ireland	109,868	28	South Africa	32,693
14	South Korea	99,049	29	New Zealand	29,867
15	Japan	98,195	30	Portugal	29,105

Busiest airports

Total passengers, m, 2013

1	Atlanta, Hartsfield	94.0
2	Beijing, Capital	83.7
3	London, Heathrow	72.4
4	Tokyo, Haneda	68.9
5	Chicago, O'Hare	66.9
6	Los Angeles, Intl.	66.7
7	Dubai Intl.	66.4
8	Paris, Charles de Gaulle	62.1
9	Dallas, Ft Worth	60.4
10	Jakarta, Soekarno-Hatta	59.7
11	Hong Kong, Intl.	59.6
12	Frankfurt, Main	58.0
13	Singapore, Changi	53.7
14	Amsterdam, Schipol	52.6
	Denver, Intl.	52.6

Total cargo, m tonnes, 2013

1	Hong Kong, Intl.	4.16
2	Memphis, Intl.	4.14
3	Shanghai, Pudong Intl.	2.93
4	Seoul, Incheon	2.46
5	Dubai, Intl.	2.44
6	Anchorage, Intl.	2.42
7	Louisville, Standiford Fld.	2.22
8	Frankfurt, Main	2.09
9	Tokyo, Narita	2.02
10	Miami, Intl.	1.95
11	Paris, Charles de Gaulle	1.88
12	Singapore, Changi	1.86
13	Beijing, Capital	1.84
14	Los Angeles, Intl.	1.74
15	Taiwan, Taoyuan Intl.	1.57

Average daily aircraft movements, take-offs and landings, 2013

1	Atlanta, Hartsfield	2,496	13	Amsterdam, Schiphol	1,206
2	Chicago, O'Hare	2,420	14	Phoenix, Skyharbor Intl.	1,194
3	Dallas, Ft Worth	1,858	15	Philadelphia, Intl.	1,186
4	Los Angeles, Intl.	1,685	16	Minneapolis, St Paul	1,185
5	Denver, Intl.	1,596	17	Toronto, Pearson Intl.	1,182
6	Beijing, Capital	1,556	17	Detroit, Metro	1,166
7	Charlotte/Douglas, Intl.	1,529	19	San Francisco	1,155
8	Las Vegas, McCarran Intl.	1,427	20	Newark	1,133
9	Houston, George Bush Intercontinental	1,387	21	Istanbul Ataturk	1,113
				New York, JFK	1,113
10	Paris, Charles de Gaulle	1,310	23	Tokyo, Haneda	1,099
11	Frankfurt, Main	1,295	24	Miami	1,094
12	London, Heathrow	1,293	25	Mexico City, Intl.	1,085

a Air passenger–km data refer to the distance travelled by aircraft of national origin.

Longest railway networks
'000 km, 2012 or latest

1	United States	228.2		21	Sweden	9.9
2	Russia	84.2		22	Turkey	9.6
3	China	66.3		23	Czech Republic	9.5
4	India	64.5		24	Iran	8.4
5	Canada	64.3		25	Hungary	7.9
6	South Africa	40.3		26	Pakistan	7.8
7	Germany	33.5		27	Finland	5.9
8	Australia	33.3		28	Belarus	5.5
9	France	30.0			Chile	5.5
10	Brazil	29.8		30	Thailand	5.3
11	Mexico	26.7		31	Egypt	5.2
12	Argentina	25.0		32	Austria	5.0
13	Ukraine	21.6		33	Algeria	4.7
14	Japan	20.1			Indonesia	4.7
15	Poland	19.6		35	Sudan	4.3
16	Italy	17.1		36	Norway	4.2
17	United Kingdom	16.4			Uzbekistan	4.2
18	Spain	15.7		38	Bulgaria	4.1
19	Kazakhstan	14.3		39	Serbia	3.8
20	Romania	10.8		40	South Korea	3.7

Most rail passengers
Km per person per year, 2012 or latest

1	Switzerland	2,274		13	Belgium	1,004
2	Japan	1,912		14	Belarus	945
3	Denmark	1,365		15	Slovakia	901
4	France	1,301		16	India	809
5	Austria	1,233		17	Taiwan	791
6	Kazakhstan	1,095		18	Finland	747
7	Ukraine	1,074		19	Luxembourg	746
8	Germany	1,047		20	Sweden	682
9	United Kingdom	1,038		21	Czech Republic	658
10	Mongolia	1,030		22	Italy	638
11	Netherlands	1,024		23	China	593
12	Russia	1,014		24	Hungary	589

Most rail freight
Million tonnes-km per year, 2012 or latest

1	United States	2,524,585		13	Belarus	48,351
2	China	2,518,310		14	Poland	32,904
3	Russia	2,222,388		15	France	31,616
4	India	625,723		16	Mongolia	23,561
5	Canada	352,535		17	Iran	22,604
6	Brazil	267,700		18	Uzbekistan	22,482
7	Ukraine	237,722		19	Austria	21,683
8	Kazakhstan	235,846		20	Japan	20,255
9	South Africa	113,342		21	Latvia	16,930
10	Germany	105,894		22	Lithuania	14,172
11	Mexico	69,185		23	Slovakia	14,116
12	Australia	58,649		24	Argentina	12,111

Transport: shipping

Merchant fleets
Number of vessels, by country of domicile, January 2013

1	China	5,313	11	Indonesia	1,530
2	Japan	3,991	12	United Kingdom	1,237
3	Germany	3,833	13	Netherlands	1,207
4	Greece	3,695	14	Denmark	991
5	United States	1,943	15	Italy	884
6	Norway	1,908	16	Vietnam	841
7	Singapore	1,888	17	Taiwan	814
8	Russia	1,727	18	India	742
9	Turkey	1,580	19	United Arab Emirates	699
10	South Korea	1,576	20	Malaysia	614

Deadweight tonnage, by country of domicile, m, January 2013

1	Greece	244.9	11	Denmark	40.7
2	Japan	223.8	12	Bermuda	32.9
3	China	190.1	13	Turkey	29.1
4	Germany	125.8	14	Italy	25.3
5	South Korea	75.1	15	Hong Kong	24.3
6	Singapore	64.2	16	India	22.4
7	United States	58.3	17	United Arab Emirates	19.5
8	United Kingdom	50.3	18	Malaysia	19.4
9	Norway	46.0		Russia	19.4
10	Taiwan	44.3	20	Netherlands	16.7

Shipbuilding
Deliveries[a], '000 dwt, 2013

1	China	44,090	11	Norway	160
2	South Korea	33,320	12	Russia	150
3	Japan	24,760		United States	150
4	Philippines	2,460	14	Netherlands	130
5	Vietnam	870	15	Germany	110
6	Taiwan	540	16	Indonesia	80
7	India	410	17	Spain	70
8	Romania	380	18	Malaysia	60
9	Brazil	230		Poland	60
10	Turkey	190		Singapore	60

Order books, % of world total by gross tonnage[b], by country of ownership, Jan. 2014

1	China	14.7	11	Taiwan	2.3
2	Greece	14.6	12	United States	2.1
3	Norway	7.6	13	Switzerland	1.7
4	Italy	6.4	14	Kuwait	1.5
5	Japan	5.5	15	Bermuda	1.0
	South Korea	5.5	16	Denmark	0.9
7	Germany	5.3	17	Malaysia	0.7
8	Singapore	4.7	18	Belgium	0.4
9	Hong Kong	2.8		Thailand	0.4
10	United Kingdom	2.6	20	Croatia	0.1

a Sea-going propelled merchant ships of 100 gross tons and above.
b Sea-going cargo-carrying vessels.

Tourism

Most tourist arrivals
Number of arrivals, '000, 2012

1	France	83,018	21	Netherlands	11,680
2	United States	66,969	22	Egypt	11,196
3	China	57,725	23	South Korea	11,140
4	Spain	57,701	24	Sweden	10,914
5	Italy	43,360	25	Croatia	10,369
6	Turkey	35,698	26	Hungary	10,353
7	Germany	30,408	27	Morocco	9,375
8	United Kingdom	29,282	28	South Africa	9,188
9	Russia	25,736	29	United Arab Emirates	8,977
10	Malaysia	25,033	30	Bulgaria	8,936
11	Austria	24,151	31	Czech Republic	8,908
12	Hong Kong	23,770	32	Switzerland	8,566
13	Mexico	23,403	33	Japan	8,368
14	Ukraine	23,013	34	Indonesia	8,044
15	Thailand	22,354	35	Portugal	7,696
16	Canada	16,311	36	Belgium	7,505
17	Greece	15,518	37	Taiwan	7,311
18	Poland	14,840	38	Vietnam	6,848
19	Saudi Arabia	13,664	39	India	6,649
20	Macau	13,577	40	Australia	6,146

Biggest tourist spenders
$m, 2012

1	United States	89,002	13	Belgium	20,146
2	Germany	81,235	14	Hong Kong	20,129
3	China	56,816	15	South Korea	19,526
4	United Kingdom	52,919	16	Singapore	19,331
5	France	41,821	17	Netherlands	18,780
6	Canada	36,115	18	Norway	16,543
7	Russia	35,324	19	Switzerland	15,831
8	Australia	29,198	20	Sweden	15,252
9	Japan	29,151	21	India	13,048
10	Italy	26,776	22	United Arab Emirates	12,442
11	Brazil	22,321	23	Iran	12,150
12	Spain	21,263	24	Saudi Arabia	11,531

Largest tourist receipts
$m, 2012

1	United States	126,214	13	Malaysia	20,250
2	Spain	55,916	14	Singapore	19,261
3	France	53,697	15	Austria	18,894
4	China	50,028	16	India	17,971
5	Macau	43,707	17	Canada	17,401
6	Italy	41,185	18	Switzerland	16,581
7	Germany	38,114	19	Sweden	15,427
8	United Kingdom	36,373	20	Japan	14,576
9	Hong Kong	32,089	21	South Korea	14,231
10	Australia	31,534	22	Netherlands	13,887
11	Thailand	30,092	23	Greece	12,879
12	Turkey	25,653	24	Mexico	12,739

Education

Primary enrolment
Number enrolled as % of relevant age group

Highest

1	Gabon	165
2	Madagascar	145
3	Malawi	141
4	Angola	140
5	Burundi	137
6	Nepal	135
7	Russia	134
8	Togo	133
9	Sierra Leone	131
10	China	128
11	Cambodia	124
	Timor-Leste	124
13	Benin	123
	Laos	123
15	Syria	122

Lowest

1	Eritrea	42
2	Papua New Guinea	60
3	Niger	71
4	Saudi Arabia	84
5	Burkina Faso	85
	Gambia, The	85
	Nigeria	85
8	Puerto Rico	87
9	Mali	88
10	Bermuda	89
11	Macedonia	90
12	Equatorial Guinea	91
	Guinea	91
14	Oman	93
	Senegal	93

Highest secondary enrolment
Number enrolled as % of relevant age group

1	Australia	133
2	Spain	131
3	Netherlands	128
4	Denmark	120
	New Zealand	120
6	Ireland	118
7	Saudi Arabia	114
8	Norway	113
9	Qatar	112
10	Greece	111
	Liechtenstein	111

12	France	110
	Portugal	110
14	Estonia	109
	Iceland	109
16	Brunei	108
17	Finland	107
	Lithuania	107
19	Belarus	106
	Belgium	106
	Hong Kong	106

Highest tertiary enrolment[a]
Number enrolled as % of relevant age group

1	South Korea	98
2	Finland	96
3	United States	95
4	Belarus	94
5	Puerto Rico	86
	Slovenia	86
7	Australia	83
	Spain	83
9	Iceland	81
	New Zealand	81

11	Ukraine	80
12	Argentina	79
13	Venezuela	78
14	Lithuania	77
15	Netherlands	76
16	Russia	75
17	Chile	74
	Denmark	74
	Sweden	74

Notes: Latest available year 2008–13. The gross enrolment ratios shown are the actual number enrolled as a percentage of the number of children in the official primary age group. They may exceed 100 when children outside the primary age group are receiving primary education.

a Tertiary education includes all levels of post-secondary education including courses leading to awards not equivalent to a university degree, courses leading to a first university degree and postgraduate courses.

Least literate
% adult population

1	Guinea	25.3	15	Timor-Leste	58.3
2	Mali	33.4	16	Mauritania	58.6
3	Chad	35.4	17	Togo	60.4
4	Sierra Leone	43.3	18	Malawi	61.3
5	Senegal	49.7	19	Papua New Guinea	62.4
6	Mozambique	50.6	20	Madagascar	64.5
7	Gambia, The	51.1	21	Yemen	65.3
	Nigeria	51.1	22	Rwanda	65.9
9	Pakistan	54.9	23	Morocco	67.1
10	Guinea-Bissau	55.3	24	Tanzania	67.8
11	Central African Rep.	56.6	25	Angola	70.4
12	Côte d'Ivoire	56.9	26	Cameroon	71.3
13	Nepal	57.4	27	Ghana	71.5
14	Bangladesh	57.7	28	Uganda	73.2

Top universities[b]
2013

1	Harvard, US	13	Cornell, US
2	Stanford, US	14	California, San Diego, US
3	California, Berkeley, US	15	Pennsylvania, US
4	Massachusetts Institute of Technology, US	16	Washington, US
5	Cambridge, UK	17	The Johns Hopkins, Baltimore, US
6	California Institute of Technology, US	18	California, San Francisco, US
7	Princeton, US	19	Wisconsin – Madison, US
8	Columbia, US	20	Swiss Federal Institute of Technology Zurich
9	Chicago, US	21	Tokyo, Japan
10	Oxford, UK	22	University College London, UK
11	Yale, US	23	Michigan – Ann Arbor, US
12	California, Los Angeles, US	24	Imperial College London, UK

Education spending
% of GDP

Highest

			Lowest		
1	Lesotho	13.0	1	Myanmar	0.8
2	Cuba	12.8	2	Central African Rep.	1.2
3	Botswana	9.5	3	Zambia	1.3
4	Timor-Leste	9.4	4	Monaco	1.6
5	Denmark	8.7	5	Sri Lanka	1.7
6	Moldova	8.4	6	Georgia	2.0
	Namibia	8.4	7	Liechtenstein	2.1
8	Swaziland	8.3		Pakistan	2.1
9	Ghana	8.1	9	Bangladesh	2.2
10	Iceland	7.6		Dominican Rep.	2.2
11	New Zealand	7.4		Lebanon	2.2
12	Cyprus	7.3	12	Chad	2.3
13	Sweden	7.0	13	Congo-Brazzaville	2.5

b Based on academic peer review, employer review, faculty/student ratio, research strength and international factors.

Life expectancy

Highest life expectancy
Years, 2010–15

1	Monaco[a]	89.6		Greece	80.7
2	Japan	83.5	26	Ireland	80.6
3	Hong Kong	83.3	27	Finland	80.5
4	Andorra[a]	82.7		Luxembourg	80.5
5	Switzerland	82.5	29	Belgium	80.4
6	Australia	82.4		United Kingdom	80.4
7	Italy	82.3	31	Macau	80.3
8	Singapore	82.2	32	Channel Islands	80.2
9	Iceland	82.0	33	Virgin Islands (US)	80.0
	Spain	82.0	34	Chile	79.8
11	France	81.7		Costa Rica	79.8
	Israel	81.7		Cyprus	79.8
	Liechtenstein[a]	81.7		Lebanon	79.8
	Sweden	81.7		Portugal	79.8
15	Canada	81.4		Taiwan[a]	79.8
	Norway	81.4	40	Malta	79.7
	South Korea	81.4	41	Réunion	79.5
18	Martinique	81.3		Slovenia	79.5
19	Austria	81.0	43	Denmark	79.3
	Bermuda[a]	81.0	44	Cuba	79.2
	New Zealand	81.0	45	United States	78.9
22	Netherlands	80.9	46	Puerto Rico	78.8
23	Guadeloupe	80.8	47	Guam	78.7
24	Germany	80.7	48	Brunei	78.4

Highest male life expectancy
Years, 2010–15

1	Monaco[a]	85.7		Sweden	79.7
2	Andorra[a]	80.5	11	Italy	79.5
3	Hong Kong	80.3		Liechtenstein[a]	79.5
4	Australia	80.2	13	Canada	79.3
	Iceland	80.2		Norway	79.3
6	Switzerland	80.1	15	New Zealand	79.1
7	Japan	80.0	16	Netherlands	78.9
8	Israel	79.8	17	Spain	78.8
9	Singapore	79.7			

Highest female life expectancy
Years, 2010–15

1	Monaco[a]	93.6	10	Singapore	84.6
2	Japan	86.9		South Korea	84.6
3	Hong Kong	86.4	12	Liechtenstein[a]	84.4
4	Spain	85.2		Martinique	84.4
5	France	85.1	14	Bermuda[a]	84.3
6	Andorra[a]	84.9	15	Guadeloupe	84.0
	Italy	84.9	16	Iceland	83.8
	Switzerland	84.9		Sweden	83.8
9	Australia	84.7	18	Finland	83.6

a 2013 estimates.

Lowest life expectancy
Years, 2010–15

1	Sierra Leone	45.3	26	Congo-Brazzaville	58.6
2	Botswana	47.4	27	Gambia, The	58.7
3	Swaziland	49.2	28	Uganda	59.0
4	Lesotho	49.5	29	Benin	59.2
5	Congo-Kinshasa	49.8	30	Zimbabwe	59.8
6	Central African Rep.	49.9	31	Liberia	60.3
7	Mozambique	50.2	32	Afghanistan	60.7
8	Côte d'Ivoire	50.5	33	Ghana	61.0
9	Chad	51.0	34	Tanzania	61.4
10	Angola	51.7	35	Mauritania	61.5
11	Nigeria	52.3	36	Kenya	61.6
12	Equatorial Guinea	52.9	37	Sudan	61.9
13	Burundi	53.9	38	Papua New Guinea	62.3
14	Guinea-Bissau	54.2	39	Eritrea	62.6
15	Mali	54.8	40	Haiti	63.0
16	Cameroon	54.9		Yemen	63.0
	Somalia	54.9	42	Ethiopia	63.3
18	South Sudan	55.0		Gabon	63.3
19	Malawi	55.1		Senegal	63.3
20	Guinea	55.9	45	Rwanda	63.6
21	Burkina Faso	56.1	46	Namibia	64.3
22	Togo	56.4	47	Madagascar	64.5
23	South Africa	57.1	48	Myanmar	65.1
24	Zambia	57.7	49	Turkmenistan	65.4
25	Niger	58.1	50	India	66.3

Lowest male life expectancy
Years, 2010–15

1	Sierra Leone	45.1	11	Equatorial Guinea	51.5
2	Botswana	48.0	12	Burundi	52.0
	Central African Rep.	48.0		Nigeria	52.0
4	Congo-Kinshasa	48.1	14	Guinea-Bissau	52.7
5	Lesotho	49.2	15	Somalia	53.3
	Mozambique	49.2	16	Cameroon	53.7
7	Côte d'Ivoire	49.7	17	South Sudan	53.9
	Swaziland	49.7	18	Malawi	54.9
9	Chad	50.1		Mali	54.9
10	Angola	50.2		South Africa	54.9

Lowest female life expectancy
Years, 2010–15

1	Sierra Leone	45.6	10	Nigeria	52.6
2	Botswana	46.5	11	Angola	53.2
3	Swaziland	48.5	12	Equatorial Guinea	54.5
4	Lesotho	49.6	13	Mali	54.7
5	Côte d'Ivoire	51.4	14	Malawi	55.2
6	Mozambique	51.5	15	Guinea	55.7
7	Congo-Kinshasa	51.6		Guinea-Bissau	55.7
8	Central African Rep.	51.8	17	Burundi	55.8
9	Chad	51.9			

Death rates and infant mortality

Highest death rates
Number of deaths per 1,000 population, 2010–15

#	Country	Rate		#	Country	Rate
1	Sierra Leone	17.4			Italy	10.1
2	Botswana	17.0			Kazakhstan	10.1
3	Ukraine	16.8		50	Belgium	10.0
4	Bulgaria	15.8			Bosnia & Herz.	10.0
5	Belarus	15.7		52	Gambia, The	9.8
	Latvia	15.7			Japan	9.8
7	Congo-Kinshasa	15.5			Slovenia	9.8
	Russia	15.5		55	Benin	9.6
9	Central African Rep.	15.0			Finland	9.6
10	Lesotho	14.9			Macedonia	9.6
11	Chad	14.5			Sweden	9.6
12	Côte d'Ivoire	14.3			Trinidad & Tobago	9.6
13	Mozambique	14.2		60	Austria	9.4
14	Angola	14.1			Uganda	9.4
	Moldova	14.1			United Kingdom	9.4
	Swaziland	14.1			Uruguay	9.4
17	Lithuania	13.9		64	Gabon	9.2
18	Estonia	13.6			North Korea	9.2
19	Hungary	13.4		66	Barbados	9.1
	Nigeria	13.4			Channel Islands	9.1
21	Equatorial Guinea	13.3		68	Ghana	9.1
22	Mali	13.2		69	Liberia	9.0
23	Burundi	12.9			Monaco[a]	9.0
	South Africa	12.9			Zimbabwe	9.0
25	Guinea-Bissau	12.6		72	France	8.9
26	Romania	12.5		73	Armenia	8.7
27	Croatia	12.4			Mauritania	8.7
	Serbia	12.4			Spain	8.7
	Somalia	12.4		76	Haiti	8.6
30	South Sudan	12.0			Netherlands	8.6
31	Cameroon	11.9			Tanzania	8.6
32	Guinea	11.6		79	Myanmar	8.5
33	Georgia	11.5		80	Norway	8.4
	Malawi	11.5			Sudan	8.4
35	Burkina Faso	11.2		82	Kenya	8.3
36	Niger	11.1			Malta	8.3
37	Germany	10.9			United States	8.3
38	Togo	10.7		85	Switzerland	8.2
39	Czech Republic	10.6		86	Bermuda[a]	8.1
40	Poland	10.5			Puerto Rico	8.1
41	Greece	10.4		88	Afghanistan	8.0
	Montenegro	10.4		89	India	7.9
	Zambia	10.4			Luxembourg	7.9
44	Congo-Brazzaville	10.3			Mauritius	7.9
	Portugal	10.3		92	Martinique	7.8
	Slovakia	10.3			Turkmenistan	7.8
47	Denmark	10.1				

Note: Both death and, in particular, infant mortality rates can be underestimated in certain countries where not all deaths are officially recorded.

Highest infant mortality
Number of deaths per 1,000 live births, 2010–15

1	New Caledonia	131.0	23	Togo	66.4
2	Sierra Leone	116.7	24	Zambia	65.5
3	Congo-Kinshasa	108.6	25	Pakistan	65.1
4	Angola	96.2	26	Swaziland	64.6
5	Chad	95.8	27	Congo-Brazzaville	63.6
6	Guinea-Bissau	93.9	28	Liberia	61.2
7	Central African Rep.	93.3	29	Lesotho	60.1
8	Equatorial Guinea	88.9	30	Uganda	57.0
9	Burundi	87.0	31	Tajikistan	56.8
10	Mali	86.7	32	Yemen	56.2
11	Malawi	86.1	33	Gambia, The	55.3
12	Somalia	79.5	34	Sudan	55.0
13	South Sudan	78.0	35	Niger	53.6
14	Nigeria	76.3	36	Kenya	51.6
15	Côte d'Ivoire	75.3	37	Ghana	51.1
16	Mozambique	74.3	38	Rwanda	49.8
17	Cameroon	73.5	39	Ethiopia	49.7
	Guinea	73.5	40	Senegal	49.3
19	Mauritania	71.7	41	Myanmar	48.9
20	Burkina Faso	69.8	42	Tanzania	48.7
21	Benin	68.7	43	Papua New Guinea	47.6
22	Afghanistan	67.3	44	Turkmenistan	46.7

Lowest death rates
No. deaths per 1,000 pop., 2010–15

1	United Arab Emirates	1.0
2	Qatar	1.4
3	Bahrain	2.3
4	Oman	2.8
5	Kuwait	2.9
6	Brunei	3.1
7	Saudi Arabia	3.3
8	West Bank & Gaza	3.5
9	French Guiana	3.6
10	Jordan	3.7
11	Syria	3.9
12	Costa Rica	4.2
	Libya	4.2
14	Lebanon	4.4
15	Mexico	4.5
16	Nicaragua	4.6
17	Honduras	4.7
	Malaysia	4.7
	Singapore	4.7
20	Guam	4.8
	Macau	4.8
22	Ecuador	4.9
	Panama	4.9

Lowest infant mortality
No. deaths per 1,000 live births, 2010–15

1	Iceland	1.8
	Monaco[a]	1.8
	Singapore	1.8
4	Hong Kong	1.9
5	Luxembourg	2.0
6	Japan	2.2
7	Finland	2.3
	Sweden	2.3
9	Bermuda[a]	2.5
10	Czech Republic	2.6
	Norway	2.6
12	Italy	2.8
	Portugal	2.8
	Slovenia	2.8
15	Ireland	2.9
16	Austria	3.1
	Germany	3.1
	Spain	3.1
19	Belgium	3.2
	France	3.2
21	Israel	3.3
22	Denmark	3.4
	South Korea	3.4

a 2013 estimates.

Death and disease

Diabetes

% of population aged 20–79,
2013 age-standardised estimate[a]

1	Saudi Arabia	23.9
2	Kuwait	23.1
3	Qatar	22.9
4	French Polynesia	22.4
5	Bahrain	21.8
6	Guam	19.5
	New Caledonia	19.5
8	United Arab Emirates	19.0
9	Egypt	16.8
10	Réunion	15.4
11	Lebanon	15.0
12	Turkey	14.9
13	Mauritius	14.8
14	Martinique	14.3
15	Bahamas	14.2
	Oman	14.2

Malaria

Deaths per 100,000 population,
estimate, 2010

1	Burkina Faso	191
2	Sierra Leone	177
3	Chad	172
4	Central African Rep.	169
5	Guinea	144
6	Mali	138
7	Nigeria	131
8	Mozambique	125
9	Congo-Kinshasa	119
10	Côte d'Ivoire	116
11	Guinea-Bissau	108
12	Benin	104
13	Niger	100
14	Congo-Brazzaville	93
15	Liberia	86
16	Gambia, The	83

Cancer

Deaths per 100,000 population,
2012 age-standardised estimate[a]

1	Mongolia	161.0
2	Hungary	152.1
3	Armenia	150.3
4	Serbia	147.8
5	Uruguay	144.8
6	Zimbabwe	142.7
7	Macedonia	141.6
8	Kazakhstan	140.2
9	Montenegro	139.0
10	Croatia	136.7
11	Kenya	135.3
12	French Polynesia	134.4
13	Uganda	134.2
14	Poland	131.0
15	Timor-Leste	129.7
16	Lithuania	129.0
17	Latvia	128.8
	Turkey	128.8
19	New Caledonia	127.3
20	Romania	127.1
21	Slovakia	125.8
22	North Korea	125.5
23	Slovenia	125.4
24	Papua New Guinea	125.1

Tuberculosis

Incidence per 100,000 population,
2012

1	Swaziland	1,349
2	South Africa	1,003
3	Sierra Leone	674
4	Namibia	655
5	Lesotho	630
6	Zimbabwe	562
7	Mozambique	552
8	Timor-Leste	498
9	Gabon	428
10	Zambia	427
11	Cambodia	411
12	North Korea	409
13	Botswana	408
14	Congo-Brazzaville	381
15	Myanmar	377
16	Central African Rep.	367
17	Mauritania	350
18	Papua New Guinea	348
19	Congo-Kinshasa	327
20	Angola	316
21	Liberia	304
22	Somalia	286
23	Gambia, The	284
24	Kenya	272

a Assumes that every country and region has the same age profile (the age profile of the world population has been used).
Note: Statistics are not available for all countries. The number of cases diagnosed and reported depends on the quality of medical practice and administration and can be under-reported in a number of countries.

Measles immunisation
Lowest % of children aged 12–23 months, 2012

1	Nigeria	42
2	Somalia	46
3	Central African Rep.	49
4	Equatorial Guinea	51
5	Guinea	58
	Haiti	58
7	Mali	59
8	Syria	61
9	South Sudan	62
	Timor-Leste	62
11	Chad	64
12	Azerbaijan	66
	Ethiopia	66
14	Papua New Guinea	67
15	Afghanistan	68
16	Guinea-Bissau	69
	Iraq	69
	Madagascar	69

DPT[a] immunisation
Lowest % of children aged 12–23 months, 2012

1	Equatorial Guinea	33
2	Nigeria	41
3	Somalia	42
4	Chad	45
	Syria	45
6	Central African Rep.	47
7	Guinea	59
	South Sudan	59
9	Haiti	60
10	Ethiopia	61
11	Papua New Guinea	63
12	Indonesia	64
13	Timor-Leste	67
14	South Africa	68
15	Iraq	69
16	Afghanistan	71
17	Congo-Kinshasa	72
	India	72

HIV/AIDS
Prevalence among population aged 15–49, %, 2012

1	Swaziland	26.5
2	Lesotho	23.1
3	Botswana	23.0
4	South Africa	17.9
5	Zimbabwe	14.7
6	Namibia	13.3
7	Zambia	12.7
8	Mozambique	11.1
9	Malawi	10.8
10	Uganda	7.2
11	Equatorial Guinea	6.2
12	Kenya	6.1
13	Tanzania	5.1
14	Cameroon	4.5
15	Gabon	4.0
16	Guinea-Bissau	3.9
17	Bahamas	3.3
18	Côte d'Ivoire	3.2
19	Nigeria	3.1
20	Rwanda	2.9
	Togo	2.9
22	Congo-Brazzaville	2.8
23	Chad	2.7
	South Sudan	2.7
25	Angola	2.3

AIDS
Estimated deaths per 100,000 pop., 2011

1	Lesotho	638
2	Swaziland	566
3	South Africa	535
4	Zimbabwe	457
5	Mozambique	310
6	Malawi	285
7	Zambia	232
8	Central African Rep.	229
9	Namibia	223
10	Botswana	207
11	Tanzania	181
	Uganda	181
13	Cameroon	172
14	Gabon	166
15	Kenya	148
16	Togo	145
17	Nigeria	132
18	Côte d'Ivoire	113
19	Congo-Brazzaville	112
20	South Sudan	108
21	Bahamas	107
	Equatorial Guinea	107
23	Chad	104
24	Burundi	67
25	Ghana	61

a Diptheria, pertussis and tetanus

Health

Highest health spending
As % of GDP, 2012

1	United States	17.9
2	Liberia	15.5
3	Sierra Leone	15.1
4	Netherlands	12.4
5	France	11.7
	Moldova	11.7
7	Lesotho	11.6
8	Austria	11.5
9	Germany	11.3
	Switzerland	11.3
11	Denmark	11.2
12	Canada	10.9
	Cuba	10.9
14	Belgium	10.8
15	Rwanda	10.7
16	Serbia	10.5
17	New Zealand	10.3
	Paraguay	10.3
19	Costa Rica	10.1
	Japan	10.1
21	Bosnia & Herz.	9.9
22	Jordan	9.8
23	Spain	9.6
	Sweden	9.6
25	Portugal	9.4
	United Kingdom	9.4

Lowest health spending
As % of GDP, 2012

1	Myanmar	1.8
2	Turkmenistan	2.0
3	Qatar	2.2
4	Brunei	2.3
5	Kuwait	2.5
6	Eritrea	2.6
	South Sudan	2.6
8	Chad	2.8
	United Arab Emirates	2.8
10	Laos	2.9
11	Indonesia	3.0
12	Pakistan	3.1
13	Congo-Kinshasa	3.2
	Saudi Arabia	3.2
15	Sri Lanka	3.3
16	Syria	3.4
17	Angola	3.5
	Gabon	3.5
19	Bangladesh	3.6
	Iraq	3.6
	Oman	3.6
22	Central African Rep.	3.8
	Ethiopia	3.8
24	Bahrain	3.9
	Libya	3.9
	Malaysia	3.9
	Thailand	3.9

Highest pop. per doctor
2012 or latest[a]

1	Tanzania	125,000
2	Liberia	71,429
3	Malawi	52,632
	Niger	52,632
5	Ethiopia	45,455
	Sierra Leone	45,455
7	Somalia	28,571
8	Gambia, The	26,316
9	Mozambique	25,000
10	Guinea-Bissau	22,222
11	Burkina Faso	21,277
12	Central African Rep.	20,833
13	Papua New Guinea	18,868
	Togo	18,868
15	Rwanda	17,857
16	Benin	16,949
	Senegal	16,949
18	Zimbabwe	16,129

Lowest pop. per doctor
2012 or latest[a]

1	Qatar	129
2	Monaco	140
3	Cuba	149
4	Greece	162
5	Austria	207
6	Russia	232
7	Georgia	236
8	Lithuania	243
9	Italy	244
10	Hungary	253
11	Switzerland	254
12	Andorra	256
13	Portugal	259
14	Bulgaria	262
15	Germany	263
16	Sweden	265
17	Belarus	266
18	Norway	267

a 2009–12

Obesity[a]

% of adult population aged 20 and over, 2013

Male			Female		
1	Qatar	44.0	1	Kuwait	58.6
2	Kuwait	43.4	2	Libya	57.2
3	United States	31.7	3	Qatar	54.7
4	Bahrain	31.0	4	Egypt	48.4
5	Bahamas	30.9	5	Bahamas	47.7
6	Libya	30.2	6	Jordan	45.6
7	Saudi Arabia	30.0	7	Saudi Arabia	44.4
8	Malta	29.0	8	Bahrain	42.9
9	New Zealand	28.1	9	South Africa	42.0
10	Australia	27.5	10	Syria	39.9
11	Jordan	27.5	11	Iraq	37.5
12	United Arab Emirates	27.1	12	Oman	36.9
13	Iceland	26.9	13	Trinidad & Tobago	36.2

Food supply

Average per person per day, 2012 or latest

Highest calories available			Lowest calories available		
1	Austria	3,844	1	Congo-Kinshasa	1,590
2	United States	3,763	2	Burundi	1,596
3	Belgium	3,728	3	Eritrea	1,666
4	Turkey	3,682	4	Somalia	1,844
5	Greece	3,661	5	Zambia	1,845
6	Ireland	3,628	6	Haiti	1,962

Highest fat as % of calories[b]			Lowest fat as % of calories[b]		
1	Australia	42	1	Bangladesh	10
2	France	41		Burundi	10
	Spain	41	3	Ethiopia	11
4	Austria	40		Rwanda	11

Hunger Index[c]

2013 ranking[d]

1	Burundi	38.8	14	Mozambique	21.5
2	Eritrea	35.0	15	India	21.3
3	Timor-Leste	29.6	16	Tanzania	20.6
4	Sudan	27.0	17	Congo-Kinshasa	20.5
5	Chad	26.9	18	Niger	20.3
6	Yemen	26.5	19	Bangladesh	19.4
7	Ethiopia	25.7	20	Pakistan	19.3
8	Madagascar	25.2	21	Uganda	19.2
9	Zambia	24.1	22	Angola	19.1
10	Central African Rep.	23.3	23	Laos	18.7
	Haiti	23.3	24	Namibia	18.4
12	Sierra Leone	22.8	25	Kenya	18.0
13	Burkina Faso	22.2		North Korea	18.0

a Defined as body mass index of 30 or more – see page 248.   b Fat as a percentage of total daily energy intake is recommended at between 15–30%.   c Compiled using prevalence of undernourishment in the population (2010–12), underweight children under five (2008-12) and under five mortality (2011)   d Over 10 is serious, over 20 alarming and over 30 extremely alarming.

Marriage and divorce

Highest marriage rates
Number of marriages per 1,000 population, 2012 or latest available year

1	Tajikistan	12.3	23	Jamaica	7.5
2	Iran	11.6	24	Cyprus	7.3
3	Bahamas	11.2		Singapore	7.3
	Egypt	11.2	26	Georgia	6.8
	Indonesia	11.2		Macedonia	6.8
6	Kyrgyzstan	10.7		Moldova	6.8
7	Jordan	10.3		United States	6.8
8	Uzbekistan	10.1	30	Macau	6.7
9	Kazakhstan	9.7	31	South Korea	6.6
10	Algeria	9.6	32	Lithuania	6.5
	China	9.6	33	Kuwait	6.4
12	Russia	9.2		Tunisia	6.4
13	Albania	8.9	35	Israel	6.3
14	Guam	8.7		Turkmenistan	6.3
	West Bank & Gaza	8.7	37	Malta	6.1
16	Bermuda	8.6		Ukraine	6.1
17	Azerbaijan	8.5	39	Armenia	6.0
18	Costa Rica	8.3	40	Ecuador	5.6
	Hong Kong	8.3		Philippines	5.6
20	Belarus	8.1	42	Australia	5.5
21	Mauritius	8.0		Latvia	5.5
	Turkey	8.0	44	Taiwan	5.4

Lowest marriage rates
Number of marriages per 1,000 population, 2012 or latest available year

1	United Arab Emirates	1.8	21	Belgium	3.6
2	Qatar	1.9		Hungary	3.6
3	French Guiana	2.5		New Caledonia	3.6
4	Uruguay	2.8		Réunion	3.6
5	Bulgaria	2.9	25	Andorra	3.7
6	Colombia	3.0		France	3.7
7	Argentina	3.1		Panama	3.7
8	Martinique	3.2	28	Netherlands	4.2
9	Peru	3.3	29	Czech Republic	4.3
	Portugal	3.3	30	Dominican Rep.	4.4
11	Italy	3.4		Estonia	4.4
	Luxembourg	3.4	32	Saudi Arabia	4.5
	Monaco	3.4		United Kingdom	4.5
	Mongolia	3.4	34	Austria	4.6
	Slovenia	3.4		Canada	4.6
16	Chile	3.5		Croatia	4.6
	Guadeloupe	3.5		Iceland	4.6
	South Africa	3.5		Ireland	4.6
	Spain	3.5		New Zealand	4.6
	Venezuela	3.5			

Note: The data are based on latest available figures (no earlier than 2008) and hence will be affected by the population age structure at the time. Marriage rates refer to registered marriages only and, therefore, reflect the customs surrounding registry and efficiency of administration.

Highest divorce rates
Number of divorces per 1,000 population, 2012 or latest available year

1	Guam	5.3		South Korea	2.3
2	Russia	4.7	28	Australia	2.2
3	Belarus	4.1		Canada	2.2
4	Puerto Rico	3.8		Hungary	2.2
5	Latvia	3.6		Macau	2.2
6	Lithuania	3.3		Spain	2.2
7	Moldova	3.0		Switzerland	2.2
8	Denmark	2.8	34	France	2.1
	United States	2.8		Netherlands	2.1
10	Bermuda	2.7		United Kingdom	2.1
	Kazakhstan	2.7	37	Austria	2.0
12	Cuba	2.6		Kuwait	2.0
	Hong Kong	2.6		Norway	2.0
	Jordan	2.6		Slovakia	2.0
15	Belgium	2.5	41	Egypt	1.9
	Costa Rica	2.5		Iran	1.9
	Czech Republic	2.5		New Zealand	1.9
	Luxembourg	2.5	44	China	1.8
	Portugal	2.5		Dominican Rep.	1.8
	Sweden	2.5		Japan	1.8
	Taiwan	2.5		Singapore	1.8
22	Finland	2.4	48	Albania	1.7
	Liechtenstein	2.4		Israel	1.7
24	Cyprus	2.3		Kyrgyzstan	1.7
	Estonia	2.3		Poland	1.7
	Germany	2.3			

Lowest divorce rates
Number of divorces per 1,000 population, 2012 or latest available year

1	Malta	0.1		Serbia	1.0
2	Guatemala	0.2	23	Mongolia	1.1
	Vietnam	0.2		Thailand	1.1
4	Bosnia & Herz.	0.4		Tunisia	1.1
5	United Arab Emirates	0.5		Ukraine	1.1
6	Qatar	0.6	27	Azerbaijan	1.2
	South Africa	0.6		Bahamas	1.2
	Uzbekistan	0.6		Ecuador	1.2
9	Indonesia	0.7		New Caledonia	1.2
	Ireland	0.7		Slovenia	1.2
11	Brazil	0.8		Turkmenistan	1.2
	Mexico	0.8	33	Croatia	1.3
	Montenegro	0.8		Greece	1.3
	Venezuela	0.8	35	Mauritius	1.4
15	Jamaica	0.9	36	Romania	1.5
	Macedonia	0.9		West Bank & Gaza	1.5
	Saudi Arabia	0.9	38	Bulgaria	1.6
	Tajikistan	0.9		Georgia	1.6
19	Armenia	1.0		Iceland	1.6
	Italy	1.0		Monaco	1.6
	Panama	1.0		Turkey	1.6

Households, living costs and giving

Number of households
Biggest, m, 2012

1	China	432.0	14	France	27.7
2	India	252.3	15	Italy	24.9
3	United States	121.1	16	Vietnam	24.7
4	Indonesia	62.6	17	Iran	21.9
5	Brazil	59.6	18	Philippines	21.3
6	Russia	56.3		Thailand	21.3
7	Japan	52.5	20	Egypt	20.7
8	Germany	40.6	21	Ethiopia	20.0
9	Bangladesh	35.8	22	Ukraine	19.9
10	Nigeria	35.7	23	Turkey	19.3
11	Pakistan	30.1	24	Spain	18.1
12	Mexico	29.4	25	South Korea	17.9
13	United Kingdom	27.9	26	Poland	14.8

Household occupation

Single occupation, % of total, 2012			*With 6+ occupants, % of total, 2012*		
1	Sweden	47.1	1	Kuwait	60.8
2	Norway	40.1	2	Pakistan	58.3
3	Denmark	39.8	3	United Arab Emirates	57.3
4	Finland	39.5	4	Saudi Arabia	47.2
5	Germany	38.8	5	Algeria	44.8
6	Switzerland	38.0	6	Turkmenistan	43.6
7	Slovakia	37.3	7	Jordan	39.0
8	Netherlands	36.6	8	Morocco	38.9
9	Austria	36.5	9	Nigeria	37.7
10	Estonia	35.5	10	India	37.5
11	France	34.5	11	Philippines	32.2
12	United Kingdom	34.4	12	Tunisia	31.3
13	Czech Republic	33.6	13	Cameroon	30.1
	Ukraine	33.6	14	Azerbaijan	27.9

Average household size, people

Biggest, 2012			*Smallest, 2012*		
1	Senegal	9.6	1	Germany	2.0
2	Guinea	8.8	2	Denmark	2.1
3	Angola	8.6		Finland	2.1
4	Gambia, The	8.3		Sweden	2.1
5	Chad	8.0	5	Estonia	2.2
	Equatorial Guinea	8.0		Lithuania	2.2
7	Gabon	7.9		Norway	2.2
8	Mauritania	7.8		Switzerland	2.2
9	Oman	7.0			
10	Guinea-Bissau	6.9			
11	Congo-Kinshasa	6.8			
	Kuwait	6.8			
	Pakistan	6.8			

a The cost of living index shown is compiled by the Economist Intelligence Unit for use by companies in determining expatriate compensation: it is a comparison of the cost of maintaining a typical international lifestyle in the country rather than a comparison of the purchasing power of a citizen of the country. The index is based on typical urban prices an international executive and family will face abroad. The prices

Cost of living[a]
December 2013, US = 100

Highest			Lowest		
1	Singapore	130	1	Pakistan	40
2	France	129	2	India	43
3	Norway	128	3	Nepal	44
4	Australia	120		Syria	44
5	Japan	118	5	Algeria	53
	Switzerland	118	6	Panama	55
	Venezuela	118		Romania	55
8	Denmark	117	8	Saudi Arabia	57
9	Finland	114	9	Oman	58
10	Hong Kong	113		Sri Lanka	58
11	South Korea	108	11	Paraguay	59
	United Kingdom	108	12	Kuwait	61
13	Austria	105		Qatar	61
14	New Zealand	104		South Africa	61
15	Israel	103	15	Kazakhstan	62
16	Ireland	101		Nigeria	62
	Sweden	101		Philippines	62
18	United States	100	18	Bahrain	63
19	Spain	99		Bulgaria	63
20	Belgium	98		Egypt	63
	Canada	98	21	Bangladesh	64
	Italy	98		Ecuador	64
	New Caledonia	98		Uzbekistan	64
24	Germany	95		Zambia	64
			25	Cambodia	65

World Giving Index[b]
Top givers, % of population, 2013

1	United States	61	17	Hong Kong	44
2	Canada	58		Iceland	44
	Myanmar	58		Indonesia	44
	New Zealand	58		Italy	44
5	Ireland	57		Nigeria	44
	United Kingdom	57	22	Costa Rica	43
7	Australia	55		Cyprus	43
8	Netherlands	54		Germany	43
9	Qatar	51	25	Denmark	42
10	Norway	48		Haiti	42
	Sri Lanka	48		Luxembourg	42
12	Malta	47		Turkmenistan	42
	Switzerland	47	29	Colombia	41
14	Libya	46		Guatemala	41
15	Austria	45		Israel	41
16	Philippines	45			

are for products of international comparable quality found in a supermarket or department store. Prices found in local markets and bazaars are not used unless the available merchandise is of the specified quality and the shopping area itself is safe for executive and family members. New York City prices are used as the base, so United States = 100.

b Three criteria are used to assess giving: in the previous month those surveyed either gave money to charity, gave time to those in need or helped a stranger.

Telephones, computers and broadband

Telephones
Telephone lines per 100 people, 2012

1	Monaco	121.7	16	Liechtenstein	50.4
2	Bermuda	105.8	17	Greece	49.1
3	Taiwan	68.7	18	Andorra	48.9
4	France	61.5	19	Israel	47.0
5	South Korea	61.4	20	Belarus	46.9
6	Hong Kong	61.3	21	Australia	45.4
7	Germany	60.5	22	United States	44.4
8	Switzerland	56.5	23	Ireland	43.9
9	Iceland	55.2	24	Sweden	43.8
10	Malta	53.7	25	Denmark	43.4
11	United Kingdom	52.9	26	Netherlands	43.0
12	Luxembourg	50.9		Portugal	43.0
13	Barbados	50.8	28	New Zealand	42.2
14	Canada	50.7	29	Belgium	41.9
15	Japan	50.5		Spain	41.9

Mobile telephones
Subscribers per 100 people, 2012

1	Macau	289.8	18	Botswana	153.8
2	Hong Kong	229.2	19	Singapore	152.1
3	Saudi Arabia	187.4	20	Argentina	151.9
4	Kazakhstan	185.8	21	United Arab Emirates	149.6
5	Russia	182.9	22	Bulgaria	148.1
6	Montenegro	181.3	23	Vietnam	147.7
7	Gabon	179.5	24	Uruguay	147.1
8	Panama	178.0	25	Luxembourg	145.4
9	Finland	172.3	26	Malaysia	141.3
10	Lithuania	165.1	27	Trinidad & Tobago	140.8
11	Bahrain	161.2	28	Poland	140.3
12	Austria	160.5	29	Bermuda	139.5
13	Estonia	160.4	30	Chile	138.2
14	Italy	159.8	31	Guatemala	137.8
15	Oman	159.3	32	El Salvador	137.3
16	Kuwait	156.9	33	United Kingdom	135.3
17	Libya	155.8	34	South Africa	130.6

Mobile broadband
Subscribers per 100 people, 2012

1	Singapore	123.3	14	United Kingdom	72.0
2	Japan	113.1	15	Iceland	71.7
3	Finland	106.5	16	Bahrain	67.1
4	South Korea	106.0	17	Israel	65.5
5	Sweden	101.3	18	New Zealand	65.2
6	Australia	96.2	19	Ireland	64.2
7	Denmark	87.5	20	Netherlands	61.0
8	Norway	84.6	21	Malta	57.6
9	United States	74.7	22	Oman	56.7
10	Hong Kong	73.5	23	Austria	55.5
11	Luxembourg	72.6	24	Spain	53.2
12	Estonia	72.5	25	Russia	52.9
13	Qatar	72.1	26	Croatia	52.3

Computers
Computers per 100 people, 2012

1	Canada	132.6		26	Spain	59.6
2	Netherlands	123.5		27	Slovenia	58.5
3	Switzerland	105.3		28	Belgium	54.9
4	United Kingdom	101.8		29	Macau	50.8
5	Sweden	99.4		30	Latvia	50.2
6	United States	99.3		31	Czech Republic	49.6
7	Taiwan	95.3		32	Macedonia	49.0
8	Germany	89.4		33	Malta	47.8
9	Denmark	87.9		34	Cyprus	45.9
10	France	86.6		35	New Caledonia	41.9
11	Australia	86.4		36	Israel	39.6
12	Austria	83.9		37	Costa Rica	37.6
13	Iceland	81.7		38	Malaysia	37.3
14	Singapore	81.3		39	Bermuda	34.8
15	Norway	79.3		40	Kuwait	34.4
16	Hong Kong	79.1		41	Croatia	34.3
17	Luxembourg	78.4		42	Estonia	33.5
18	Slovakia	77.2		43	Lithuania	32.4
19	Ireland	71.4		44	Mongolia	32.1
20	Finland	68.6		45	United Arab Emirates	30.6
21	Japan	66.9		46	Hungary	29.6
22	South Korea	66.6		47	Mauritius	28.6
23	New Zealand	65.8		48	Serbia	28.0
24	Italy	62.4		49	Namibia	27.7
25	Bahrain	60.8		50	French Guiana	27.2

Broadband
Subscribers per 100 people, 2012

1	Monaco	43.3		23	Belarus	26.9
2	Switzerland	39.9		24	Macau	26.0
3	Netherlands	39.8		25	Estonia	25.5
4	Denmark	38.8		26	Singapore	25.4
5	France	37.5		27	Israel	25.3
6	South Korea	37.2		28	Austria	25.0
7	Norway	36.3		29	Spain	24.4
8	Andorra	34.3		30	Australia	24.3
	Iceland	34.3			Slovenia	24.3
10	United Kingdom	34.0		32	Greece	24.1
11	Germany	33.7		33	Taiwan	23.9
12	Belgium	33.3		34	Latvia	23.3
13	Canada	32.5		35	Barbados	23.1
14	Luxembourg	32.4		36	Hungary	22.9
15	Sweden	32.3		37	Ireland	22.7
16	Malta	32.0		38	Portugal	22.5
17	Hong Kong	31.2		39	Italy	22.1
18	Liechtenstein	30.5		40	Lithuania	21.1
19	Finland	30.3		41	Croatia	20.7
20	United States	28.3		42	Guadeloupe	19.9
21	New Zealand	27.8		43	Cyprus	19.2
22	Japan	27.7		44	New Caledonia	18.9

The internet and music

Internet hosts

	By country, January 2014			Per 1,000 pop., January 2014	
1	United States[a]	592,529,894	1	United States[a]	1,876.3
2	Japan	74,641,810	2	Iceland	1,307.3
3	Brazil	36,887,717	3	Monaco	877.8
4	Germany	34,194,659	4	Netherlands	857.2
5	Italy	26,052,423	5	Finland	834.4
6	China	22,158,030	6	Australia	703.4
7	Mexico	19,232,985	7	New Zealand	702.4
8	Australia	16,108,223	8	Switzerland	700.8
9	France	15,769,166	9	Norway	675.3
10	Russia	15,387,813	10	Sweden	651.1
11	Netherlands	14,314,981	11	Netherlands Antilles	604.9
12	Argentina	14,038,087	12	Estonia	593.7
13	Poland	13,376,783	13	Japan	590.5
14	Canada	9,682,093	14	Luxembourg	511.3
15	United Kingdom	8,632,179	15	Belgium	498.1
16	India	7,458,755	16	Denmark	497.1
17	Turkey	7,224,244	17	Liechtenstein	435.8
18	Taiwan	6,541,347	18	Austria	432.3
19	Sweden	6,185,898	19	Italy	427.1
20	Switzerland	5,396,243	20	Germany	417.0
21	Colombia	5,394,946	21	Bermuda	403.2
22	Belgium	5,379,700	22	Singapore	397.9
23	Finland	4,505,502	23	Lithuania	368.8
24	Spain	4,235,161	24	Portugal	364.7
25	Portugal	3,902,123	25	Poland	349.3
26	Thailand	3,694,788	26	Argentina	341.6
27	Austria	3,631,645	27	Israel	339.0
28	South Africa	3,594,058	28	Andorra	334.6

Music sales

	Total including downloads, $m, 2013			$ per head, 2013	
1	United States	4,474	1	Japan	23.7
2	Japan	3,012	2	Norway	23.5
3	Germany	1,365	3	United Kingdom	20.6
4	United Kingdom	1,304	4	Sweden	20.2
5	France	956	5	Australia	19.3
6	Australia	431	6	Denmark	17.0
7	Canada	424	7	Germany	16.8
8	Italy	239	8	Austria	14.6
9	Brazil	228	9	France	14.5
10	South Korea	211		Switzerland	14.5
11	Netherlands	206	11	United States	14.1
12	Sweden	194	12	Finland	12.9
13	Spain	151	13	Canada	12.3
14	Mexico	135	14	Netherlands	12.2
15	Austria	120	15	New Zealand	11.9
	Norway	120	16	Belgium	11.0
17	Switzerland	116	17	Ireland	9.5
18	Belgium	114	18	Hong Kong	5.5

a Includes all hosts ending ".com", ".net" and ".org", which exaggerates the numbers.

Facebook users

'000, May 2013			Per 1,000 pop., May 2013	
1	United States	158,923	1	Monaco	984
2	Brazil	71,865	2	Iceland	744
3	India	63,793	3	Taiwan	578
4	Indonesia	47,971	4	Norway	565
5	Mexico	42,571	5	Chile	558
6	Turkey	32,775	6	Bahamas	552
7	United Kingdom	31,130	7	Malta	551
8	Philippines	30,285	8	Hong Kong	547
9	France	25,392	9	Denmark	534
10	Germany	24,970	10	Cyprus	533
11	Italy	23,345	11	Brunei	523
12	Argentina	21,298	12	Argentina	522
13	Thailand	18,550	13	Singapore	520
14	Colombia	18,328	14	Canada	519
15	Canada	17,809	15	New Zealand	517
16	Spain	16,941	16	Uruguay	516
17	Egypt	13,981	17	Australia	510
18	Japan	13,820	18	Montenegro	509
19	Vietnam	13,817	19	United States	508
20	Taiwan	13,418	20	Sweden	504
21	Malaysia	13,347	21	United Kingdom	499
22	Australia	11,535	22	Ireland	492
23	Poland	10,679	23	Israel	490
24	Peru	10,455	24	Macedonia	478
25	Venezuela	9,912	25	Belgium	465

Internet users

Per 100 population, 2012				
1	Iceland	96.2	23	Belgium	82.0
2	Norway	95.0	24	Austria	81.0
3	Sweden	94.0		United States	81.0
4	Denmark	93.0	26	Slovakia	80.0
	Netherlands	93.0	27	Kuwait	79.2
6	Luxembourg	92.0	28	Japan	79.1
7	Bermuda	91.3	29	Estonia	79.0
8	Finland	91.0		Ireland	79.0
9	New Zealand	89.5	31	Taiwan	76.0
10	Liechtenstein	89.4	32	Czech Republic	75.0
11	Qatar	88.1	33	Singapore	74.2
12	Bahrain	88.0	34	Latvia	74.0
13	Monaco	87.0	35	Israel	73.4
	United Kingdom	87.0	36	Barbados	73.3
15	Canada	86.8	37	Hong Kong	72.8
16	Andorra	86.4	38	Hungary	72.0
17	Switzerland	85.2		Spain	72.0
18	United Arab Emirates	85.0	40	Bahamas	71.7
19	South Korea	84.1	41	Malta	70.0
20	Germany	84.0		Slovenia	70.0
21	France	83.0	43	Lithuania	68.0
22	Australia	82.3	44	Malaysia	65.8

Going out

Cinema attendances
Total visits, m, 2012

1	India	3,204.2
2	United States	1,242.8
3	China	333.3
4	France	225.4
5	Mexico	196.2
6	United Kingdom	173.8
7	South Korea	170.6
8	Russia	168.7
9	Japan	146.2
10	Brazil	133.6
11	Germany	129.5
12	Italy	110.5
13	Spain	95.9
14	Australia	94.7
15	Philippines	75.2
16	Indonesia	59.8
17	Malaysia	50.6
18	Turkey	45.2
19	Poland	38.1
20	Colombia	33.8
21	Netherlands	32.9
22	Venezuela	31.5
23	Argentina	29.4

Visits per head, 2012

1	Iceland	5.0
2	Singapore	4.3
3	Australia	4.1
4	United States	3.9
5	France	3.5
	Ireland	3.5
	South Korea	3.5
8	United Kingdom	2.8
9	Luxembourg	2.6
10	India	2.5
11	Denmark	2.3
12	Norway	2.2
13	Austria	2.1
	Belgium	2.1
15	Malta	2.0
	Netherlands	2.0
	Spain	2.0
	Switzerland	2.0
19	Italy	1.8
	Sweden	1.8
21	Belarus	1.7
	Malaysia	1.7
	Mexico	1.7

Most popular art galleries and museums
Total visits, m, 2013

1	Louvre, Paris	9.33
2	British Museum, London	6.70
3	Metropolitan Museum of Art, New York	6.23
4	National Gallery, London	6.03
5	Vatican Museums, Vatican City	5.46
6	Tate Modern, London	4.88
7	National Palace Museum, Taipei	4.50
8	National Gallery of Art, Washington, DC	4.09
9	Centre Pompidou, Paris	3.75
10	Musée d'Orsay, Paris	3.50
11	Victoria and Albert Museum, London	3.29
12	Reina Sofía, Madrid	3.19
13	Museum of Modern Art, New York	3.07
14	National Museum of Korea, Seoul	3.05
15	State Hermitage Museum, St Petersburg	2.90

Most popular theme parks
Total visits, m, 2013

1	Magic Kingdom[a]	18.59
2	Tokyo Disneyland	17.21
3	Disneyland, Anaheim	16.20
4	Tokyo DisneySea	14.08
5	Epcot[a]	11.23
6	Disneyland Park, Disneyland Paris	10.43
7	Disney's Animal Kingdom[a]	10.20
8	Disney's Hollywood Studios[a]	10.11
9	Universal Studios Japan, Osaka	10.10
10	Disney California Adventure Park, Anaheim	8.51
11	Islands of Adventure, Universal Orlando	8.14
12	Ocean Park, Hong Kong	7.48
13	Hong Kong Disneyland	7.40
	Lotte World, Seoul	7.40
15	Everland, Yongin	7.30
16	Universal Studios, Universal Orlando	7.06

a Walt Disney World, Florida

The press

Daily newspapers
Copies per '000 population, 2012

1	Luxembourg	670	15	Malta	250
2	Hong Kong	516	16	United Kingdom	234
3	Liechtenstein	500	17	Germany	223
4	Kuwait	417	18	Denmark	216
5	Switzerland	385	19	Belarus	191
6	Japan	380		Lithuania	191
7	Sweden	376	21	Slovenia	170
8	Austria	372	22	Bulgaria	167
9	Norway	356	23	Moldova	159
10	Finland	349	24	Canada	158
11	South Korea	324	25	Taiwan	156
12	Iceland	323	26	France	155
13	Singapore	287	27	Hungary	151
14	Netherlands	258	28	Estonia	148

Press freedom[a]
Scores, 1=best, 100=worst, 2013

Most free			Least free		
1	Finland	6.40	1	Eritrea	84.83
2	Netherlands	6.46	2	North Korea	81.96
3	Norway	6.52	3	Turkmenistan	80.81
4	Luxembourg	6.70	4	Syria	77.04
5	Andorra	6.82	5	Somalia	73.19
6	Liechtenstein	7.02	6	China	72.91
7	Denmark	7.43	7	Vietnam	72.36
8	Iceland	8.50	8	Iran	72.29
9	New Zealand	8.55	9	Sudan	71.88
10	Sweden	8.98	10	Laos	71.22
11	Estonia	9.63	11	Cuba	70.92
12	Austria	10.01	12	Equatorial Guinea	67.95
13	Czech Republic	10.07	13	Yemen	67.26
14	Germany	10.23	14	Uzbekistan	61.01
15	Switzerland	10.47	15	Sri Lanka	59.13
16	Ireland	10.87	16	Saudi Arabia	58.30
17	Jamaica	10.90	17	Bahrain	58.26
18	Canada	10.99	18	Rwanda	56.57
19	Poland	11.03	19	Kazakhstan	54.94
20	Slovakia	11.39	20	Azerbaijan	52.87
21	Costa Rica	12.23	21	Egypt	51.89
22	Namibia	12.50	22	Pakistan	51.46
23	Belgium	12.80	23	Belarus	47.82
24	Cyprus	14.45	24	Swaziland	46.76
25	Uruguay	16.08	25	Gambia, The	46.42
26	Ghana	16.29	26	Turkey	45.87
27	Australia	16.91	27	Iraq	45.44
28	Portugal	17.73	28	Mexico	45.04

a Based on data for deaths and violence against journalists, and attacks on organisations, plus 73 questions on topics such as media independence, monopolies, legal status and censorship, answered by journalists and media experts.

Nobel prize winners: 1901–2013

Peace (two or more)

1	United States	19
2	United Kingdom	11
3	France	9
4	Sweden	5
5	Belgium	4
	Germany	4
7	Austria	3
	Norway	3
	South Africa	3
	Switzerland	3
11	Argentina	2
	Egypt	2
	Israel	2
	Russia	2

Economics[a]

1	United States	37
2	United Kingdom	9
3	Norway	2
	Sweden	2
5	Denmark	1
	France	1
	Germany	1
	Israel	1
	Netherlands	1
	Russia	1

Literature (three or more)

1	France	15
2	United States	12
3	United Kingdom	11
4	Germany	8
5	Sweden	7
6	Italy	5
	Spain	5
8	Norway	3
	Poland	3
	Russia	3

Medicine (three or more)

1	United States	55
2	United Kingdom	24
3	Germany	15
4	France	8
5	Sweden	7
6	Switzerland	6
7	Austria	5
	Denmark	5
9	Australia	3
	Belgium	3
	Italy	3

Physics

1	United States	52
2	United Kingdom	21
3	Germany	19
4	France	10
5	Netherlands	6
	Russia	6
7	Japan	5
8	Sweden	4
	Switzerland	4
10	Austria	3
	Italy	3
12	Canada	2
	Denmark	2
14	Australia	1
	Belgium	1
	China	1
	India	1
	Ireland	1
	Pakistan	1
	Poland	1

Chemistry

1	United States	47
2	United Kingdom	23
3	Germany	15
4	France	7
5	Switzerland	6
6	Japan	5
	Sweden	5
8	Canada	4
9	Israel	3
10	Argentina	1
	Austria	1
	Belgium	1
	Czech Republic	1
	Denmark	1
	Finland	1
	Italy	1
	Netherlands	1
	Norway	1
	Russia	1

a Since 1969.
Notes: Prizes by country of residence at time awarded. When prizes have been shared in the same field, one credit given to each country.

Olympics

Winter games, medals won, 2014

		Gold	Silver	Bronze
1	Russia	13	11	9
2	Norway	11	5	10
3	Canada	10	10	5
4	United States	9	7	12
5	Netherlands	8	7	9
6	Germany	8	6	5
7	Switzerland	6	3	2
8	Belarus	5	0	1
9	Austria	4	8	5
10	France	4	4	7
11	Poland	4	1	1
12	China	3	4	2
13	South Korea	3	3	2
14	Sweden	2	7	6
15	Czech Republic	2	4	2
16	Slovenia	2	2	4
17	Japan	1	4	3
18	Finland	1	3	1
19	United Kingdom	1	1	2
20	Ukraine	1	0	1
21	Slovakia	1	0	0
22	Italy	0	2	6
23	Latvia	0	2	2
24	Australia	0	2	1
25	Croatia	0	1	0

Winter games, overall medals won, 1924–2014

		Gold	Silver	Bronze
1	Norway	118	111	100
2	United States	96	102	83
3	Germany	86	84	58
4	Soviet Union (1952–88)	78	57	59
5	Canada	62	55	53
6	Austria	59	78	81
7	Sweden	50	40	54
8	Switzerland	50	40	48
9	Russia	49	40	35
10	Finland	42	62	57
11	East Germany (1968–88)	39	36	35
12	Netherlands	37	38	35
13	Italy	37	34	43
14	France	31	31	45
15	South Korea	26	17	10
16	China	12	22	19
17	West Germany (1968–88)	11	15	13
18	Japan	10	15	18
19	United Kingdom	10	4	12
20	Unified Team[a] (1992)	9	6	8

a Former Soviet states of Armenia, Belarus, Kazakhstan, Russia, Ukraine and Uzbekistan.

Drinking and smoking

Beer drinkers

Retail sales, litres per head of population, 2012

1	Czech Republic	144.1
2	Germany	106.5
3	Estonia	103.5
4	Ireland	102.3
5	Austria	100.4
6	Poland	99.3
7	Lithuania	95.4
8	Slovenia	91.7
9	Belgium	86.8
10	Romania	86.3
11	Luxembourg	85.7
12	Finland	82.3
13	Croatia	79.0
14	United States	75.9
15	Latvia	74.7
16	United Kingdom	71.8
17	Slovakia	71.7
18	Hungary	71.3
19	Bulgaria	71.2
	Russia	71.2
21	Australia	70.3
22	South Africa	69.1
23	Brazil	69.0

Wine drinkers

Retail sales, litres per head of population, 2012

1	Luxembourg	61.3
2	Portugal	43.2
3	Italy	40.5
4	France	38.7
5	Slovenia	38.3
6	Switzerland	35.7
7	Monaco	34.5
8	Liechtenstein	33.0
9	Austria	31.8
10	Denmark	31.2
11	Belgium	27.1
12	Greece	26.2
13	Germany	25.6
14	Netherlands	25.1
15	Argentina	24.9
16	Australia	24.0
17	Sweden	22.5
18	New Zealand	22.2
19	Hungary	21.9
20	United Kingdom	21.8
21	Spain	20.9
22	Belarus	19.7
23	Czech Republic	18.5

Cannabis use

15–64 year olds, at least once in past year, %, 2011 or latest

1	Italy	14.6
	New Zealand	14.6
3	Nigeria	14.3
4	United States	14.0
5	Bermuda	10.9
	Canada	10.9
7	Australia	10.3
8	Czech Republic	9.7
9	Poland	9.6
	Spain	9.6
11	Israel	8.9
12	Brazil	8.8
13	France	8.4
14	Uruguay	8.3
15	Netherlands	7.0
16	United Kingdom	6.9
17	Egypt	6.2
18	Ireland	6.0
19	Lithuania	5.6
20	Bahamas	5.5
21	Denmark	5.4
	Sierra Leone	5.4

Smoking

Av. ann. consumption of cigarettes per head per day, 2013

1	Belarus	7.4
2	Lebanon	7.1
3	Moldova	6.8
	Russia	6.8
5	Serbia	6.4
	Slovenia	6.4
7	Bosnia & Herz.	5.5
8	Czech Republic	5.4
9	Macedonia	5.2
10	China	5.1
11	South Korea	4.9
12	Greece	4.8
13	Georgia	4.7
	Ukraine	4.7
15	Austria	4.4
	Bulgaria	4.4
17	Azerbaijan	4.3
	Kuwait	4.3
	Taiwan	4.3
20	Japan	4.2
21	Armenia	3.9

Crime and punishment

Murders

Homicides per 100,000 pop., 2011 or latest

1	Honduras	91.4
2	El Salvador	69.9
3	Virgin Islands (US)	52.6
4	Venezuela	47.8
5	Jamaica	41.1
6	Guatemala	38.6
7	Lesotho	38.0
8	Bahamas	34.7
9	Colombia	33.6
10	South Africa	30.0
11	Puerto Rico	26.5
12	Trinidad & Tobago	26.4
13	Dominican Rep.	24.8
14	Brazil	23.4
15	Mexico	22.8
16	Panama	20.3
17	Ecuador	15.4
18	Namibia	13.9
19	Nicaragua	12.5
20	Bermuda	12.3

Robberies

Per 100,000 pop., 2011 or latest

1	Belgium	1,806
2	Argentina	974
3	Spain	867
4	Costa Rica	855
5	Mexico	655
6	Brazil	553
7	Chile	533
8	Nicaragua	491
9	Uruguay	442
10	Honduras	320
11	Trinidad & Tobago	276
12	Panama	271
13	Paraguay	206
14	France	192
15	Portugal	191
16	Peru	170
17	Jamaica	141
18	Barbados	140
19	Colombia	135
20	Botswana	121

Prisoners

Total prison pop., latest available year

1	United States	2,228,224
2	China	1,701,344
3	Russia	674,100
4	Brazil	548,003
5	India	385,135
6	Thailand	292,227
7	Mexico	246,334
8	Iran	217,000
9	South Africa	156,370
10	Indonesia	154,000
11	Turkey	151,312
12	Vietnam	130,180
13	Ukraine	124,473
14	Colombia	119,815
15	Philippines	110,925
16	Ethiopia	93,044
17	United Kingdom	94,946
18	Poland	80,582
19	Pakistan	74,944
20	Morocco	72,816
21	Bangladesh	69,968
22	Peru	67,597
23	France	67,050
24	Spain	66,783
25	Japan	64,932
26	Taiwan	63,727

Per 100,000 pop., latest available year

1	United States	707
2	Virgin Islands (US)	535
3	Barbados	529
4	Cuba	510
5	Rwanda	492
6	Russia	470
7	Bahamas	453
8	El Salvador	424
9	Bermuda	417
10	Thailand	413
11	Panama	383
12	Trinidad & Tobago	362
13	Belarus	335
	Puerto Rico	335
15	Lithuania	329
16	Costa Rica	314
17	Latvia	304
18	South Africa	294
19	Kazakhstan	290
20	Uruguay	289
21	Iran	284
	Swaziland	284
23	Ukraine	276
24	Bahrain	275
25	Brazil	274
	Mongolia	274

War and peace

Defence spending
As % of GDP, 2013

1	Afghanistan	13.8	13	Myanmar	4.2
2	Oman	11.7	14	Iran	4.1
3	Saudi Arabia	8.0	15	United States	3.7
4	Iraq	7.2	16	Jordan	3.6
5	Israel	6.0		Namibia	3.6
6	South Sudan	5.3	18	Morocco	3.5
7	Bahrain	5.0	19	Singapore	3.4
	Libya	5.0	20	Zimbabwe	3.2
9	Angola	4.8	21	Russia	3.1
10	Algeria	4.7	22	Sudan	3.0
	Yemen	4.7	23	Sri Lanka	2.8
12	Armenia	4.3	24	Côte d'Ivoire	2.7

Defence spending

	$bn, 2013			*Per head, $, 2013*	
1	United States	600.4	1	Oman	2,931
2	China[a]	112.2	2	Saudi Arabia	2,211
3	Russia	68.2	3	Israel	1,967
4	Saudi Arabia	59.6	4	United States	1,896
5	United Kingdom	57.0	5	Singapore	1,807
6	France	52.4	6	Kuwait	1,642
7	Japan	51.0	7	Norway	1,593
8	Germany	44.2	8	Australia	1,166
9	India	36.3	9	Bahrain	1,088
10	Brazil	34.7	10	Brunei	1,002
11	South Korea	31.8	11	United Kingdom	900
12	Australia	26.0	12	Denmark	812
13	Italy	25.2	13	Libya	795
14	Iran	17.7	14	France	794
15	Iraq	16.9	15	Sweden	727

Armed forces
'000, 2014[b]

		Regulars	Reserves			Regulars	Reserves
1	China	2,333	510	14	Thailand	361	200
2	United States	1,492	844	15	Brazil	318	1,340
3	India	1,325	1,155	16	Taiwan	290	1,657
4	North Korea	1,190	600	17	Colombia	281	62
5	Russia	845	2,000	18	Iraq	271	0
6	South Korea	655	4,500	19	Mexico	270	87
7	Pakistan	644	0	20	Japan	247	56
8	Iran	523	350	21	Sudan	244	0
9	Turkey	511	379	22	Saudi Arabia	234	0
10	Vietnam	482	5,000	23	France	222	30
11	Egypt	439	479	24	South Sudan	210	0
12	Myanmar	406	0	25	Eritrea	202	120
13	Indonesia	396	400	26	Morocco	196	150

a Official budget only at market exchange rates.   b Estimates.

Arms exporters
$m, 2013

1	Russia	8,283
2	United States	6,153
3	China	1,837
4	France	1,489
5	United Kingdom	1,394
6	Germany	972
7	Italy	807
8	Israel	773
9	Spain	605
10	Ukraine	589
11	Sweden	505
12	Belarus	338
13	South Korea	307
14	Netherlands	302
15	Switzerland	205
16	Canada	199
17	Poland	131
18	Romania	108
19	Finland	94
20	Turkey	82

Arms importers
$m, 2013

1	India	5,581
2	United Arab Emirates	2,245
3	China	1,534
4	Saudi Arabia	1,486
5	Pakistan	1,002
6	Azerbaijan	921
7	Indonesia	774
8	United States	759
9	Bangladesh	672
10	Taiwan	633
11	Turkey	604
12	Egypt	501
13	Oman	490
14	Venezuela	476
15	United Kingdom	438
16	Thailand	373
17	Vietnam	369
18	Myanmar	362
19	Syria	361
20	Israel	348

Global Peace Index[a]

Most peaceful, 2014

1	Iceland	1.189
2	Denmark	1.193
3	Austria	1.200
4	New Zealand	1.236
5	Switzerland	1.258
6	Finland	1.297
7	Canada	1.306
7	Japan	1.316
9	Belgium	1.354
10	Norway	1.371
11	Czech Republic	1.381
	Sweden	1.381
13	Ireland	1.384
14	Slovenia	1.398
15	Australia	1.414
16	Germany	1.423
17	Portugal	1.425
18	Slovakia	1.467
19	Netherlands	1.475
20	Hungary	1.482
21	Qatar	1.491
22	Poland	1.532
23	Mauritius	1.544
24	Singapore	1.545

Least peaceful, 2014

1	Syria	3.650
2	Afghanistan	3.416
3	South Sudan	3.397
4	Iraq	3.377
5	Somalia	3.368
6	Sudan	3.362
7	Central African Rep.	3.331
8	Congo-Kinshasa	3.213
9	Pakistan	3.107
10	North Korea	3.071
11	Russia	3.039
12	Nigeria	2.710
13	Colombia	2.701
14	Israel	2.689
15	Zimbabwe	2.662
16	Yemen	2.629
17	Lebanon	2.620
18	Guinea-Bissau	2.591
19	Egypt	2.571
	India	2.571
21	Chad	2.558
22	Ukraine	2.546
23	Côte d'Ivoire	2.520
24	Ethiopia	2.502

a Ranks 162 countries using 22 indicators which gauge the level of safety and security in society, the extent of domestic or international conflict and the degree of militarisation.

Environment

Environmental Performance Index[a]
Scores, 2012

Best			Worst		
1	Switzerland	87.7	1	Somalia	15.5
2	Luxembourg	83.3	2	Mali	18.4
3	Australia	82.4	3	Haiti	19.0
4	Singapore	81.8	4	Lesotho	20.8
5	Czech Republic	81.5	5	Afghanistan	21.6
6	Germany	80.5	6	Sierra Leone	21.7
7	Spain	79.8	7	Liberia	24.0
8	Austria	78.3	8	Sudan	24.6
9	Sweden	78.1	9	Congo-Kinshasa	25.0
10	Norway	78.0	10	Bangladesh	25.6
11	Netherlands	77.8	11	Burundi	25.8
12	United Kingdom	77.4		Eritrea	25.8
13	Denmark	76.9	13	Madagascar	26.7
14	Iceland	76.5	14	Mauritania	27.2

% change in score, 2002–12

Best			Worst		
1	Niger	45.9	1	Bahrain	-4.1
2	Timor-Leste	45.4	2	Qatar	-1.3
3	Kuwait	23.0	3	United Arab Emirates	-1.0
4	Sierra Leone	21.8	4	Brunei	-0.8
5	Namibia	18.7		Zambia	-0.8
6	Congo	18.3	6	Jordan	-0.1
7	El Salvador	17.8	7	Yemen	0.2
8	Eritrea	17.1	8	Lebanon	0.3
9	Estonia	15.9		Turkmenistan	0.3
10	Uruguay	15.6	10	Dominican Rep.	0.5
11	Madagascar	15.5		Finland	0.5
12	Slovenia	15.2		Sudan	0.5
13	Kenya	14.0	13	Burundi	0.6
14	Afghanistan	12.2	14	Israel	0.7

Poorest air quality
Average particulate matter concentration in urban areas[b], micrograms per cubic metre, 2010

1	Mongolia	275.4	13	India	105.4
2	Botswana	197.9	14	Zimbabwe	103.0
3	Pakistan	184.1	15	Kuwait	93.3
4	Senegal	148.0	16	Macedonia	91.1
5	Nigeria	144.9	17	Ghana	88.3
6	United Arab Emirates	131.7	18	Ethiopia	88.0
7	North Korea	127.0	19	Cambodia	86.9
8	Bangladesh	126.7	20	China	85.2
9	Egypt	125.4	21	Honduras	84.5
10	Iran	124.6	22	Bosnia & Herz.	84.0
11	Saudi Arabia	112.2	23	Yemen	80.3
12	Nepal	109.0	24	Tunisia	78.7

a An overall rank on scores from 0–100 over various indicators that include environmental, public health and ecosystem vitality.　b Particulates less than 10 microns in diameter. Data are weighted for the size of a country's urban population.

Biggest emitters of carbon dioxide
Million tonnes, 2010

1	China	8,286.9	26	Egypt	204.8
2	United States	5,433.1	27	Venezuela	201.7
3	India	2,008.8	28	Netherlands	182.1
4	Russia	1,740.8	29	Argentina	180.5
5	Japan	1,170.7	30	United Arab Emirates	167.6
6	Germany	745.4	31	Pakistan	161.4
7	Iran	571.6	32	Vietnam	150.2
8	South Korea	567.6	33	Algeria	123.5
9	Canada	499.1	34	Iraq	114.7
10	United Kingdom	493.5	35	Czech Republic	111.8
11	Saudi Arabia	464.5	36	Belgium	108.9
12	South Africa	460.1	37	Uzbekistan	104.4
13	Mexico	443.7	38	Kuwait	93.7
14	Indonesia	434.0	39	Greece	86.7
15	Brazil	419.8	40	Philippines	81.6
16	Italy	406.3	41	Nigeria	78.9
17	Australia	373.1	42	Romania	78.7
18	France	361.3	43	Colombia	75.7
19	Poland	317.3	44	Chile	72.3
20	Ukraine	304.8	45	North Korea	71.6
21	Turkey	298.0	46	Israel	70.7
22	Thailand	295.3	47	Qatar	70.5
23	Spain	269.7	48	Austria	66.9
24	Kazakhstan	248.7	49	Belarus	62.2
25	Malaysia	216.8	50	Syria	61.9

Largest amount of carbon dioxide emitted per person
Tonnes, 2010

1	Qatar	40.3	23	Belgium	10.0
2	Trinidad & Tobago	38.2	24	Libya	9.8
3	Kuwait	31.3	25	Israel	9.3
4	Brunei	22.9	26	Japan	9.2
5	Luxembourg	21.4		South Africa	9.2
6	Oman	20.4	28	Germany	9.1
7	United Arab Emirates	19.9	29	Ireland	8.9
8	Bahrain	19.3	30	Denmark	8.3
9	United States	17.6		Poland	8.3
10	Saudi Arabia	17.0	32	Bosnia & Herz.	8.1
11	Australia	16.9	33	Austria	8.0
12	New Caledonia	15.7	34	United Kingdom	7.9
13	Kazakhstan	15.2	35	Greece	7.7
14	Canada	14.6		Iran	7.7
15	Estonia	13.7		Malaysia	7.7
16	Russia	12.2	38	Slovenia	7.5
17	Norway	11.7	39	Bermuda	7.3
18	Finland	11.5	40	New Zealand	7.2
	South Korea	11.5	41	Cyprus	7.0
20	Netherlands	11.0	42	Venezuela	6.9
21	Czech Republic	10.6	43	Bahamas	6.8
22	Turkmenistan	10.5			

Renewable sources of energy[a]
As % of electricity production, 2011

1	Denmark	40.2	14	Lithuania	14.9
2	El Salvador	31.3	15	Philippines	14.6
3	Iceland	27.3	16	Italy	12.4
4	Guatemala	27.1	17	Sweden	11.7
5	Portugal	24.2	18	Netherlands	10.9
6	Kenya	23.3	19	Austria	10.7
7	Nicaragua	22.4	20	Uruguay	9.3
8	New Zealand	19.5	21	Belgium	9.2
9	Spain	19.2	22	Estonia	8.9
10	Costa Rica	18.7	23	United Kingdom	7.9
11	Germany	17.6	24	Chile	7.6
12	Ireland	17.1	25	Greece	7.0
13	Finland	15.9		Luxembourg	7.0

Population with access to an improved water source
Lowest %, 2010

1	Somalia	31.5	16	Togo	58.8
2	Papua New Guinea	38.8	17	Kenya	60.1
3	Congo-Kinshasa	46.0	18	Zambia	61.7
4	Madagascar	47.6	19	Haiti	62.4
5	Ethiopia	47.8	20	Nigeria	62.6
	Mozambique	47.8	21	Mali	63.6
7	Mauritania	49.6	22	Cambodia	66.0
8	Chad	49.7	23	Central African Rep.	67.2
9	Niger	50.5	24	Laos	67.5
10	Angola	52.6	25	Timor-Leste	67.7
11	Tanzania	53.4	26	Tajikistan	69.7
12	Yemen	54.6	27	Guinea-Bissau	69.9
13	Sudan	54.9	28	Rwanda	70.1
14	Afghanistan	57.1	29	Swaziland	70.3
15	Sierra Leone	57.9	30	Turkmenistan	70.8

Population with access to improved sanitation
Lowest %, 2010

1	Niger	8.6	16	Mozambique	19.8
2	Malawi	10.3	17	Central African Rep.	20.7
3	Chad	11.5	18	Côte d'Ivoire	21.1
	Togo	11.5		Ethiopia	21.1
5	Tanzania	11.6	20	Mali	21.3
6	Sierra Leone	12.8	21	Sudan	22.4
7	Madagascar	13.4	22	Somalia	23.4
8	Benin	13.7	23	Haiti	23.9
	Ghana	13.7	24	Mauritania	26.5
10	Congo-Brazzaville	14.3	25	Afghanistan	28.0
11	Liberia	16.3	26	Nigeria	28.5
12	Burkina Faso	17.4	27	Lesotho	28.7
13	Guinea	17.9	28	Kenya	29.1
14	Guinea-Bissau	18.4	29	Congo-Kinshasa	30.0
15	Papua New Guinea	18.7	30	Namibia	31.5

a Includes geothermal, solar, municipal waste, biofuels, but not hydroelectric.

Number of species under threat
2012
Mammals

1	Indonesia	185	9	Australia	55
2	Mexico	101		Peru	55
3	India	95	11	Colombia	54
4	Brazil	82		Vietnam	54
5	China	75	13	Myanmar	46
6	Malaysia	71	14	Ecuador	45
7	Madagascar	65		Laos	45
8	Thailand	57			

Birds

1	Brazil	152	10	Philippines	74
2	Peru	124	11	New Zealand	70
3	Indonesia	122	12	Mexico	61
4	Colombia	112	13	Bolivia	53
5	Ecuador	94	14	Australia	51
6	China	87	15	Argentina	50
7	Russia	83	16	Thailand	47
8	India	80	17	Malaysia	45
9	United States	78		Vietnam	45

Fish

1	United States	236	10	Thailand	96
2	India	213	11	Madagascar	87
3	Tanzania	175		South Africa	87
4	Mexico	154	13	Brazil	84
5	Indonesia	145		Congo-Kinshasa	84
6	China	121	15	Greece	75
7	Cameroon	112	16	Vietnam	73
8	Australia	106	17	Philippines	72
9	Malawi	101	18	Malaysia	71

Biggest nationally protected land area[a]
As % of total land, 2012

1	New Caledonia	61.3	16	Greece	34.7
2	Slovenia	54.5	17	Poland	34.2
3	Venezuela	53.0	18	Trinidad & Tobago	32.6
4	Germany	48.0	19	Tanzania	32.2
5	Brunei	44.0	20	Saudi Arabia	31.3
6	Namibia	43.2	21	Guatemala	30.9
7	Liechtenstein	43.1	22	Nicaragua	30.8
8	Hong Kong	41.9	23	Congo-Brazzaville	30.4
9	Cyprus	40.9	24	Spain	29.0
10	Luxembourg	39.7	25	Guinea	28.1
11	Zambia	37.8	26	United Kingdom	27.9
12	Botswana	37.2	27	New Zealand	27.3
13	Bulgaria	36.6	28	Zimbabwe	27.2
14	Slovakia	36.1	29	Costa Rica	26.9
15	Monaco	35.9	30	Guam	26.8

a Scientific reserves with limited access, national parks, nature reserves and protected landscapes.

Largest forests
Sq km, 2011

1	Russia	8,091,500
2	Brazil	5,173,276
3	Canada	3,101,340
4	United States	3,044,048
5	China	2,096,239
6	Congo-Kinshasa	1,538,236
7	Australia	1,483,760
8	Indonesia	937,470
9	India	685,790
10	Peru	678,420
11	Mexico	646,468
12	Colombia	603,980
13	Angola	583,552
14	Bolivia	568,884
15	Sudan	550,752
16	Zambia	493,014
17	Venezuela	459,874
18	Mozambique	388,106
19	Tanzania	330,246
20	Myanmar	314,634
21	Argentina	291,602
22	Papua New Guinea	285,838
23	Sweden	282,030
24	Japan	249,878
25	Central African Rep.	225,750
26	Congo-Brazzaville	223,990
27	Finland	221,570
28	Gabon	220,000
29	Malaysia	203,692
30	Cameroon	196,960

Most forest
% of land area, 2011

1	Suriname	94.6
2	Gabon	85.4
3	Finland	72.9
4	Brunei	71.8
5	Guinea-Bissau	71.6
6	Sweden	68.7
7	Japan	68.6
8	Congo-Kinshasa	67.9
	Laos	67.9
10	Zambia	66.3
11	Congo-Brazzaville	65.6
12	South Korea	64.0
13	Puerto Rico	63.2
14	Papua New Guinea	63.1
15	Slovenia	62.3
16	Malaysia	62.0
17	Brazil	61.2
18	Equatorial Guinea	57.5
19	Virgin Islands (US)	57.4
20	Cambodia	56.5
21	Fiji	55.7
22	Colombia	54.4
23	Latvia	54.1
24	Peru	53.0
25	Bolivia	52.5
26	Estonia	52.1
	Venezuela	52.1
28	Indonesia	51.7
29	Costa Rica	51.5
30	Bahamas	51.4

Biggest changes in forested land
%, 2000–11

Deforestation

1	Togo	-45.0
2	Nigeria	-34.3
3	Mauritania	-25.2
4	Uganda	-25.1
5	Pakistan	-22.3
6	Sudan	-21.9
7	Ghana	-20.8
8	Honduras	-20.7
9	Nicaragua	-20.2
10	North Korea	-20.1
11	Zimbabwe	-19.0
12	Ecuador	-18.4
13	Armenia	-15.2
14	El Salvador	-14.9
15	Guatemala	-14.4
	Timor-Leste	-14.4

Forestation

1	Iceland	67.4
2	French Polynesia	52.4
3	Bahrain	35.0
4	Kuwait	30.4
5	Rwanda	29.4
6	Uruguay	26.7
7	Tunisia	22.2
8	Puerto Rico	20.9
9	Moldova	20.6
10	Egypt	19.7
11	Cuba	19.3
12	Vietnam	18.9
13	China	18.4
14	Bulgaria	18.0
15	Ireland	17.8
16	Syria	15.0

Country profiles

ALGERIA

Area	2,381,741 sq km	Capital	Algiers
Arable as % of total land	3.2	Currency	Algerian dinar (AD)

People

Population	36.5m	Life expectancy: men	69.4 yrs
Pop. per sq km	15.0	women	72.6 yrs
Average annual growth		Adult literacy	...
in pop. 2010–15	1.8%	Fertility rate (per woman)	2.8
Pop. under 15	27.8%	Urban population	76.2%
Pop. over 60	7.4%		per 1,000 pop.
No. of men per 100 women	101.9	Crude birth rate	24.6
Human Development Index	71.7	Crude death rate	5.9

The economy

GDP	AD15,843bn	GDP per head	$5,350
GDP	$206bn	GDP per head in purchasing	
Av. ann. growth in real		power parity (USA=100)	16.3
GDP 2007–12	2.6%	Economic freedom index	50.8

Origins of GDP		Components of GDP	
	% of total		% of total
Agriculture	9	Private consumption	33
Industry, of which:	49	Public consumption	20
manufacturing	...	Investment	37
Services	42	Exports	37
		Imports	-28

Structure of employment

	% of total		% of labour force
Agriculture	10.8	Unemployed 2012	9.8
Industry	30.9	Av. ann. rate 2000–12	16.9
Services	58.4		

Energy

	m TOE		
Total output	145.8	Net energy imports as %	
Total consumption	41.9	of energy use	-248
Consumption per head			
kg oil equivalent	1,108		

Inflation and finance

Consumer price		av. ann. increase 2008–13	
inflation 2013[a]	3.3%	Narrow money (M1)	10.7%
Av. ann. inflation 2008–13[a]	5.2%	Broad money	11.4%
Treasury bill rate, Dec. 2013	0.24%		

Exchange rates

	end 2013		2013
AD per $	78.15	Effective rates	2005 = 100
AD per SDR	120.36	– nominal	89.60
AD per €	107.78	– real	90.96

Trade

Principal exports	$bn fob	Principal imports	$bn cif
Hydrocarbons	70.6	Capital goods	12.6
Semi-finished goods	0.6	Semi-finished goods	10.0
Raw materials	0.2	Food	8.5
		Consumer goods	9.6
Total incl. others	**71.7**	Total incl. others	**50.4**

Main export destinations	% of total	Main origins of imports	% of total
Italy	16.1	France	12.8
United States	15.0	China	11.8
Spain	10.9	Italy	10.3
France	8.5	Spain	8.6

Balance of payments, reserves and debt, $bn

Visible exports fob	71.6	Change in reserves	9.2
Visible imports fob	-51.5	Level of reserves	
Trade balance	20.0	end Dec.	200.6
Invisibles inflows	7.7	No. months of import cover	34.3
Invisibles outflows	-18.6	Official gold holdings, m oz	5.6
Net transfers	3.2	Foreign debt	5.6
Current account balance	12.3	– as % of GDP	2.3
– as % of GDP	6.0	– as % of total exports	7.0
Capital balance	2.3	Debt service ratio	1.1
Overall balance	12.0		

Health and education

Health spending, % of GDP	5.2	Education spending, % of GDP	4.3
Doctors per 1,000 pop.	1.2	Enrolment, %: primary	117
Hospital beds per 1,000 pop.	...	secondary	98
Improved-water source access,		tertiary	31
% of pop.	84		

Society

No. of households	6.5m	Cost of living, Dec. 2013	
Av. no. per household	5.7	New York = 100	53
Marriages per 1,000 pop.	9.6	Cars per 1,000 pop.	...
Divorces per 1,000 pop.	...	Colour TV households, % with:	
Religion, % of pop.		cable	...
Muslim	97.9	satellite	93.1
Non-religious	1.8	Telephone lines per 100 pop.	8.3
Christian	0.2	Mobile telephone subscribers	
Hindu	<0.1	per 100 pop.	98
Jewish	<0.1	Broadband subs per 100 pop.	2.9
Other	<0.1	Internet hosts per 1,000 pop.	0.2

a Estimate.

ARGENTINA

Area	2,766,889 sq km	Capital	Buenos Aires
Arable as % of total land	13.9	Currency	Peso (P)

People

Population	41.1m	Life expectancy: men	72.5 yrs
Pop. per sq km	14.7	women	79.8 yrs
Average annual growth		Adult literacy	98.9%
in pop. 2010–15	0.9%	Fertility rate (per woman)	2.2
Pop. under 15	24.2%	Urban population	93.1%
Pop. over 60	15.1%		per 1,000 pop.
No. of men per 100 women	95.8	Crude birth rate	16.8
Human Development Index	80.8	Crude death rate	7.7

The economy

GDP	P2,164bn	GDP per head	$11,570
GDP	$476bn	GDP per head in purchasing	
Av. ann. growth in real		power parity (USA=100)	34.6
GDP 2007–12	5.4%	Economic freedom index	44.6

Origins of GDP		Components of GDP	
	% of total		% of total
Agriculture	9	Private consumption	59
Industry, of which:	31	Public consumption	17
manufacturing	20	Investment	22
Services	60	Exports	20
		Imports	-17

Structure of employment

	% of total		% of labour force
Agriculture	0.6	Unemployed 2012	7.2
Industry	23.4	Av. ann. rate 2000–12	11.4
Services	75.3		

Energy

	m TOE		
Total output	77.2	Net energy imports as %	
Total consumption	80.1	of energy use	4
Consumption per head			
kg oil equivalent	1,967		

Inflation and finance

Consumer price		av. ann. increase 2008–13	
inflation 2013[a]	10.6%	Narrow money (M1)	29.5%
Av. ann. inflation 2008–13[a]	9.4%	Broad money	27.4%
Money market rate, Dec. 2013	19.67%		

Exchange rates

	end 2013		2013
P per $	6.50	Effective rates	2005 = 100
P per SDR	10.01	– nominal	...
P per €	8.96	– real	...

Trade

Principal exports		Principal imports	
	$bn fob		*$bn cif*
Processed agricultural products	27.7	Intermediate goods	20.0
Manufactures	27.6	Capital goods	11.9
Primary products	19.2	Fuels	9.3
Fuels	6.9	Consumer goods	7.3
Total	**81.2**	Total incl. others	**68.5**

Main export destinations		Main origins of imports	
	% of total		*% of total*
Brazil	20.1	Brazil	26.1
China	6.2	China	14.5
Chile	6.1	United States	12.4
United States	4.9	Germany	5.4

Balance of payments, reserves and debt, $bn

Visible exports fob	80.9	Change in reserves	-3.1
Visible imports fob	-65.6	Level of reserves	
Trade balance	15.3	end Dec.	43.2
Invisibles inflows	17.3	No. months of import cover	5.3
Invisibles outflows	-32.2	Official gold holdings, m oz	2.0
Net transfers	-0.4	Foreign debt	121.0
Current account balance	0.0	– as % of GDP	20.0
– as % of GDP	0.0	– as % of total exports	122.5
Capital balance	-0.6	Debt service ratio	13.3
Overall balance	-3.4		

Health and education

Health spending, % of GDP	8.5	Education spending, % of GDP	6.3
Doctors per 1,000 pop.	3.2	Enrolment, %: primary	118
Hospital beds per 1,000 pop.	4.7	secondary	92
Improved-water source access,		tertiary	79
% of pop.	99		

Society

No. of households	12.8m	Cost of living, Dec. 2013	
Av. no. per household	3.2	New York = 100	71
Marriages per 1,000 pop.	3.1	Cars per 1,000 pop.	...
Divorces per 1,000 pop.	...	Colour TV households, % with:	
Religion, % of pop.		cable	64.8
Christian	85.2	satellite	14.4
Non-religious	12.2	Telephone lines per 100 pop.	23.5
Other	1.1	Mobile telephone subscribers	
Muslim	1.0	per 100 pop.	152
Jewish	0.5	Broadband subs per 100 pop.	10.9
Hindu	<0.1	Internet hosts per 1,000 pop.	341.6

a Estimate.

AUSTRALIA

Area	7,682,300 sq km	Capital	Canberra
Arable as % of total land	6.2	Currency	Australian dollar (A$)

People

Population	22.9m	Life expectancy: men		80.2 yrs
Pop. per sq km	2.9	women		84.7 yrs
Average annual growth		Adult literacy		...
in pop. 2010–15	1.3%	Fertility rate (per woman)		1.9
Pop. under 15	19.1%	Urban population		89.8%
Pop. over 60	19.8%			per 1,000 pop.
No. of men per 100 women	99.3	Crude birth rate		13.2
Human Development Index	93.3	Crude death rate		6.6

The economy

GDP	A$1,475bn	GDP per head	$67,440
GDP	$1,532bn	GDP per head in purchasing	
Av. ann. growth in real		power parity (USA=100)	84.7
GDP 2007–12	2.7%	Economic freedom index	82.0

Origins of GDP		**Components of GDP**	
	% of total		% of total
Agriculture	2	Private consumption	54
Industry, of which:	28	Public consumption	18
manufacturing	8	Investment	28
Services	69	Exports	21
		Imports	-21

Structure of employment

	% of total		% of labour force
Agriculture	3.3	Unemployed 2012	5.2
Industry	21.1	Av. ann. rate 2000–12	5.4
Services	75.5		

Energy

	m TOE		
Total output	296.7	Net energy imports as %	
Total consumption	122.9	of energy use	-141
Consumption per head			
kg oil equivalent	5,505		

Inflation and finance

Consumer price		av. ann. increase 2008–13	
inflation 2013	2.5%	Narrow money (M1)	4.2%
Av. ann. inflation 2008–13	2.4%	Broad money	7.4%
Money market rate, Dec. 2013	2.50%	H'hold saving rate, 2013	10.4%

Exchange rates

	end 2013		2013
A$ per $	1.13	Effective rates	2005 = 100
A$ per SDR	1.73	– nominal	117.60
A$ per €	1.56	– real	108.70

Trade

Principal exports	$bn fob	Principal imports	$bn cif
Crude materials	89.3	Machinery & transport equip.	99.2
Fuels	72.8	Mineral fuels	42.3
Food	26.2	Miscellaneous manufactured	
Manufactured goods	14.3	articles	30.1
		Manufactured goods	26.8
Total incl. others	**256.5**	Total incl. others	**250.8**

Main export destinations	% of total	Main origins of imports	% of total
China	29.6	China	20.2
Japan	19.4	United States	12.9
South Korea	8.1	Japan	8.7
India	4.9	Singapore	6.6

Balance of payments, reserves and aid, $bn

Visible exports fob	258.0	Overall balance	2.5
Visible imports fob	-270.3	Change in reserves	2.4
Trade balance	-12.3	Level of reserves	
Invisibles inflows	101.6	end Dec.	49.1
Invisibles outflows	-151.3	No. months of import cover	1.4
Net transfers	-2.3	Official gold holdings, m oz	2.6
Current account balance	-64.3	Aid given	5.40
– as % of GDP	-4.2	– as % of GDP	0.35
Capital balance	66.9		

Health and education

Health spending, % of GDP	8.9	Education spending, % of GDP	5.6
Doctors per 1,000 pop.	3.3	Enrolment, %: primary	104
Hospital beds per 1,000 pop.	3.9	secondary	133
Improved-water source access,		tertiary	83
% of pop.	100		

Society

No. of households	8.3m	Cost of living, Dec. 2013	
Av. no. per household	2.7	New York = 100	120
Marriages per 1,000 pop.	5.5	Cars per 1,000 pop.	560
Divorces per 1,000 pop.	2.2	Colour TV households, % with:	
Religion, % of pop.		cable	24.9
Christian	67.3	satellite	33.7
Non-religious	24.2	Telephone lines per 100 pop.	45.4
Other	4.2	Mobile telephone subscribers	
Muslim	2.4	per 100 pop.	105.6
Hindu	1.4	Broadband subs per 100 pop.	24.3
Jewish	0.5	Internet hosts per 1,000 pop.	703.4

AUSTRIA

Area	83,855 sq km	Capital	Vienna
Arable as % of total land	16.5	Currency	Euro (€)

People

Population	8.4m	Life expectancy: men	78.5 yrs
Pop. per sq km	100.0	women	83.5 yrs
Average annual growth		Adult literacy	...
in pop. 2010–15	0.4%	Fertility rate (per woman)	1.5
Pop. under 15	14.5%	Urban population	68.5%
Pop. over 60	23.7%		per 1,000 pop.
No. of men per 100 women	95.3	Crude birth rate	9.5
Human Development Index	88.1	Crude death rate	9.4

The economy

GDP	€307bn	GDP per head	$46,820
GDP	$395bn	GDP per head in purchasing	
Av. ann. growth in real		power parity (USA=100)	85.3
GDP 2007–12	0.6%	Economic freedom index	72.4

Origins of GDP		Components of GDP	
	% of total		% of total
Agriculture	2	Private consumption	55
Industry, of which:	29	Public consumption	19
manufacturing	18	Investment	23
Services	70	Exports	57
		Imports	-54

Structure of employment

	% of total		% of labour force
Agriculture	4.9	Unemployed 2012	4.3
Industry	26.2	Av. ann. rate 2000–12	4.3
Services	68.9		

Energy

	m TOE		
Total output	11.5	Net energy imports as %	
Total consumption	33.0	of energy use	65
Consumption per head			
kg oil equivalent	3,920		

Inflation and finance

Consumer price		av. ann. increase 2008–13	
inflation 2013	2.1%	Euro area:	
Av. ann. inflation 2008–13	2.1%	Narrow money (M1)	6.0%
Deposit rate, h'holds, Dec. 2013	0.75%	Broad money	0.8%
		H'hold saving rate, 2013	6.6%

Exchange rates

	end 2013		2013
€ per $	0.73	Effective rates	2005 = 100
€ per SDR	1.12	– nominal	101.70
		– real	101.20

Trade

Principal exports	$bn fob	Principal imports	$bn cif
Machinery & transport equip.	62.9	Machinery & transport equip.	58.0
Chemicals & related products	21.1	Mineral fuels & lubricants	21.8
Food, drink & tobacco	11.7	Chemicals & related products	21.3
Raw materials	5.3	Food, drink & tobacco	12.2
Total incl. others	**165.0**	**Total incl. others**	**176.8**

Main export destinations	% of total	Main origins of imports	% of total
Germany	30.7	Germany	41.9
Italy	6.8	Italy	6.5
France	4.5	Switzerland	5.1
Switzerland	4.4	Netherlands	3.9
EU27	62.9	EU27	75.9

Balance of payments, reserves and aid, $bn

Visible exports fob	159.2	Overall balance	1.2
Visible imports fob	-163.4	Change in reserves	2.4
Trade balance	-4.2	Level of reserves	
Invisibles inflows	98.5	end Dec.	27.2
Invisibles outflows	-82.1	No. months of import cover	1.3
Net transfers	-2.7	Official gold holdings, m oz	9.0
Current account balance	9.5	Aid given	1.11
– as % of GDP	2.4	– as % of GDP	0.28
Capital balance	-8.8		

Health and education

Health spending, % of GDP	11.5	Education spending, % of GDP	5.9
Doctors per 1,000 pop.	4.8	Enrolment, %: primary	101
Hospital beds per 1,000 pop.	7.6	secondary	98
Improved-water source access,		tertiary	71
% of pop.	100		

Society

No. of households	3.7m	Cost of living, Dec. 2013	
Av. no. per household	2.3	New York = 100	105
Marriages per 1,000 pop.	4.6	Cars per 1,000 pop.	543
Divorces per 1,000 pop.	2	Colour TV households, % with:	
Religion, % of pop.		cable	38.6
Christian	80.4	satellite	54.3
Non-religious	13.5	Telephone lines per 100 pop.	39.7
Muslim	5.4	Mobile telephone subscribers	
Other	0.5	per 100 pop.	160.5
Jewish	0.2	Broadband subs per 100 pop.	25.0
Hindu	<0.1	Internet hosts per 1,000 pop.	432.3

BANGLADESH

Area	143,998 sq km	Capital	Dhaka
Arable as % of total land	58.6	Currency	Taka (Tk)

People

Population	152.4m	Life expectancy: men	69.8 yrs
Pop. per sq km	1,045.1	women	71.3 yrs
Average annual growth		Adult literacy	57.7%
in pop. 2010–15	1.2%	Fertility rate (per woman)	2.2
Pop. under 15	30.0%	Urban population	30.4%
Pop. over 60	7.0%		per 1,000 pop.
No. of men per 100 women	102.6	Crude birth rate	20.3
Human Development Index	55.8	Crude death rate	5.7

The economy

GDP	Tk9,181bn	GDP per head	$750
GDP	$116bn	GDP per head in purchasing	
Av. ann. growth in real		power parity (USA=100)	3.6
GDP 2007–12	6.2%	Economic freedom index	54.1

Origins of GDP		Components of GDP	
	% of total		% of total
Agriculture	18	Private consumption	77
Industry, of which:	28	Public consumption	6
manufacturing	18	Investment	27
Services	54	Exports	23
		Imports	-32

Structure of employment

	% of total		% of labour force
Agriculture	...	Unemployed 2012	4.5
Industry	...	Av. ann. rate 2000–12	4.2
Services	...		

Energy

			m TOE
Total output	26.1	Net energy imports as %	
Total consumption	31.3	of energy use	17
Consumption per head			
kg oil equivalent	205		

Inflation and finance

Consumer price		av. ann. increase 2008–13	
inflation 2013	7.5%	Narrow money (M1)	14.7%
Av. ann. inflation 2008–13	7.6%	Broad money	18.0%
Deposit rate, Dec. 2013	10.68%		

Exchange rates

	end 2013		2013
Tk per $	77.75	Effective rates	2005 = 100
Tk per SDR	119.74	– nominal	...
Tk per €	107.23	– real	...

Trade

Principal exports[a]		Principal imports[a]	
	$bn fob		$bn cif
Clothing	15.1	Fuels	4.9
Jute goods	0.7	Textiles & yarns	3.0
Leather	0.6	Iron & steel	2.3
Fish & fish products	0.5	Cotton	2.2
Total incl. others	**22.2**	Total incl. others	**34.2**

Main export destinations		Main origins of imports	
	% of total		% of total
United States	16.6	China	17.8
Germany	13.4	India	13.8
United Kingdom	8.6	Malaysia	5.0
France	5.2	Singapore	4.6

Balance of payments, reserves and debt, $bn

Visible exports fob	24.9	Change in reserves	3.6
Visible imports fob	-32.2	Level of reserves	
Trade balance	-7.3	end Dec.	12.8
Invisibles inflows	2.9	No. months of import cover	3.9
Invisibles outflows	-7.6	Official gold holdings, m oz	0.4
Net transfers	14.5	Foreign debt	26.1
Current account balance	2.6	– as % of GDP	22.5
– as % of GDP	2.2	– as % of total exports	62.4
Capital balance	1.6	Debt service ratio	3.6
Overall balance	3.5		

Health and education

Health spending, % of GDP	3.6	Education spending, % of GDP	2.2
Doctors per 1,000 pop.	0.4	Enrolment, %: primary	114
Hospital beds per 1,000 pop.	0.6	secondary	51
Improved-water source access,		tertiary	13
% of pop.	85		

Society

No. of households	35.8m	Cost of living, Dec. 2013	
Av. no. per household	4.3	New York = 100	64
Marriages per 1,000 pop.	...	Cars per 1,000 pop.	2
Divorces per 1,000 pop.	...	Colour TV households, % with:	
Religion, % of pop. of pop.		cable	...
Muslim	89.8	satellite	...
Hindu	9.1	Telephone lines per 100 pop.	0.6
Other	0.9	Mobile telephone subscribers	
Christian	0.2	per 100 pop.	62.8
Jewish	<0.1	Broadband subs per 100 pop.	0.4
Non-religious	<0.1	Internet hosts per 1,000 pop.	0.9

a Fiscal years ending June 30 2012.

BELGIUM

Area	30,520 sq km	Capital	Brussels
Arable as % of total land	27.3	Currency	Euro (€)

People

Population	10.8m	Life expectancy: men		77.9 yrs
Pop. per sq km	348.4	women		83.0 yrs
Average annual growth		Adult literacy		...
in pop. 2010–15	0.4%	Fertility rate (per woman)		1.9
Pop. under 15	17.0%	Urban population		97.6%
Pop. over 60	24.0%			per 1,000 pop.
No. of men per 100 women	96	Crude birth rate		11.7
Human Development Index	88.1	Crude death rate		10.0

The economy

GDP	€376bn	GDP per head	$43,430
GDP	$483bn	GDP per head in purchasing	
Av. ann. growth in real		power parity (USA=100)	78.4
GDP 2007–12	0.4%	Economic freedom index	69.9

Origins of GDP		**Components of GDP**	
	% of total		% of total
Agriculture	1	Private consumption	53
Industry, of which:	22	Public consumption	25
manufacturing	13	Investment	21
Services	77	Exports	86
		Imports	-85

Structure of employment

	% of total		% of labour force
Agriculture	1.2	Unemployed 2012	7.5
Industry	21.8	Av. ann. rate 2000–12	7.6
Services	77.1		

Energy

	m TOE		
Total output	18.2	Net energy imports as %	
Total consumption	59.1	of energy use	69
Consumption per head			
kg oil equivalent	5,349		

Inflation and finance

Consumer price		av. ann. increase 2008–13	
inflation 2013	1.2%	Euro area:	
Av. ann. inflation 2008–13	1.9%	Narrow money (M1)	6.0%
Treasury bill rate, Dec. 2013	0.04%	Broad money	0.8%
		H'hold saving rate, 2013	9.9%

Exchange rates

	end 2013		2013
€ per $	0.73	Effective rates	2005 = 100
€ per SDR	1.12	– nominal	103.80
		– real	102.10

Trade

Principal exports	
	$bn fob
Chemicals & related products	129.9
Machinery & transport equip.	91.7
Mineral fuels & lubricants	50.8
Food, drink & tobacco	38.4
Total incl. others	**446.9**

Principal imports	
	$bn cif
Chemicals & related products	101.5
Machinery & transport equip.	97.6
Mineral fuels & lubricants	75.5
Food, drink & tobacco	32.9
Total incl. others	**439.8**

Main export destinations	
	% of total
Germany	17.4
France	15.5
Netherlands	12.5
United Kingdom	7.0
EU27	70.0

Main origins of imports	
	% of total
Netherlands	20.6
Germany	14.1
France	10.5
United States	6.1
EU27	67.5

Balance of payments, reserves and aid, $bn

Visible exports fob	301.8	Overall balance	0.7
Visible imports fob	-315.5	Change in reserves	1.6
Trade balance	-13.7	Level of reserves	
Invisibles inflows	161.9	end Dec.	30.7
Invisibles outflows	-147.9	No. months of import cover	0.8
Net transfers	-9.6	Official gold holdings, m oz	7.3
Current account balance	-9.4	Aid given	2.31
– as % of GDP	-1.9	– as % of GDP	0.48
Capital balance	9.0		

Health and education

Health spending, % of GDP	10.8	Education spending, % of GDP	6.6
Doctors per 1,000 pop.	3.0	Enrolment, %: primary	104
Hospital beds per 1,000 pop.	6.5	secondary	106
Improved-water source access,		tertiary	69
% of pop.	100		

Society

No. of households	4.8m	Cost of living, Dec. 2013	
Av. no. per household	2.3	New York = 100	98
Marriages per 1,000 pop.	3.6	Cars per 1,000 pop.	500
Divorces per 1,000 pop.	2.5	Colour TV households, % with:	
Religion, % of pop.		cable	74.2
Christian	64.2	satellite	5.9
Non-religious	29.0	Telephone lines per 100 pop.	41.9
Muslim	5.9	Mobile telephone subscribers	
Other	0.6	per 100 pop.	111.3
Jewish	0.3	Broadband subs per 100 pop.	33.3
Hindu	<0.1	Internet hosts per 1,000 pop.	498.1

BRAZIL

Area	8,511,965 sq km	Capital	Brasilia
Arable as % of total land	8.5	Currency	Real (R)

People

Population	198.4m	Life expectancy: men	70.2 yrs
Pop. per sq km	23.1	women	77.5 yrs
Average annual growth		Adult literacy	90.4%
in pop. 2010–15	0.9%	Fertility rate (per woman)	1.8
Pop. under 15	24.1%	Urban population	85.7%
Pop. over 60	11.2%		per 1,000 pop.
No. of men per 100 women	96.9	Crude birth rate	15.1
Human Development Index	74.4	Crude death rate	6.5

The economy

GDP	R4,403bn	GDP per head	$11,340
GDP	$2,253bn	GDP per head in purchasing	
Av. ann. growth in real		power parity (USA=100)	22.6
GDP 2007–12	3.2%	Economic freedom index	56.9

Origins of GDP		**Components of GDP**	
	% of total		% of total
Agriculture	5	Private consumption	62
Industry, of which:	26	Public consumption	21
manufacturing	13	Investment	18
Services	68	Exports	13
		Imports	-14

Structure of employment

	% of total		% of labour force
Agriculture	15.3	Unemployed 2012	6.9
Industry	21.9	Av. ann. rate 2000–12	8.4
Services	62.7		

Energy

			m TOE
Total output	249.2	Net energy imports as %	
Total consumption	270.0	of energy use	8
Consumption per head			
kg oil equivalent	1,371		

Inflation and finance

Consumer price		av. ann. increase 2008–13	
inflation 2013	6.2%	Narrow money (M1)	9.1%
Av. ann. inflation 2008–13	5.6%	Broad money	14.9%
Money market rate, Dec. 2013	9.90%		

Exchange rates

	end 2013		2013
R per $	2.34	Effective rates	2005 = 100
R per SDR	3.61	– nominal	104.46
R per €	3.23	– real	125.73

Trade

Principal exports		Principal imports	
	$bn fob		$bn cif
Primary products	113.5	Intermediate products &	
Manufactured products	90.7	raw materials	99.9
Semi-manufactured products	33.0	Capital goods	48.6
		Consumer goods	39.4
		Fuels & lubricants	35.3
Total incl. others	**242.6**	Total	**223.2**

Main export destinations		Main origins of imports	
	% of total		% of total
China	17.0	China	16.9
United States	11.1	United States	16.1
Argentina	7.4	Argentina	8.1
Netherlands	6.2	Germany	7.0

Balance of payments, reserves and debt, $bn

Visible exports fob	242.6	Change in reserves	21.1
Visible imports fob	-223.1	Level of reserves	
Trade balance	19.4	end Dec.	373.1
Invisibles inflows	50.8	No. months of import cover	12.8
Invisibles outflows	-127.3	Official gold holdings, m oz	2.2
Net transfers	2.8	Foreign debt	440.5
Current account balance	-54.2	– as % of GDP	19.6
– as % of GDP	-2.4	– as % of total exports	148.9
Capital balance	72.8	Debt service ratio	15.4
Overall balance	18.9		

Health and education

Health spending, % of GDP	9.3	Education spending, % of GDP	5.8
Doctors per 1,000 pop.	1.8	Enrolment, %: primary	...
Hospital beds per 1,000 pop.	2.3	secondary	...
Improved-water source access,		tertiary	...
% of pop.	98		

Society

No. of households	59.6m	Cost of living, Dec. 2013	
Av. no. per household	3.3	New York = 100	76
Marriages per 1,000 pop.	5.1	Cars per 1,000 pop.	...
Divorces per 1,000 pop.	0.8	Colour TV households, % with:	
Religion, % of pop.		cable	11.3
Christian	88.9	satellite	16.9
Non-religious	7.9	Telephone lines per 100 pop.	22.3
Other	3.1	Mobile telephone subscribers	
Hindu	<0.1	per 100 pop.	125
Jewish	<0.1	Broadband subs per 100 pop.	9.2
Muslim	<0.1	Internet hosts per 1,000 pop.	185.9

BULGARIA

Area	110,994 sq km	Capital	Sofia
Arable as % of total land	29.9	Currency	Lev (BGL)

People

Population	7.4m	Life expectancy: men	69.9 yrs
Pop. per sq km	66.7	women	77.2 yrs
Average annual growth		Adult literacy	98.4%
in pop. 2010–15	-0.8%	Fertility rate (per woman)	1.5
Pop. under 15	13.7%	Urban population	75.3%
Pop. over 60	26.4%		per 1,000 pop.
No. of men per 100 women	93.6	Crude birth rate	9.6
Human Development Index	77.7	Crude death rate	15.8

The economy

GDP	BGL77.6bn	GDP per head	$6,980
GDP	$51.0bn	GDP per head in purchasing	
Av. ann. growth in real		power parity (USA=100)	31.0
GDP 2007–12	0.7%	Economic freedom index	65.7

Origins of GDP		**Components of GDP**	
	% of total		% of total
Agriculture	6	Private consumption	64
Industry, of which:	30	Public consumption	16
manufacturing	17	Investment	24
Services	63	Exports	67
		Imports	-70

Structure of employment

	% of total		% of labour force
Agriculture	6.4	Unemployed 2012	12.3
Industry	31.3	Av. ann. rate 2000–12	11.7
Services	62.2		

Energy

		m TOE	
Total output	12.4	Net energy imports as %	
Total consumption	19.2	of energy use	36
Consumption per head			
kg oil equivalent	2,615		

Inflation and finance

		av. ann. change 2006–11	
Consumer price			
inflation 2013	0.4%	Narrow money (M1)	6.4%
Av. ann. inflation 2008–13	2.3%	Broad money	8.0%
Money market rate, Dec. 2013	0.02%		

Exchange rates

	end 2013		2013
BGL per $	1.42	Effective rates	2005 = 100
BGL per SDR	2.19	– nominal	108.94
BGL per €	1.96	– real	123.85

Trade

Principal exports	$bn fob	Principal imports	$bn cif
Other metals	3.0	Crude oil & natural gas	6.2
Clothing & footwear	1.9	Chemicals, plastics & rubber	2.2
Chemicals, plastics & rubber	1.2	Machinery & equipment	2.2
Iron & steel	0.9	Textiles	1.4
Total incl. others	**26.7**	**Total incl. others**	**31.1**

Main export destinations	% of total	Main origins of imports	% of total
Germany	10.3	Russia	21.7
Turkey	8.9	Germany	11.7
Italy	8.5	Italy	7.0
Romania	8.0	Romania	6.9
EU27	58.5	EU27	58.6

Balance of payments, reserves and debt, $bn

Visible exports fob	26.7	Change in reserves	3.3
Visible imports fob	-31.1	Level of reserves	
Trade balance	-4.5	end Dec.	20.5
Invisibles inflows	8.3	No. months of import cover	6.5
Invisibles outflows	-7.0	Official gold holdings, m oz	1.3
Net transfers	2.7	Foreign debt	50.8
Current account balance	-0.5	– as % of GDP	102.9
– as % of GDP	-1.0	– as % of total exports	139.2
Capital balance	2.5	Debt service ratio	12.4
Overall balance	2.7	Aid given	0.04
		– as % of GDP	0.08

Health and education

Health spending, % of GDP	7.4	Education spending, % of GDP	4.1
Doctors per 1,000 pop.	3.8	Enrolment, %: primary	101
Hospital beds per 1,000 pop.	6.4	secondary	93
Improved-water source access,		tertiary	60
% of pop.	99		

Society

No. of households	2.9m	Cost of living, Dec. 2013	
Av. no. per household	2.5	New York = 100	63
Marriages per 1,000 pop.	2.9	Cars per 1,000 pop.	383
Divorces per 1,000 pop.	1.6	Colour TV households, % with:	
Religion, % of pop.		cable	48.2
Christian	82.1	satellite	28.8
Muslim	13.7	Telephone lines per 100 pop.	29.3
Non-religious	4.2	Mobile telephone subscribers	
Hindu	<0.1	per 100 pop.	148.1
Jewish	<0.1	Broadband subs per 100 pop.	18.0
Other	<0.1	Internet hosts per 1,000 pop.	130.9

CAMEROON

Area	475,442 sq km	Capital	Yaoundé
Arable as % of total land	13.1	Currency	CFA franc (CFAfr)

People

Population	20.5m	Life expectancy: men	57.3 yrs
Pop. per sq km	42.1	women	56.0 yrs
Average annual growth		Adult literacy	71.3%
in pop. 2010–15	2.5%	Fertility rate (per woman)	4.8
Pop. under 15	43.0%	Urban population	54.4%
Pop. over 60	4.9%		per 1,000 pop.
No. of men per 100 women	99.7	Crude birth rate	37.5
Human Development Index	50.4	Crude death rate	11.9

The economy

GDP	CFAfr12,927bn	GDP per head	$1,170
GDP	$25.3bn	GDP per head in purchasing	
Av. ann. growth in real		power parity (USA=100)	4.5
GDP 2007–12	3.5%	Economic freedom index	52.6

Origins of GDP		**Components of GDP**	
	% of total		% of total
Agriculture	26	Private consumption	70
Industry, of which:	33	Public consumption	14
manufacturing	...	Investment	19
Services	41	Exports	29
		Imports	-32

Structure of employment

	% of total		% of labour force
Agriculture	53.3	Unemployed 2012	3.8
Industry	12.6	Av. ann. rate 2000–12	4.8
Services	34.1		

Energy

	m TOE		
Total output	8.2	Net energy imports as %	
Total consumption	6.7	of energy use	-22
Consumption per head			
kg oil equivalent	318		

Inflation and finance

Consumer price			av. ann. change 2006–11
inflation 2013[a]	2.1%	Narrow money (M1)	8.6%
Av. ann. inflation 2008–13[a]	2.3%	Broad money	8.6%
Deposit rate, Dec. 2013	2.75%		

Exchange rates

	end 2013		2013
CFAfr per $	475.64	Effective rates	2005 = 100
CFAfr per SDR	732.49	– nominal	105.70
CFAfr per €	655.96	– real	102.10

Trade

Principal exports	$bn fob	Principal imports	$bn cif
Fuels	2.5	Manufactures	3.4
Foodstuffs	0.8	Fuels	2.1
Agricultural products	0.7	Foodstuffs	1.3
Total incl. others	**4.5**	Total incl. others	**7.1**

Main export destinations	% of total	Main origins of imports	% of total
China	15.2	China	18.7
Netherlands	9.7	France	14.9
Spain	9.1	Nigeria	12.3
India	8.6	Belgium	5.2

Balance of payments, reserves and debt, $bn

Visible exports fob	5.8	Change in reserves	0.2
Visible imports fob	-6.0	Level of reserves	
Trade balance	-0.3	end Dec.	3.4
Invisibles inflows	1.8	No. months of import cover	4.6
Invisibles outflows	-2.8	Official gold holdings, m oz	0.0
Net transfers	0.3	Foreign debt	3.7
Current account balance	-1.0	– as % of GDP	14.5
– as % of GDP	-3.8	– as % of total exports	47.1
Capital balance	1.2	Debt service ratio	3.9
Overall balance	0.1		

Health and education

Health spending, % of GDP	5.1	Education spending, % of GDP	3.2
Doctors per 1,000 pop.	0.1	Enrolment, %: primary	111
Hospital beds per 1,000 pop.	1.3	secondary	50
Improved-water source access,		tertiary	12
% of pop.	74		

Society

No. of households	4.2m	Cost of living, Dec. 2013	
Av. no. per household	4.8	New York = 100	...
Marriages per 1,000 pop.	...	Cars per 1,000 pop.	14
Divorces per 1,000 pop.	...	Colour TV households, % with:	
Religion, % of pop.		cable	...
Christian	70.3	satellite	2.4
Muslim	18.3	Telephone lines per 100 pop.	3.4
Other	6.0	Mobile telephone subscribers	
Non-religious	5.3	per 100 pop.	60.4
Hindu	<0.1	Broadband subs per 100 pop.	0.6
Jewish	<0.1	Internet hosts per 1,000 pop.	0.7

a Estimate.

CANADA

Area[a]	9,970,610 sq km	Capital	Ottawa
Arable as % of total land	4.7	Currency	Canadian dollar (C$)

People

Population	34.7m	Life expectancy: men	79.3 yrs
Pop. per sq km	3.4	women	83.5 yrs
Average annual growth		Adult literacy	...
in pop. 2010–15	1.0%	Fertility rate (per woman)	1.7
Pop. under 15	16.4%	Urban population	81.1%
Pop. over 60	21.2%		per 1,000 pop.
No. of men per 100 women	98.4	Crude birth rate	11.2
Human Development Index	90.2	Crude death rate	7.5

The economy

GDP	C$1,778bn	GDP per head	$51,210
GDP	$1,780bn	GDP per head in purchasing	
Av. ann. growth in real		power parity (USA=100)	79.8
GDP 2007–12	1.1%	Economic freedom index	80.2

Origins of GDP[b]

	% of total
Agriculture	2
Industry, of which:	27
manufacturing	...
Services	71

Components of GDP

	% of total
Private consumption	57
Public consumption	21
Investment	23
Exports	30
Imports	-32

Structure of employment

	% of total		% of labour force
Agriculture	2.4	Unemployed 2012	7.2
Industry	21.5	Av. ann. rate 2000–12	7.1
Services	76.5		

Energy

	m TOE		
Total output	409.0	Net energy imports as %	
Total consumption	251.8	of energy use	-62
Consumption per head			
kg oil equivalent	7,303		

Inflation and finance

		av. ann. increase 2008–13	
Consumer price inflation 2013	1.0%	Narrow money (M1)	8.8%
Av. ann. inflation 2008–13	1.5%	Broad money	6.2%
Money market rate, Dec. 2013	1.00%	H'hold saving rate, 2013	5.2%

Exchange rates

	end 2013		2013
C$ per $	1.06	Effective rates	2005 = 100
C$ per SDR	1.64	– nominal	110.50
C$ per €	1.46	– real	105.80

Trade

Principal exports		Principal imports	
	$bn fob		*$bn cif*
Energy products	105.2	Consumer goods	93.1
Motor vehicles & parts	68.5	Motor vehicles & parts	82.9
Metal & mineral products	54.4	Electronic & electrical equip.	55.5
Consumer goods	48.6	Energy products	45.8
Total incl. others	**462.9**	Total incl. others	**474.9**

Main export destinations		Main origins of imports	
	% of total		*% of total*
United States	74.5	United States	50.6
China	4.3	China	11.0
United Kingdom	4.1	Mexico	5.5
Japan	2.3	Japan	3.5
EU27	8.5	EU27	10.6

Balance of payments, reserves and aid, $bn

Visible exports fob	462.9	Overall balance	1.7
Visible imports fob	-474.9	Change in reserves	2.7
Trade balance	-12.0	Level of reserves	
Invisibles inflows	156.9	end Dec.	68.5
Invisibles outflows	-203.6	No. months of import cover	1.2
Net transfers	-3.5	Official gold holdings, m oz	0.1
Current account balance	-62.3	Aid given	5.65
– as % of GDP	-3.5	– as % of GDP	0.31
Capital balance	65.5		

Health and education

Health spending, % of GDP	10.9	Education spending, % of GDP	5.4
Doctors per 1,000 pop.	2.1	Enrolment, %: primary	99
Hospital beds per 1,000 pop.	2.7	secondary	102
Improved-water source access,		tertiary	...
% of pop.	74		

Society

No. of households	13.5m	Cost of living, Dec. 2013	
Av. no. per household	2.6	New York = 100	98
Marriages per 1,000 pop.	4.6	Cars per 1,000 pop.	461
Divorces per 1,000 pop.	2.2	Colour TV households, % with:	
Religion, % of pop.		cable	66.4
Christian	69.0	satellite	22.2
Non-religious	23.7	Telephone lines per 100 pop.	50.7
Other	2.8	Mobile telephone subscribers	
Muslim	2.1	per 100 pop.	80.1
Hindu	1.4	Broadband subs per 100 pop.	32.5
Jewish	1.0	Internet hosts per 1,000 pop.	279.0

a Including freshwater.   b 2009

CHILE

Area	756,945 sq km	Capital	Santiago
Arable as % of total land	1.8	Currency	Chilean peso (Ps)

People

Population	17.4m	Life expectancy: men	77.0 yrs
Pop. per sq km	22.9	women	82.6 yrs
Average annual growth		Adult literacy	95.6%
in pop. 2010–15	0.9%	Fertility rate (per woman)	1.8
Pop. under 15	21.1%	Urban population	90.0%
Pop. over 60	14.2%		per 1,000 pop.
No. of men per 100 women	97.8	Crude birth rate	14.0
Human Development Index	82.2	Crude death rate	5.5

The economy

GDP	130.5trn pesos	GDP per head	$15,450
GDP	$270bn	GDP per head in purchasing	
Av. ann. growth in real		power parity (USA=100)	41.5
GDP 2007–12	3.9%	Economic freedom index	78.7

Origins of GDP		Components of GDP	
	% of total		% of total
Agriculture	4	Private consumption	63
Industry, of which:	36	Public consumption	12
manufacturing	11	Investment	25
Services	61	Exports	34
		Imports	-34

Structure of employment

	% of total		% of labour force
Agriculture	10.3	Unemployed 2012	6.4
Industry	23.4	Av. ann. rate 2000–12	8.2
Services	66.4		

Energy

	m TOE		
Total output	9.9	Net energy imports as %	
Total consumption	33.6	of energy use	71
Consumption per head			
kg oil equivalent	1,940		

Inflation and finance

Consumer price		av. ann. increase 2008–13	
inflation 2013	1.8%	Narrow money (M1)	15.2%
Av. ann. inflation 2008–13	2.2%	Broad money	18.4%
Money market rate, Dec. 2013	4.50%	H'hold saving rate, 2013	8.8%

Exchange rates

	end 2013		2013
Ps per $	523.76	Effective rates	2005 = 100
Ps per SDR	806.59	– nominal	102.80
Ps per €	722.32	– real	104.50

Trade

Principal exports		Principal imports	
	$bn fob		*$bn cif*
Copper	42.2	Intermediate goods	43.4
Fresh fruit	4.3	Consumer goods	19.9
Paper products	3.3	Capital goods	16.2
Total incl. others	**78.9**	Total	**79.5**

Main export destinations		Main origins of imports	
	% of total		*% of total*
China	22.9	United States	23.4
United States	12.2	China	18.2
Japan	10.6	Argentina	6.6
South Korea	5.7	Brazil	6.5
Brazil	5.5	Germany	3.6

Balance of payments, reserves and debt, $bn

Visible exports fob	78.0	Change in reserves	-0.3
Visible imports fob	-75.5	Level of reserves	
Trade balance	2.5	end Dec.	41.6
Invisibles inflows	19.6	No. months of import cover	4.6
Invisibles outflows	-33.4	Official gold holdings, m oz	0.0
Net transfers	2.2	Foreign debt	116.9
Current account balance	-9.1	– as % of GDP	43.6
– as % of GDP	-3.4	– as % of total exports	120.2
Capital balance	9.1	Debt service ratio	20.1
Overall balance	-0.4		

Health and education

Health spending, % of GDP	7.2	Education spending, % of GDP	4.5
Doctors per 1,000 pop.	1.0	Enrolment, %: primary	101
Hospital beds per 1,000 pop.	2.1	secondary	89
Improved-water source access,		tertiary	74
% of pop.	99		

Society

No. of households	5.7m	Cost of living, Dec. 2013	
Av. no. per household	3.0	New York = 100	76
Marriages per 1,000 pop.	3.5	Cars per 1,000 pop.	
Divorces per 1,000 pop.	...	Colour TV households, % with:	
Religion, % of pop.		cable	34.2
Christian	89.4	satellite	5.2
Non-religious	8.6	Telephone lines per 100 pop.	18.8
Other	1.9	Mobile telephone subscribers	
Jewish	0.1	per 100 pop.	138.2
Hindu	<0.1	Broadband subs per 100 pop.	12.4
Muslim	<0.1	Internet hosts per 1,000 pop.	149.0

CHINA

Area	9,560,900 sq km	Capital	Beijing
Arable as % of total land	12.0	Currency	Yuan

People

Population	1,353.6m	Life expectancy:	men	74.0 yrs
Pop. per sq km	140.9		women	76.6 yrs
Average annual growth		Adult literacy		95.1%
in pop. 2010–15	0.6%	Fertility rate (per woman)		1.7
Pop. under 15	18.0%	Urban population		55.6%
Pop. over 60	13.9%			per 1,000 pop.
No. of men per 100 women	108.0	Crude birth rate		11.9
Human Development Index	71.9	Crude death rate		7.2

The economy

GDP	Yuan51.9trn	GDP per head	$6,090
GDP	$8,227bn	GDP per head in purchasing	
Av. ann. growth in real		power parity (USA=100)	17.6
GDP 2007–12	9.3%	Economic freedom index	52.5

Origins of GDP		Components of GDP	
	% of total		% of total
Agriculture	10	Private consumption	35
Industry, of which:	45	Public consumption	14
manufacturing	32	Investment	49
Services	45	Exports	27
		Imports	-25

Structure of employment

	% of total		% of labour force
Agriculture	34.8	Unemployed 2012	4.5
Industry	29.5	Av. ann. rate 2000–12	4.3
Services	35.7		

Energy

	m TOE		
Total output	2,432.5	Net energy imports as %	
Total consumption	2,727.7	of energy use	11
Consumption per head			
kg oil equivalent	2,029		

Inflation and finance

Consumer price		av. ann. increase 2008–13	
inflation 2013	2.6%	Narrow money (M1)	18.1%
Av. ann. inflation 2008–13	2.6%	Broad money	19.8%
Deposit rate, Dec. 2013	3.00%		

Exchange rates

	end 2013		2013
Yuan per $	6.10	Effective rates	2005 = 100
Yuan per SDR	9.40	– nominal	128.42
Yuan per €	8.41	– real	189.28

Trade

Principal exports		Principal imports	
	$bn fob		*$bn cif*
Electrical goods	240.2	Electrical machinery	307.7
Telecoms equipment	235.4	Petroleum & products	263.6
Office machinery	220.1	Metal ores & scrap	158.7
Clothing & apparel	159.6	Professional instruments	87.3
Total incl. others	**2,049.0**	Total incl. others	**1,818.6**

Main export destinations		Main origins of imports	
	% of total		*% of total*
United States	17.2	Japan	9.8
Hong Kong	15.8	South Korea	9.2
Japan	7.4	Taiwan	7.3
South Korea	4.3	United States	7.1
EU27	16.4	EU27	10.4

Balance of payments, reserves and debt, $bn

Visible exports fob	1,971	Change in reserves	133
Visible imports fob	-1,653	Level of reserves	
Trade balance	318	end Dec.	3,387
Invisibles inflows	357	No. months of import cover	19.0
Invisibles outflows	-485	Official gold holdings, m oz	33.9
Net transfers	3	Foreign debt	754
Current account balance	193	– as % of GDP	8.9
– as % of GDP	2.3	– as % of total exports	31.9
Capital balance	-17	Debt service ratio	3.3
Overall balance	97		

Health and education

Health spending, % of GDP	5.4	Education spending, % of GDP	...
Doctors per 1,000 pop.	1.9	Enrolment, %: primary	128
Hospital beds per 1,000 pop.	3.8	secondary	89
Improved-water source access,		tertiary	27
% of pop.	92		

Society

No. of households	432.0m	Cost of living, Dec. 2013	
Av. no. per household	3.1	New York = 100	88
Marriages per 1,000 pop.	9.6	Cars per 1,000 pop.	...
Divorces per 1,000 pop.	1.8	Colour TV households, % with:	
Religion, % of pop.		cable	50.0
Non-religious	52.2	satellite	...
Other	22.7	Telephone lines per 100 pop.	20.2
Buddhist	18.2	Mobile telephone subscribers	
Christian	5.1	per 100 pop.	80.8
Muslim	1.8	Broadband subs per 100 pop.	12.7
Jewish	<0.1	Internet hosts per 1,000 pop.	16.4

Note: Data excludes Special Administrative Regions ie, Hong Kong and Macau.

COLOMBIA

Area	1,141,748 sq km	Capital	Bogota
Arable as % of total land	1.9	Currency	Colombian peso (peso)

People

Population	47.6m	Life expectancy: men	70.3 yrs
Pop. per sq km	41.1	women	77.6 yrs
Average annual growth		Adult literacy	93.6%
in pop. 2010–15	1.3%	Fertility rate (per woman)	2.3
Pop. under 15	27.7%	Urban population	76.4%
Pop. over 60	9.5%		per 1,000 pop.
No. of men per 100 women	96.8	Crude birth rate	18.9
Human Development Index	71.1	Crude death rate	5.6

The economy

GDP	664trn pesos	GDP per head	$7,750
GDP	$370bn	GDP per head in purchasing	
Av. ann. growth in real		power parity (USA=100)	20.2
GDP 2007–12	4.0%	Economic freedom index	70.7

Origins of GDP		Components of GDP	
	% of total		% of total
Agriculture	7	Private consumption	62
Industry, of which:	38	Public consumption	17
manufacturing	13	Investment	23
Services	56	Exports	18
		Imports	-20

Structure of employment

	% of total		% of labour force
Agriculture	16.9	Unemployed 2012	10.4
Industry	20.9	Av. ann. rate 2000–12	12.4
Services	62.2		

Energy

	m TOE		
Total output	120.5	Net energy imports as %	
Total consumption	31.6	of energy use	-281
Consumption per head			
kg oil equivalent	671		

Inflation and finance

Consumer price			av. ann. increase 2008–13
inflation 2013[a]	2.0%	Narrow money (M1)	11.7%
Av. ann. inflation 2008–13[a]	3.0%	Broad money	13.6%
Money market rate, Dec. 2013	3.24%		

Exchange rates

	end 2013		2013
Peso per $	1,922.60	Effective rates	2005 = 100
Peso per SDR	2,960.70	– nominal	128.10
Peso per €	2,651.46	– real	121.40

Trade

Principal exports		Principal imports	
	$bn fob		*$bn cif*
Petroleum & products	31.5	Intermediate goods & raw	
Coal	7.8	materials	23.9
Coffee	1.9	Capital goods	18.9
Nickel	0.9	Consumer goods	11.8
Total incl. others	**60.1**	Total incl. others	**59.1**

Main export destinations		Main origins of imports	
	% of total		*% of total*
United States	36.9	United States	24.0
Italy	5.6	China	16.2
Spain	4.9	Mexico	10.8
Panama	4.8	Brazil	4.7

Balance of payments, reserves and debt, $bn

Visible exports fob	61.3	Change in reserves	5.1
Visible imports fob	-56.6	Level of reserves	
Trade balance	4.7	end Dec.	37.0
Invisibles inflows	8.9	No. months of import cover	5.1
Invisibles outflows	-30.0	Official gold holdings, m oz	0.3
Net transfers	4.6	Foreign debt	79.1
Current account balance	-11.8	– as % of GDP	21.4
– as % of GDP	-3.2	– as % of total exports	108.4
Capital balance	17.3	Debt service ratio	21.3
Overall balance	5.3		

Health and education

Health spending, % of GDP	6.8	Education spending, % of GDP	4.4
Doctors per 1,000 pop.	1.5	Enrolment, %: primary	107
Hospital beds per 1,000 pop.	1.5	secondary	93
Improved-water source access,		tertiary	45
% of pop.	91		

Society

No. of households	12.9m	Cost of living, Dec. 2013	
Av. no. per household	3.7	New York = 100	83
Marriages per 1,000 pop.	3	Cars per 1,000 pop.	...
Divorces per 1,000 pop.	...	Colour TV households, % with:	
Religion, % of pop.		cable	57.0
Christian	92.5	satellite	7.4
Non-religious	6.6	Telephone lines per 100 pop.	13
Other	0.8	Mobile telephone subscribers	
Hindu	<0.1	per 100 pop.	102.9
Jewish	<0.1	Broadband subs per 100 pop.	8.2
Muslim	<0.1	Internet hosts per 1,000 pop.	113.3

a Estimate.

CÔTE D'IVOIRE

| Area | 322,463 sq km | Capital | Abidjan/Yamoussoukro |
| Arable as % of total land | 9.1 | Currency | CFA franc (CFAfr) |

People

Population	20.6m	Life expectancy: men	49.7 yrs
Pop. per sq km	62.7	women	51.4 yrs
Average annual growth		Adult literacy	56.9%
in pop. 2010–15	2.3%	Fertility rate (per woman)	4.9
Pop. under 15	41.3%	Urban population	54.2%
Pop. over 60	5.1%		per 1,000 pop.
No. of men per 100 women	103.9	Crude birth rate	36.9
Human Development Index	45.2	Crude death rate	14.3

The economy

GDP	CFAfr12,600bn	GDP per head	$1,240
GDP	$24.7bn	GDP per head in purchasing	
Av. ann. growth in real		power parity (USA=100)	3.9
GDP 2007–12	2.5%	Economic freedom index	57.7

Origins of GDP		**Components of GDP**	
	% of total		% of total
Agriculture	27	Private consumption	67
Industry, of which:	21	Public consumption	14
manufacturing	...	Investment	14
Services	52	Exports	52
		Imports	-47

Structure of employment

	% of total		% of labour force
Agriculture	...	Unemployed 2012	4.0
Industry	...	Av. ann. rate 2000–12	4.1
Services	...		

Energy

	m TOE		
Total output	11.9	Net energy imports as %	
Total consumption	11.2	of energy use	-6
Consumption per head			
kg oil equivalent	579		

Inflation and finance

Consumer price		av. ann. change 2008–13	
inflation 2013[a]	2.6%	Narrow money (M1)	12.9%
Av. ann. inflation 2008–13[a]	2.2%	Broad money	12.8%
Repurchase rate, Dec. 2013	3.50%		

Exchange rates

	end 2013		2013
CFAfr per $	475.64	Effective rates	2005 = 100
CFAfr per SDR	732.49	– nominal	104.90
CFAfr per €	655.96	– real	103.40

Trade

Principal exports[b]		**Principal imports**[b]	
	$bn fob		*$bn cif*
Petroleum products	4.9	Fuels & lubricants	3.3
Cocoa beans & butter	3.4	Capital equipment & raw	2.4
Timber	0.3	materials	
Coffee	0.2	Foodstuffs	1.3
Total incl. others	**11.3**	Total incl. others	**8.3**

Main export destinations		**Main origins of imports**	
	% of total		*% of total*
Netherlands	8.8	Nigeria	25.0
United States	8.1	France	11.0
Nigeria	8.0	China	7.2
Germany	7.5	India	3.9
France	4.5	Colombia	3.6

Balance of payments, reserves and debt, $bn

Visible exports fob	12.5	Change in reserves	-0.7
Visible imports fob	-6.6	Level of reserves	
Trade balance	5.9	end Dec.	3.6
Invisibles inflows	1.2	No. months of import cover	4.6
Invisibles outflows	-2.8	Official gold holdings, m oz	0.0
Net transfers	0.5	Foreign debt	9.9
Current account balance	2.6	– as % of GDP	41.7
– as % of GDP	10.7	– as % of total exports	72.5
Capital balance	-1.7	Debt service ratio	9.9
Overall balance	0.9		

Health and education

Health spending, % of GDP	7.1	Education spending, % of GDP	4.6
Doctors per 1,000 pop.	0.1	Enrolment, %: primary	94
Hospital beds per 1,000 pop.	...	secondary	0
Improved-water source access,		tertiary	...
% of pop.	80		

Society

No. of households	3.7m	Cost of living, Dec. 2013	
Av. no. per household	5.3	New York = 100	71
Marriages per 1,000 pop.	...	Cars per 1,000 pop.	17
Divorces per 1,000 pop.	...	Colour TV households, % with:	
Religion, % of pop.	...	cable	...
		satellite	...
		Telephone lines per 100 pop.	1.4
		Mobile telephone subscribers	
		per 100 pop.	91.2
		Broadband subs per 100 pop.	...
		Internet hosts per 1,000 pop.	1.6

a Estimate.   b 2011

CZECH REPUBLIC

Area	78,864 sq km	Capital	Prague
Arable as % of total land	41.0	Currency	Koruna (Kc)

People

Population	10.6m	Life expectancy: men	74.5 yrs
Pop. per sq km	132.9	women	80.6 yrs
Average annual growth		Adult literacy	...
in pop. 2010–15	0.4%	Fertility rate (per woman)	1.6
Pop. under 15	14.9%	Urban population	73.4%
Pop. over 60	23.7%		per 1,000 pop.
No. of men per 100 women	96.3	Crude birth rate	11.0
Human Development Index	86.1	Crude death rate	10.6

The economy

GDP	Kc3,846bn	GDP per head	$18,690
GDP	$196bn	GDP per head in purchasing	
Av. ann. growth in real		power parity (USA=100)	53.2
GDP 2007–12	0.3%	Economic freedom index	72.2

Origins of GDP

	% of total
Agriculture	2
Industry, of which:	37
manufacturing	25
Services	60

Components of GDP

	% of total
Private consumption	51
Public consumption	21
Investment	23
Exports	78
Imports	-72

Structure of employment

	% of total		% of labour force
Agriculture	3.1	Unemployed 2012	7.0
Industry	38.1	Av. ann. rate 2000–12	7.1
Services	58.8		

Energy

	m TOE		
Total output	32.1	Net energy imports as %	
Total consumption	43.4	of energy use	26
Consumption per head			
kg oil equivalent	4,138		

Inflation and finance

		av. ann. increase 2008–13	
Consumer price			
inflation 2013	1.4%	Narrow money (M1)	8.4%
Av. ann. inflation 2008–13	1.8%	Broad money	3.0%
Money market rate, Dec. 2013	0.38%	H'hold saving rate, 2013	3.9%

Exchange rates

	end 2013		2013
Kc per $	19.89	Effective rates	2005 = 100
Kc per SDR	30.64	– nominal	110.09
Kc per €	27.43	– real	112.65

Trade

Principal exports		Principal imports	
	$bn fob		$bn cif
Machinery & transport equip.	88.0	Machinery & transport equip.	58.0
Semi-manufactures	27.2	Semi-manufactures	25.2
Chemicals	9.7	Chemicals	15.7
Raw materials & fuels	8.5	Raw materials & fuels	15.3
Total incl. others	**157.2**	Total incl. others	**141.5**

Main export destinations		Main origins of imports	
	% of total		% of total
Germany	31.4	Germany	29.3
Slovakia	9.0	Poland	7.7
Poland	6.1	Slovakia	7.4
France	5.1	China	6.3
EU27	81.0	EU27	75.3

Balance of payments, reserves and debt, $bn

Visible exports fob	127.1	Change in reserves	4.6
Visible imports fob	-120.1	Level of reserves	
Trade balance	6.9	end Dec.	44.9
Invisibles inflows	31.1	No. months of import cover	3.4
Invisibles outflows	-39.4	Official gold holdings, m oz	0.4
Net transfers	-1.1	Foreign debt	101.8
Current account balance	-2.6	– as % of GDP	51.8
– as % of GDP	-1.3	– as % of total exports	63.3
Capital balance	6.5	Debt service ratio	11.6
Overall balance	4.2	Aid given	0.22
		– as % of GDP	0.11

Health and education

Health spending, % of GDP	7.7	Education spending, % of GDP	4.2
Doctors per 1,000 pop.	3.6	Enrolment, %: primary	100
Hospital beds per 1,000 pop.	6.8	secondary	97
Improved-water source access,		tertiary	65
% of pop.	100		

Society

No. of households	4.7m	Cost of living, Dec. 2013	
Av. no. per household	2.3	New York = 100	79
Marriages per 1,000 pop.	4.3	Cars per 1,000 pop.	440
Divorces per 1,000 pop.	2.5	Colour TV households, % with:	
Religion, % of pop.		cable	24.5
Non-religious	76.4	satellite	27.0
Christian	23.3	Telephone lines per 100 pop.	19.9
Other	0.2	Mobile telephone subscribers	
Hindu	<0.1	per 100 pop.	126.9
Jewish	<0.1	Broadband subs per 100 pop.	16.4
Muslim	<0.1	Internet hosts per 1,000 pop.	333.8

DENMARK

Area	43,075 sq km	Capital	Copenhagen
Arable as % of total land	58.9	Currency	Danish krone (DKr)

People

Population	5.6m	Life expectancy: men	77.2 yrs
Pop. per sq km	130.2	women	81.4 yrs
Average annual growth		Adult literacy	...
in pop. 2010–15	0.4%	Fertility rate (per woman)	1.9
Pop. under 15	17.6%	Urban population	87.5%
Pop. over 60	24.1%		per 1,000 pop.
No. of men per 100 women	98.3	Crude birth rate	11.3
Human Development Index	90.0	Crude death rate	10.1

The economy

GDP	DKr1,826bn	GDP per head	$56,360
GDP	$315bn	GDP per head in purchasing	
Av. ann. growth in real		power parity (USA=100)	82.7
GDP 2007–12	-0.9%	Economic freedom index	76.1

Origins of GDP		Components of GDP	
	% of total		% of total
Agriculture	1	Private consumption	49
Industry, of which:	22	Public consumption	28
manufacturing	11	Investment	17
Services	77	Exports	55
		Imports	-50

Structure of employment

	% of total		% of labour force
Agriculture	2.3	Unemployed 2012	7.5
Industry	19.7	Av. ann. rate 2000–12	5.3
Services	77.5		

Energy

	m TOE		
Total output	21.0	Net energy imports as %	
Total consumption	18.0	of energy use	-17
Consumption per head			
kg oil equivalent	3,231		

Inflation and finance

Consumer price		av. ann. increase 2008–13	
inflation 2013	0.8%	Narrow money (M1)	3.1%
Av. ann. inflation 2008–13	1.9%	Broad money	1.2%
Money market rate, Sep. 2013	-0.01%	H'hold saving rate, 2013	-0.1%

Exchange rates

	end 2013		2013
DKr per $	5.41	Effective rates	2005 = 100
DKr per SDR	8.34	– nominal	102.30
DKr per €	7.46	– real	101.50

Trade

Principal exports	$bn fob	Principal imports	$bn cif
Machinery & transport equip.	24.9	Machinery & transport equip.	27.3
Food, drink & tobacco	18.9	Food, drink & tobacco	11.9
Chemicals & related products	17.9	Chemicals & related products	11.1
Mineral fuels & lubricants	10.8	Mineral fuels & lubricants	9.2
Total incl. others	**106.1**	Total incl. others	**92.3**

Main export destinations	% of total	Main origins of imports	% of total
Germany	15.5	Germany	20.8
Sweden	13.2	Sweden	13.2
United Kingdom	9.3	Netherlands	7.4
United States	6.4	Norway	6.2
EU27	63.4	EU27	70.7

Balance of payments, reserves and aid, $bn

Visible exports fob	105.4	Overall balance	1.9
Visible imports fob	-96.9	Change in reserves	4.7
Trade balance	8.5	Level of reserves	
Invisibles inflows	93.7	end Dec.	89.7
Invisibles outflows	-77.5	No. months of import cover	6.2
Net transfers	-6.0	Official gold holdings, m oz	2.1
Current account balance	18.7	Aid given	2.69
– as % of GDP	5.9	– as % of GDP	0.86
Capital balance	-17.3		

Health and education

Health spending, % of GDP	11.2	Education spending, % of GDP	8.7
Doctors per 1,000 pop.	3.4	Enrolment, %: primary	100
Hospital beds per 1,000 pop.	3.5	secondary	120
Improved-water source access,		tertiary	74
% of pop.	100		

Society

No. of households	2.6m	Cost of living, Dec. 2013	
Av. no. per household	2.1	New York = 100	117
Marriages per 1,000 pop.	5.1	Cars per 1,000 pop.	397
Divorces per 1,000 pop.	2.8	Colour TV households, % with:	
Religion, % of pop.		cable	65.3
Christian	83.5	satellite	11.8
Non-religious	11.8	Telephone lines per 100 pop.	43.4
Muslim	4.1	Mobile telephone subscribers	
Hindu	0.4	per 100 pop.	117.6
Other	0.2	Broadband subs per 100 pop.	38.8
Jewish	<0.1	Internet hosts per 1,000 pop.	497.1

EGYPT

Area	1,000,250 sq km	Capital	Cairo
Arable as % of total land	2.9	Currency	Egyptian pound (£E)

People

Population	84.0m	Life expectancy: men	68.7 yrs
Pop. per sq km	82.4	women	73.5 yrs
Average annual growth		Adult literacy	73.9%
in pop. 2010–15	1.6%	Fertility rate (per woman)	2.8
Pop. under 15	31.1%	Urban population	44.2%
Pop. over 60	8.7%		per 1,000 pop.
No. of men per 100 women	100.9	Crude birth rate	23.3
Human Development Index	68.2	Crude death rate	6.5

The economy

GDP	£E1,576bn	GDP per head	$3,260
GDP	$263bn	GDP per head in purchasing	
Av. ann. growth in real		power parity (USA=100)	12.8
GDP 2007–12	4.2%	Economic freedom index	52.9

Origins of GDP		**Components of GDP**	
	% of total		% of total
Agriculture	14	Private consumption	81
Industry, of which:	39	Public consumption	11
manufacturing	15	Investment	16
Services	46	Exports	17
		Imports	-26

Structure of employment

	% of total		% of labour force
Agriculture	29.2	Unemployed 2012	11.9
Industry	23.5	Av. ann. rate 2000–12	10.1
Services	47.1		

Energy

	m TOE		
Total output	88.2	Net energy imports as %	
Total consumption	77.6	of energy use	-14
Consumption per head			
kg oil equivalent	978		

Inflation and finance

Consumer price		*av. ann. increase 2008–13*	
inflation 2013	6.9%	Narrow money (M1)	16.5%
Av. ann. inflation 2008–13	10.9%	Broad money	11.9%
Treasury bill rate, Dec. 2013	11.00%		

Exchange rates

	end 2013		2013
£E per $	6.94	Effective rates	2005 = 100
£E per SDR	10.69	– nominal	...
£E per €	9.57	– real	...

Trade

Principal exports[a]		Principal imports[a]	
	$bn fob		*$bn cif*
Petroleum & products	11.2	Intermediate goods	16.7
Finished goods incl. textiles	10.5	Consumer goods	13.5
Semi-finished products	2.0	Fuels	10.1
Iron & steel	0.3	Capital goods	9.9
Total	**23.2**	Total incl. others	**59.9**

Main export destinations		Main origins of imports	
	% of total		*% of total*
Italy	7.9	China	9.5
India	6.9	United States	7.6
United States	6.8	Ukraine	5.3
Saudi Arabia	6.2	Turkey	5.1

Balance of payments, reserves and debt, $bn

Visible exports fob	26.8	Change in reserves	-3.0
Visible imports fob	-52.4	Level of reserves	
Trade balance	-25.5	end Dec.	15.7
Invisibles inflows	22.0	No. months of import cover	2.5
Invisibles outflows	-23.2	Official gold holdings, m oz	2.4
Net transfers	19.8	Foreign debt	40.0
Current account balance	-7.0	– as % of GDP	15.5
– as % of GDP	-2.7	– as % of total exports	62.4
Capital balance	3.3	Debt service ratio	5.0
Overall balance	-5.8		

Health and education

Health spending, % of GDP	5.0	Education spending, % of GDP	3.8
Doctors per 1,000 pop.	2.8	Enrolment, %: primary	113
Hospital beds per 1,000 pop.	0.5	secondary	86
Improved-water source access,		tertiary	29
% of pop.	99		

Society

No. of households	20.7m	Cost of living, Dec. 2013	
Av. no. per household	3.9	New York = 100	63
Marriages per 1,000 pop.	11.2	Cars per 1,000 pop.	...
Divorces per 1,000 pop.	1.9	Colour TV households, % with:	
Religion, % of pop.		cable	...
Muslim	94.9	satellite	71.6
Christian	5.1	Telephone lines per 100 pop.	10.6
Hindu	<0.1	Mobile telephone subscribers	
Jewish	<0.1	per 100 pop.	119.9
Non-religious	<0.1	Broadband subs per 100 pop.	2.8
Other	<0.1	Internet hosts per 1,000 pop.	22.2

a Year ending June 30 2012.

ESTONIA

Area	45,200 sq km	Capital	Tallinn
Arable as % of total land	14.9	Currency	Euro (€)

People

Population	1.3m	Life expectancy: men	68.9 yrs
Pop. per sq km	28.9	women	79.5 yrs
Average annual growth		Adult literacy	99.8%
in pop. 2010–15	-0.3%	Fertility rate (per woman)	1.6
Pop. under 15	15.8%	Urban population	69.7%
Pop. over 60	24.1%		per 1,000 pop.
No. of men per 100 women	85.5	Crude birth rate	10.8
Human Development Index	84.0	Crude death rate	13.6

The economy

GDP	€17.4bn	GDP per head	$16,840
GDP	$22.4bn	GDP per head in purchasing	
Av. ann. growth in real		power parity (USA=100)	47.2
GDP 2007–12	-0.8%	Economic freedom index	75.9

Origins of GDP		**Components of GDP**	
	% of total		% of total
Agriculture	4	Private consumption	52
Industry, of which:	29	Public consumption	19
manufacturing	15	Investment	28
Services	67	Exports	91
		Imports	-90

Structure of employment

	% of total		% of labour force
Agriculture	4.7	Unemployed 2012	10.1
Industry	31.1	Av. ann. rate 2000–12	10.2
Services	64.1		

Energy

	m TOE		
Total output	5.0	Net energy imports as %	
Total consumption	5.6	of energy use	10
Consumption per head			
kg oil equivalent	4,182		

Inflation and finance

Consumer price			av. ann. increase 2008–13
inflation 2013	3.5%	Euro area:	
Av. ann. inflation 2008–13	3.1%	Narrow money (M1)	6.0%
Deposit rate, h'holds, Dec. 2013	0.52%	Broad money	0.8%
		H'hold saving rate, 2013	-0.5%

Exchange rates

	end 2013		2013
€ per $	0.73	Effective rates	2005 = 100
€ per SDR	1.12	– nominal	...
		– real	...

Trade

Principal exports	$bn fob	Principal imports	$bn cif
Machinery & transport equip.	4.6	Machinery & equipment	5.1
Mineral products	2.4	Mineral products	2.7
Timber products	1.6	Chemicals	2.3
Foodstuffs	1.5	Foodstuffs	1.7
Total incl. others	**16.1**	Total incl. others	**18.1**

Main export destinations	% of total	Main origins of imports	% of total
Russia	21.1	Finland	14.4
Sweden	16.0	Germany	10.3
Finland	14.5	Sweden	10.2
Latvia	8.8	Latvia	9.2
EU27	66.0	EU27	77.4

Balance of payments, reserves and debt, $bn

Visible exports fob	14.5	Change in reserves	0.1
Visible imports fob	-15.7	Level of reserves	
Trade balance	-1.2	end Dec.	0.3
Invisibles inflows	6.7	No. months of import cover	0.2
Invisibles outflows	-6.2	Official gold holdings, m oz	0.0
Net transfers	0.3	Foreign debt	25.8
Current account balance	-0.4	– as % of GDP	115.0
– as % of GDP	-1.8	– as % of total exports	121.5
Capital balance	0.5	Debt service ratio	11.7
Overall balance	0.1	Aid given	0.02
		– as % of GDP	0.10

Health and education

Health spending, % of GDP	5.9	Education spending, % of GDP	5.7
Doctors per 1,000 pop.	3.3	Enrolment, %: primary	98
Hospital beds per 1,000 pop.	5.3	secondary	109
Improved-water source access,		tertiary	72
% of pop.	99		

Society

No. of households	0.6m	Cost of living, Dec. 2013	
Av. no. per household	2.2	New York = 100	...
Marriages per 1,000 pop.	4.4	Cars per 1,000 pop.	461
Divorces per 1,000 pop.	2.3	Colour TV households, % with:	
Religion, % of pop.		cable	47.1
Non-religious	59.6	satellite	16.6
Christian	39.9	Telephone lines per 100 pop.	34.7
Muslim	0.2	Mobile telephone subscribers	
Hindu	<0.1	per 100 pop.	160.4
Jewish	<0.1	Broadband subs per 100 pop.	25.5
Other	<0.1	Internet hosts per 1,000 pop.	593.7

FINLAND

Area	338,145 sq km	Capital	Helsinki
Arable as % of total land	7.4	Currency	Euro (€)

People

Population	5.4m	Life expectancy: men	77.3 yrs
Pop. per sq km	16.0	women	83.6 yrs
Average annual growth		Adult literacy	...
in pop. 2010–15	0.3%	Fertility rate (per woman)	1.9
Pop. under 15	16.4%	Urban population	84.2%
Pop. over 60	26.3%		per 1,000 pop.
No. of men per 100 women	96.3	Crude birth rate	11.2
Human Development Index	87.9	Crude death rate	9.6

The economy

GDP	€193bn	GDP per head	$45,720
GDP	$248bn	GDP per head in purchasing	
Av. ann. growth in real		power parity (USA=100)	75.7
GDP 2007–12	-0.7%	Economic freedom index	73.4

Origins of GDP		**Components of GDP**	
	% of total		% of total
Agriculture	3	Private consumption	56
Industry, of which:	26	Public consumption	25
manufacturing	15	Investment	20
Services	71	Exports	41
		Imports	-41

Structure of employment

	% of total		% of labour force
Agriculture	4.1	Unemployed 2012	7.6
Industry	22.7	Av. ann. rate 2000–12	8.2
Services	72.7		

Energy

	m TOE		
Total output	17.1	Net energy imports as %	
Total consumption	34.7	of energy use	51
Consumption per head			
kg oil equivalent	6,449		

Inflation and finance

Consumer price		*av. ann. increase 2008–13*	
inflation 2013	2.2%	Euro area:	
Av. ann. inflation 2008–13	2.4%	Narrow money (M1)	6.0%
Money market rate, Dec. 2013	0.28%	Broad money	0.8%
		H'hold saving rate, 2013	1.9%

Exchange rates

	end 2013		2013
€ per $	0.73	Effective rates	2005 = 100
€ per SDR	1.12	– nominal	102.90
		– real	99.40

Trade

Principal exports		Principal imports	
	$bn fob		*$bn cif*
Machinery & transport equip.	21.4	Machinery & transport equip.	21.9
Mineral fuels & lubricants	8.4	Mineral fuels & lubricants	14.9
Chemicals & related products	5.9	Chemicals & related products	8.4
Raw materials	5.4	Raw materials	5.1
Total incl. others	**73.5**	Total incl. others	**73.6**

Main export destinations		Main origins of imports	
	% of total		*% of total*
Sweden	10.9	Russia	18.3
Russia	9.7	Sweden	15.2
Germany	9.2	Germany	14.3
Netherlands	6.2	Netherlands	8.2
EU27	53.6	EU27	62.8

Balance of payments, reserves and aid, $bn

Visible exports fob	76.4	Overall balance	0.6
Visible imports fob	-72.8	Change in reserves	0.8
Trade balance	3.6	Level of reserves	
Invisibles inflows	43.1	end Dec.	11.1
Invisibles outflows	-48.1	No. months of import cover	1.1
Net transfers	-1.7	Official gold holdings, m oz	1.6
Current account balance	-3.1	Aid given	1.32
– as % of GDP	-1.3	– as % of GDP	0.53
Capital balance	23.1		

Health and education

Health spending, % of GDP	9.1	Education spending, % of GDP	6.8
Doctors per 1,000 pop.	2.9	Enrolment, %: primary	99
Hospital beds per 1,000 pop.	5.5	secondary	107
Improved-water source access,		tertiary	96
% of pop.	100		

Society

No. of households	2.6m	Cost of living, Dec. 2013	
Av. no. per household	2.1	New York = 100	114
Marriages per 1,000 pop.	5.3	Cars per 1,000 pop.	572
Divorces per 1,000 pop.	2.4	Colour TV households, % with:	
Religion, % of pop.		cable	68.5
Christian	81.6	satellite	11.1
Non-religious	17.6	Telephone lines per 100 pop.	16.5
Muslim	0.8	Mobile telephone subscribers	
Hindu	<0.1	per 100 pop.	172.3
Jewish	<0.1	Broadband subs per 100 pop.	30.3
Other	<0.1	Internet hosts per 1,000 pop.	834.4

FRANCE

Area	543,965 sq km	Capital	Paris
Arable as % of total land	33.5	Currency	Euro (€)

People

Population	63.5m	Life expectancy: men	78.2 yrs
Pop. per sq km	114.9	women	85.1 yrs
Average annual growth		Adult literacy	...
in pop. 2010–15	0.6%	Fertility rate (per woman)	2
Pop. under 15	18.2%	Urban population	87.8%
Pop. over 60	24.1%		per 1,000 pop.
No. of men per 100 women	94.8	Crude birth rate	12.3
Human Development Index	88.4	Crude death rate	8.9

The economy

GDP	€2,032bn	GDP per head	$39,770
GDP	$2,613bn	GDP per head in purchasing	
Av. ann. growth in real		power parity (USA=100)	71.1
GDP 2007–12	0.1%	Economic freedom index	63.5

Origins of GDP		Components of GDP	
	% of total		% of total
Agriculture	2	Private consumption	58
Industry, of which:	19	Public consumption	25
manufacturing	10	Investment	20
Services	79	Exports	27
		Imports	-30

Structure of employment

	% of total		% of labour force
Agriculture	2.9	Unemployed 2012	9.9
Industry	21.7	Av. ann. rate 2000–12	8.9
Services	74.9		

Energy

	m TOE		
Total output	136.1	Net energy imports as %	
Total consumption	252.8	of energy use	46
Consumption per head			
kg oil equivalent	3,868		

Inflation and finance

			av. ann. increase 2008–13
Consumer price			
inflation 2013	1.0%	Euro area:	
Av. ann. inflation 2008–13	1.5%	Narrow money (M1)	6.0%
Treasury bill rate, Dec. 2013	0.13%	Broad money	0.8%
		H'hold saving rate[a], 2013	15.6%

Exchange rates

	end 2013		2013
€ per $	0.73	Effective rates	2005 = 100
€ per SDR	1.12	– nominal	102.30
		– real	96.90

Trade

Principal exports		Principal imports	
	$bn fob		*$bn cif*
Machinery & transport equip.	212.4	Machinery & transport equip.	215.3
Chemicals & related products	105.4	Mineral fuels & lubricants	113.9
Food, drink & tobacco	67.5	Chemicals & related products	94.1
Mineral fuels & lubricants	27.1	Food, drink & tobacco	52.4
Total incl. others	**654.7**	**Total incl. others**	**568.3**

Main export destinations		Main origins of imports	
	% of total		*% of total*
Germany	14.2	Germany	22.6
Belgium	6.4	Belgium	13.2
Italy	6.4	Italy	8.9
United Kingdom	5.8	Netherlands	8.6
EU27	67.0	EU27	58.9

Balance of payments, reserves and aid, $bn

Visible exports fob	567.4	Overall balance	5.5
Visible imports fob	-643.4	Change in reserves	15.5
Trade balance	-76.1	Level of reserves	
Invisibles inflows	385.4	end Dec.	184.0
Invisibles outflows	-320.1	No. months of import cover	2.3
Net transfers	-46.4	Official gold holdings, m oz	78.3
Current account balance	-57.2	Aid given	12.03
– as % of GDP	-2.2	– as % of GDP	0.46
Capital balance	100.0		

Health and education

Health spending, % of GDP	11.7	Education spending, % of GDP	5.9
Doctors per 1,000 pop.	3.2	Enrolment, %: primary	107
Hospital beds per 1,000 pop.	6.4	secondary	110
Improved-water source access,		tertiary	57
% of pop.	100		

Society

No. of households	27.7m	Cost of living, Dec. 2013	
Av. no. per household	2.3	New York = 100	129
Marriages per 1,000 pop.	3.7	Cars per 1,000 pop.	500
Divorces per 1,000 pop.	2.1	Colour TV households, % with:	
Religion, % of pop.		cable	13.1
Christian	63.0	satellite	34.1
Non-religious	28.0	Telephone lines per 100 pop.	61.5
Muslim	7.5	Mobile telephone subscribers	
Other	1.0	per 100 pop.	97.4
Jewish	0.5	Broadband subs per 100 pop.	37.5
Hindu	<0.1	Internet hosts per 1,000 pop.	248.3

a Gross.

GERMANY

Area	357,868 sq km	Capital	Berlin
Arable as % of total land	34.1	Currency	Euro (€)

People

Population	82.0m	Life expectancy: men	78.2 yrs
Pop. per sq km	230.3	women	83.1 yrs
Average annual growth		Adult literacy	...
in pop. 2010–15	-0.1%	Fertility rate (per woman)	1.4
Pop. under 15	13.1%	Urban population	74.5%
Pop. over 60	27.1%		per 1,000 pop.
No. of men per 100 women	96.1	Crude birth rate	8.5
Human Development Index	91.1	Crude death rate	10.9

The economy

GDP	€2,666bn	GDP per head	$42,630
GDP	$3,428bn	GDP per head in purchasing	
Av. ann. growth in real		power parity (USA=100)	82.5
GDP 2007–12	0.7%	Economic freedom index	73.4

Origins of GDP		Components of GDP	
	% of total		% of total
Agriculture	1	Private consumption	58
Industry, of which:	31	Public consumption	19
manufacturing	22	Investment	17
Services	69	Exports	52
		Imports	-46

Structure of employment

	% of total		% of labour force
Agriculture	1.5	Unemployed 2012	5.4
Industry	28.2	Av. ann. rate 2000–12	8.3
Services	70.2		

Energy

	m TOE		
Total output	124.2	Net energy imports as %	
Total consumption	311.8	of energy use	60
Consumption per head			
kg oil equivalent	3,811		

Inflation and finance

Consumer price		av. ann. increase 2008–13	
inflation 2013	1.6%	Euro area:	
Av. ann. inflation 2008–13	1.5%	Narrow money (M1)	6.0%
Deposit rate, h'holds, Dec. 2013	1.03%	Broad money	0.8%
		H'hold saving rate, 2013	10.0%

Exchange rates

	end 2013		2013
€ per $	0.73	Effective rates	2005 = 100
€ per SDR	1.12	– nominal	102.60
		– real	97.30

Trade

Principal exports		Principal imports	
	$bn fob		*$bn cif*
Machinery & transport equip.	670.8	Machinery & transport equip.	386.3
Chemicals & related products	216.0	Mineral fuels & lubricants	173.7
Food, drink & tobacco	73.7	Chemicals & related products	149.0
Mineral fuels & lubricants	44.5	Food, drink & tobacco	80.5
Total incl. others	**1,411.9**	Total incl. others	**1,166.4**

Main export destinations		Main origins of imports	
	% of total		*% of total*
France	9.4	Netherlands	13.9
United Kingdom	6.7	France	7.3
Netherlands	6.4	China	6.6
United States	5.9	Belgium	6.3
EU27	56.7	EU27	63.2

Balance of payments, reserves and aid, $bn

Visible exports fob	1,462	Overall balance	1.7
Visible imports fob	-1,228	Change in reserves	14.0
Trade balance	234	Level of reserves	
Invisibles inflows	540	end Dec.	248.1
Invisibles outflows	-470	No. months of import cover	1.8
Net transfers	-49	Official gold holdings, m oz	109.0
Current account balance	255	Aid given	12.94
– as % of GDP	7.4	– as % of GDP	0.38
Capital balance	-285		

Health and education

Health spending, % of GDP	11.3	Education spending, % of GDP	5.1
Doctors per 1,000 pop.	3.8	Enrolment, %: primary	101
Hospital beds per 1,000 pop.	8.2	secondary	102
Improved-water source access,		tertiary	57
% of pop.	100		

Society

No. of households	40.6m	Cost of living, Dec. 2013	
Av. no. per household	2.0	New York = 100	95
Marriages per 1,000 pop.	4.7	Cars per 1,000 pop.	530
Divorces per 1,000 pop.	2.3	Colour TV households, % with:	
Religion, % of pop.		cable	46.0
Christian	68.7	satellite	45.1
Non-religious	24.7	Telephone lines per 100 pop.	60.5
Muslim	5.8	Mobile telephone subscribers	
Other	0.5	per 100 pop.	111.6
Jewish	0.3	Broadband subs per 100 pop.	33.7
Hindu	<0.1	Internet hosts per 1,000 pop.	417.0

GREECE

Area	131,957 sq km	Capital	Athens
Arable as % of total land	19.4	Currency	Euro (€)

People

Population	11.4m	Life expectancy: men	78.3 yrs
Pop. per sq km	86.4	women	83.0 yrs
Average annual growth		Adult literacy	97.3%
in pop. 2010–15	0.0%	Fertility rate (per woman)	1.5
Pop. under 15	14.7%	Urban population	62.4%
Pop. over 60	25.7%		per 1,000 pop.
No. of men per 100 women	97.9	Crude birth rate	9.8
Human Development Index	85.3	Crude death rate	10.4

The economy

GDP	€194bn	GDP per head	$22,460
GDP	$249bn	GDP per head in purchasing	
Av. ann. growth in real		power parity (USA=100)	50.3
GDP 2007–12	-4.4%	Economic freedom index	55.7

Origins of GDP		Components of GDP	
	% of total		% of total
Agriculture	3	Private consumption	74
Industry, of which:	16	Public consumption	18
manufacturing	10	Investment	14
Services	80	Exports	27
		Imports	-32

Structure of employment

	% of total		% of labour force
Agriculture	13.0	Unemployed 2012	24.2
Industry	16.7	Av. ann. rate 2000–12	11.6
Services	70.3		

Energy

	m TOE		
Total output	9.6	Net energy imports as %	
Total consumption	26.7	of energy use	64
Consumption per head			
kg oil equivalent	2,365		

Inflation and finance

Consumer price		av. ann. increase 2008–13	
inflation 2013	-0.9%	Euro area:	
Av. ann. inflation 2008–13	1.9%	Narrow money (M1)	6.0%
Treasury bill rate, Dec. 2013	0.54%	Broad money	0.8%

Exchange rates

	end 2013		2013
€ per $	0.73	Effective rates	2005 = 100
€ per SDR	1.12	– nominal	103.20
		– real	102.90

Trade

Principal exports		Principal imports	
	$bn fob		*$bn cif*
Mineral fuels & lubricants	13.5	Mineral fuels & lubricants	23.3
Food, drink & tobacco	5.4	Machinery & transport equip.	10.9
Chemicals & related products	3.2	Chemicals & related products	8.4
Machinery & transport equip.	3.0	Food, drink & tobacco	7.0
Total incl. others	**35.5**	Total incl. others	**63.5**

Main export destinations		Main origins of imports	
	% of total		*% of total*
Turkey	10.9	Russia	12.1
Italy	7.8	Germany	9.5
Germany	6.5	Italy	8.3
Bulgaria	5.8	Netherlands	4.7
EU27	44.1	EU27	45.7

Balance of payments, reserves and debt, $bn

Visible exports fob	28.1	Overall balance	-2.1
Visible imports fob	-53.4	Change in reserves	0.5
Trade balance	-25.3	Level of reserves	
Invisibles inflows	40.3	end Dec.	7.2
Invisibles outflows	-23.0	No. months of import cover	1.1
Net transfers	1.9	Official gold holdings, m oz	3.6
Current account balance	-6.2	Aid given	0.33
– as % of GDP	-2.5	– as % of GDP	0.13
Capital balance	4.5		

Health and education

Health spending, % of GDP	9.3	Education spending, % of GDP	...
Doctors per 1,000 pop.	6.2	Enrolment, %: primary	103
Hospital beds per 1,000 pop.	4.8	secondary	111
Improved-water source access,		tertiary	...
% of pop.	100		

Society

No. of households	4.1m	Cost of living, Dec. 2013	
Av. no. per household	2.8	New York = 100	77
Marriages per 1,000 pop.	4.9	Cars per 1,000 pop.	454
Divorces per 1,000 pop.	1.3	Colour TV households, % with:	
Religion, % of pop.		cable	0.9
Christian	88.1	satellite	13.5
Non-religious	6.1	Telephone lines per 100 pop.	49.1
Muslim	5.3	Mobile telephone subscribers	
Other	0.3	per 100 pop.	120.0
Hindu	0.1	Broadband subs per 100 pop.	24.1
Jewish	<0.1	Internet hosts per 1,000 pop.	295.0

HONG KONG

Area	1,075 sq km	Capital	Victoria
Arable as % of total land	...	Currency	Hong Kong dollar (HK$)

People

Population	7.1m	Life expectancy: men	80.3 yrs
Pop. per sq km	7,100.0	women	86.4 yrs
Average annual growth		Adult literacy	...
in pop. 2010–15	0.7%	Fertility rate (per woman)	1.1
Pop. under 15	11.7%	Urban population	100.0%
Pop. over 60	20.1%		per 1,000 pop.
No. of men per 100 women	90	Crude birth rate	9.4
Human Development Index	89.1	Crude death rate	6.2

The economy

GDP	HK$2,042bn	GDP per head	$36,800
GDP	$263bn	GDP per head in purchasing	
Av. ann. growth in real		power parity (USA=100)	98.8
GDP 2007–12	2.5%	Economic freedom index	90.1

Origins of GDP		**Components of GDP**	
	% of total		% of total
Agriculture	0	Private consumption	64
Industry, of which:	7	Public consumption	9
manufacturing	2	Investment	26
Services	93	Exports	225
		Imports	-224

Structure of employment

	% of total		% of labour force
Agriculture	0.2	Unemployed 2012	3.3
Industry	11.6	Av. ann. rate 2000–12	5.1
Services	87.7		

Energy

	m TOE		
Total output	0.1	Net energy imports as %	
Total consumption	14.9	of energy use	100
Consumption per head			
kg oil equivalent	2,106		

Inflation and finance

Consumer price		av. ann. increase 2008–13	
inflation 2013	4.3%	Narrow money (M1)	14.5%
Av. ann. inflation 2008–13	3.3%	Broad money	7.9%
Money market rate, Dec. 2013	0.06%		

Exchange rates

	end 2013		2013
HK$ per $	7.75	Effective rates	2005 = 100
HK$ per SDR	11.94	– nominal	...
HK$ per €	10.05	– real	...

Trade

Principal exports[a]		Principal imports[a]	
	$bn fob		$bn cif
Capital goods	174.5	Capital goods	179.1
Raw materials & semi-manufactures	143.3	Raw materials & semi-manufactures	165.6
Consumer goods	112.1	Consumer goods	122.1
Foodstuffs	5.1	Foodstuffs	19.5
Total incl. others	**443.1**	Total incl. others	**504.7**

Main export destinations		Main origins of imports	
	% of total		% of total
China	52.3	China	45.1
United States	9.9	Japan	8.5
Japan	4.0	Singapore	6.8
Germany	2.7	Taiwan	6.4

Balance of payments, reserves and debt, $bn

Visible exports fob	468.4	Change in reserves	32.0
Visible imports fob	-487.3	Level of reserves	
Trade balance	-18.9	end Dec.	317.4
Invisibles inflows	239.2	No. months of import cover	5.4
Invisibles outflows	-213.5	Official gold holdings, m oz	0.1
Net transfers	-2.6	Foreign debt	146.9
Current account balance	4.1	– as % of GDP	55.9
– as % of GDP	1.6	– as % of total exports	20.8
Capital balance	15.6	Debt service ratio	2.1
Overall balance	24.4		

Health and education

Health spending, % of GDP	...	Education spending, % of GDP	3.5
Doctors per 1,000 pop.	...	Enrolment, %: primary	101
Hospital beds per 1,000 pop.	...	secondary	106
Improved-water source access, % of pop.	...	tertiary	60

Society

No. of households	2.4m	Cost of living, Dec. 2013	
Av. no. per household	3.0	New York = 100	113
Marriages per 1,000 pop.	8.3	Cars per 1,000 pop.	...
Divorces per 1,000 pop.	2.6	Colour TV households, % with:	
Religion, % of pop.		cable	94.4
Non-religious	56.1	satellite	0.1
Christian	14.3	Telephone lines per 100 pop.	61.3
Other	14.2	Mobile telephone subscribers	
Buddhist	13.2	per 100 pop.	229.2
Muslim	1.8	Broadband subs per 100 pop.	31.2
Hindu	0.4	Internet hosts per 1,000 pop.	121.2

a Including re-exports.
Note: Hong Kong became a Special Administrative Region of China on July 1 1997.

HUNGARY

| Area | 93,030 sq km | Capital | Budapest |
| Arable as % of total land | 48.5 | Currency | Forint (Ft) |

People

Population	9.9m	Life expectancy: men	70.4 yrs
Pop. per sq km	107.5	women	78.5 yrs
Average annual growth		Adult literacy	99.0%
in pop. 2010–15	-0.2%	Fertility rate (per woman)	1.4
Pop. under 15	14.7%	Urban population	71.3%
Pop. over 60	23.9%		per 1,000 pop.
No. of men per 100 women	90.4	Crude birth rate	9.9
Human Development Index	81.8	Crude death rate	13.4

The economy

GDP	Ft28,048bn	GDP per head	$12,560
GDP	$125bn	GDP per head in purchasing	
Av. ann. growth in real		power parity (USA=100)	43.7
GDP 2007–12	-1.0%	Economic freedom index	67.0

Origins of GDP

	% of total
Agriculture	3
Industry, of which:	27
manufacturing	20
Services	70

Components of GDP

	% of total
Private consumption	55
Public consumption	20
Investment	17
Exports	95
Imports	-87

Structure of employment

	% of total		% of labour force
Agriculture	5.2	Unemployed 2012	10.9
Industry	29.8	Av. ann. rate 2000–12	7.9
Services	64.9		

Energy

	m TOE		
Total output	10.8	Net energy imports as %	
Total consumption	25.0	of energy use	57
Consumption per head			
kg oil equivalent	2,503		

Inflation and finance

Consumer price		av. ann. increase 2008–13	
inflation 2013	1.7%	Narrow money (M1)	7.6%
Av. ann. inflation 2008–13	4.1%	Broad money	3.1%
Treasury bill rate, Dec. 2013	2.92%	H'hold saving rate, 2013	4.0%

Exchange rates

	end 2013		2013
Ft per $	215.67	Effective rates	2005 = 100
Ft per SDR	332.13	– nominal	84.60
Ft per €	297.43	– real	101.80

Trade

Principal exports	$bn fob	Principal imports	$bn cif
Machinery & transport equip.	52.9	Machinery & transport equip.	42.0
Other manufactured goods	20.1	Chemicals & related products	19.4
Chemicals & related products	10.6	Other manufactured goods	11.9
Food, drink & tobacco	8.2	Food, drink & tobacco	10.6
Mineral fuels & lubricants	4.1	Mineral fuels & lubricants	4.8
Total incl. others	**99.6**	Total incl. others	**91.6**

Main export destinations	% of total	Main origins of imports	% of total
Germany	25.1	Germany	24.8
Romania	6.0	Russia	8.8
Slovakia	6.0	China	7.4
Austria	5.8	Austria	7.2
EU27	75.7	EU27	70.2

Balance of payments, reserves and debt, $bn

Visible exports fob	88.4	Change in reserves	-4.2
Visible imports fob	-86.5	Level of reserves	
Trade balance	1.8	end Dec.	44.7
Invisibles inflows	35.9	No. months of import cover	4.3
Invisibles outflows	-37.3	Official gold holdings, m oz	0.1
Net transfers	0.5	Foreign debt	203.8
Current account balance	0.9	– as % of GDP	173.4
– as % of GDP	0.7	– as % of total exports	136.0
Capital balance	-2.2	Debt service ratio	37.1
Overall balance	0.6	Aid given	0.12
		– as % of GDP	0.09

Health and education

Health spending, % of GDP	7.8	Education spending, % of GDP	4.9
Doctors per 1,000 pop.	4	Enrolment, %: primary	101
Hospital beds per 1,000 pop.	7.2	secondary	101
Improved-water source access, % of pop.	100	tertiary	60

Society

No. of households	4.3m	Cost of living, Dec. 2013	
Av. no. per household	2.3	New York = 100	67
Marriages per 1,000 pop.	3	Cars per 1,000 pop.	299
Divorces per 1,000 pop.	2.2	Colour TV households, % with:	
Religion, % of pop.		cable	56.4
Christian	81.0	satellite	28.5
Non-religious	18.6	Telephone lines per 100 pop.	29.7
Other	0.2	Mobile telephone subscribers	
Jewish	0.1	per 100 pop.	116.1
Hindu	<0.1	Broadband subs per 100 pop.	22.9
Muslim	<0.1	Internet hosts per 1,000 pop.	332.8

INDIA

Area	3,287,263 sq km	Capital	New Delhi
Arable as % of total land	52.9	Currency	Indian rupee (Rs)

People

Population	1,258.4m	Life expectancy: men		64.6 yrs
Pop. per sq km	377.7		women	68.1 yrs
Average annual growth		Adult literacy		...
in pop. 2010–15	1.2%	Fertility rate (per woman)		2.5
Pop. under 15	29.1%	Urban population		32.8%
Pop. over 60	8.3%			per 1,000 pop.
No. of men per 100 women	106.8	Crude birth rate		20.7
Human Development Index	58.6	Crude death rate		7.9

The economy

GDP	Rs101.1trn	GDP per head	$1,500
GDP	$1,859bn	GDP per head in purchasing	
Av. ann. growth in real		power parity (USA=100)	7.5
GDP 2007–12	6.5%	Economic freedom index	55.7

Origins of GDP		**Components of GDP**	
	% of total		% of total
Agriculture	18	Private consumption	60
Industry, of which:	26	Public consumption	12
manufacturing	14	Investment	35
Services	56	Exports	24
		Imports	-31

Structure of employment

	% of total		% of labour force
Agriculture	47.2	Unemployed 2012	3.4
Industry	24.7	Av. ann. rate 2000–12	4.0
Services	28.1		

Energy

	m TOE		
Total output	540.9	Net energy imports as %	
Total consumption	749.4	of energy use	28
Consumption per head			
kg oil equivalent	614		

Inflation and finance

			av. ann. increase 2008–13
Consumer price			
inflation 2013	9.5%	Narrow money (M1)	11.0%
Av. ann. inflation 2008–13	10.6%	Broad money	15.0%
Lending rate, Dec. 2013	10.25%		

Exchange rates

	end 2013		2013
Rs per $	61.90	Effective rates	2005 = 100
Rs per SDR	95.32	– nominal	...
Rs per €	85.37	– real	...

Trade

Principal exports[a]		Principal imports[a]	
	$bn fob		$bn cif
Engineering products	65.3	Petroleum & products	169.3
Petroleum & products	60.3	Gold & silver	55.7
Gems & jewellery	43.5	Electronic goods	31.5
Agricultural products	40.6	Machinery	27.6
Total incl. others	**300.6**	Total incl. others	**491.5**

Main export destinations		Main origins of imports	
	% of total		% of total
United Arab Emirates	12.2	China	10.7
United States	12.0	United Arab Emirates	7.8
China	5.0	Saudi Arabia	6.8
Singapore	4.9	Switzerland	6.2

Balance of payments, reserves and debt, $bn

Visible exports fob	298.3	Change in reserves	1.6
Visible imports fob	-450.2	Level of reserves	
Trade balance	-151.9	end Dec.	300.3
Invisibles inflows	155.4	No. months of import cover	5.9
Invisibles outflows	-160.4	Official gold holdings, m oz	17.9
Net transfers	65.4	Foreign debt	379.1
Current account balance	-91.5	– as % of GDP	20.4
– as % of GDP	-4.9	– as % of total exports	72.1
Capital balance	85.0	Debt service ratio	5.8
Overall balance	-4.0		

Health and education

Health spending, % of GDP	4.0	Education spending, % of GDP	3.2
Doctors per 1,000 pop.	0.7	Enrolment, %: primary	113
Hospital beds per 1,000 pop.	0.7	secondary	69
Improved-water source access,		tertiary	23
% of pop.	93		

Society

No. of households	252.3m	Cost of living, Dec. 2013	
Av. no. per household	4.9	New York = 100	43
Marriages per 1,000 pop.	...	Cars per 1,000 pop.	17
Divorces per 1,000 pop.	...	Colour TV households, % with:	
Religion, % of pop.		cable	62.5
Hindu	79.5	satellite	17.1
Muslim	14.4	Telephone lines per 100 pop.	2.5
Other	3.6	Mobile telephone subscribers	
Christian	2.5	per 100 pop.	69.9
Jewish	<0.1	Broadband subs per 100 pop.	1.2
Non-religious	<0.1	Internet hosts per 1,000 pop.	5.9

a Year ending March 31 2012.

INDONESIA

Area	1,904,443 sq km	Capital	Jakarta
Arable as % of total land	13.0	Currency	Rupiah (Rp)

People

Population	244.8m	Life expectancy: men	68.7 yrs
Pop. per sq km	127.2	women	72.8 yrs
Average annual growth		Adult literacy	92.8%
in pop. 2010–15	1.2%	Fertility rate (per woman)	2.4
Pop. under 15	28.9%	Urban population	53.7%
Pop. over 60	8.1%		per 1,000 pop.
No. of men per 100 women	99.5	Crude birth rate	18.9
Human Development Index	68.4	Crude death rate	6.3

The economy

GDP	Rp8,242trn	GDP per head	$3,560
GDP	$878bn	GDP per head in purchasing	
Av. ann. growth in real		power parity (USA=100)	9.4
GDP 2007–12	5.9%	Economic freedom index	58.5

Origins of GDP		**Components of GDP**	
	% of total		% of total
Agriculture	14	Private consumption	57
Industry, of which:	47	Public consumption	9
manufacturing	24	Investment	36
Services	39	Exports	24
		Imports	-26

Structure of employment

	% of total		% of labour force
Agriculture	35.1	Unemployed 2012	6.6
Industry	21.7	Av. ann. rate 2000–12	8.5
Services	43.2		

Energy

	m TOE		
Total output	394.6	Net energy imports as %	
Total consumption	209.0	of energy use	-89
Consumption per head			
kg oil equivalent	857		

Inflation and finance

Consumer price		av. ann. increase 2008–13	
inflation 2013	6.4%	Narrow money (M1)	14.2%
Av. ann. inflation 2008–13	5.2%	Broad money	14.5%
Money market rate, Dec. 2013	5.92%		

Exchange rates

	end 2013		2013
Rp per $	12,189.00	Effective rates	2005 = 100
Rp per SDR	18,771.00	– nominal	...
Rp per €	16,809.85	– real	...

Trade

Principal exports		Principal imports	
	$bn fob		$bn cif
Mineral fuels	63.4	Machinery & transport equip.	65.6
Machinery & transport equip.	22.8	Mineral fuels	42.7
Manufactured goods	22.3	Manufactured goods	29.8
Animal & vegetable oils	22.0	Chemicals & related products	23.7
Total incl. others	**190.0**	Total incl. others	**191.7**

Main export destinations		Main origins of imports	
	% of total		% of total
Japan	15.9	China	15.3
China	11.4	Singapore	13.6
Singapore	9.0	Japan	11.9
United States	7.8	Malaysia	6.4

Balance of payments, reserves and debt, $bn

Visible exports fob	187.3	Change in reserves	2.6
Visible imports fob	-178.7	Level of reserves	
Trade balance	8.7	end Dec.	112.8
Invisibles inflows	26.3	No. months of import cover	5.6
Invisibles outflows	-63.0	Official gold holdings, m oz	2.4
Net transfers	4.0	Foreign debt	254.9
Current account balance	-24.1	– as % of GDP	29.1
– as % of GDP	-2.7	– as % of total exports	115.4
Capital balance	24.9	Debt service ratio	16.6
Overall balance	0.2		

Health and education

Health spending, % of GDP	3.0	Education spending, % of GDP	2.8
Doctors per 1,000 pop.	0.2	Enrolment, %: primary	109
Hospital beds per 1,000 pop.	0.9	secondary	81
Improved-water source access,		tertiary	27
% of pop.	85		

Society

No. of households	62.6m	Cost of living, Dec. 2013	
Av. no. per household	3.9	New York = 100	70
Marriages per 1,000 pop.	11.2	Cars per 1,000 pop.	...
Divorces per 1,000 pop.	0.7	Colour TV households, % with:	
Religion, % of pop.		cable	6.0
Muslim	87.2	satellite	25.5
Christian	9.9	Telephone lines per 100 pop.	15.4
Hindu	1.7	Mobile telephone subscribers	
Other	1.1	per 100 pop.	114.2
Jewish	<0.1	Broadband subs per 100 pop.	1.2
Non-religious	<0.1	Internet hosts per 1,000 pop.	7.9

IRAN

Area	1,648,000 sq km	Capital	Tehran
Arable as % of total land	10.8	Currency	Rial (IR)

People

Population	75.6m	Life expectancy: men	72.1 yrs
Pop. per sq km	42.9	women	75.9 yrs
Average annual growth		Adult literacy	85.0%
in pop. 2010–15	1.3%	Fertility rate (per woman)	1.9
Pop. under 15	23.8%	Urban population	69.7%
Pop. over 60	8.1%		per 1,000 pop.
No. of men per 100 women	103.0	Crude birth rate	19.0
Human Development Index	74.9	Crude death rate	5.2

The economy

GDP	IR6,726trn	GDP per head	$7,230
GDP	$552bn	GDP per head in purchasing	
Av. ann. growth in real		power parity (USA=100)	23.7
GDP 2007–12	4.5%	Economic freedom index	40.3

Origins of GDP		Components of GDP	
	% of total		% of total
Agriculture	10	Private consumption	41
Industry, of which:	42	Public consumption	11
manufacturing	12	Investment	42
Services	51	Exports	28
		Imports	-21

Structure of employment

	% of total		% of labour force
Agriculture	21.2	Unemployed 2012	13.1
Industry	32.2	Av. ann. rate 2000–12	12.1
Services	46.5		

Energy

	m TOE		
Total output	353.7	Net energy imports as %	
Total consumption	212.1	of energy use	-67
Consumption per head			
kg oil equivalent	2,813		

Inflation and finance

Consumer price		av. ann. increase 2008–13	
inflation 2013	35.2%	Narrow money (M1)	8.4%
Av. ann. inflation 2008–13	21.7%	Broad money	7.2%
Deposit rate, 1yr, 2013	15.00%		

Exchange rates

	end 2013		2013
IR per $	24,774.00	Effective rates	2005 = 100
IR per SDR	38,152.00	– nominal	35.15
IR per €	34,165.82	– real	140.02

Trade

Principal exports[a]		Principal imports[a]	
	$bn fob		$bn cif
Oil & gas	118.2	Machinery & transport equip.	22.1
Industrial goods excl. oil &		Iron & steel	8.4
gas products	19.1	Chemicals	7.4
Agricultural & traditional goods	5.2	Foodstuffs & live animals	7.4
Metallic minerals & ores	1.0	Mineral products & fuels	1.0
Total incl. others	**144.9**	Total incl. others	**61.8**

Main export destinations		Main origins of imports	
	% of total		% of total
China	22.1	United Arab Emirates	33.3
India	11.9	China	13.8
Turkey	10.6	Turkey	11.8
South Korea	7.6	South Korea	7.4

Balance of payments[a], reserves and debt, $bn

Visible exports fob	144.9	Change in reserves	...
Visible imports fob	-77.8	Level of reserves	
Trade balance	67.1	end Dec.	...
Invisibles inflows	8.9	No. months of import cover	...
Invisibles outflows	-18.9	Official gold holdings, m oz	...
Net transfers	0.4	Foreign debt	11.5
Current account balance	59.4	– as % of GDP	2.1
– as % of GDP	10.8	– as % of total exports	10.7
Capital balance	37.3	Debt service ratio	0.5
Overall balance	75.3		

Health and education

Health spending, % of GDP	4.2	Education spending, % of GDP	3.7
Doctors per 1,000 pop.	0.9	Enrolment, %: primary	106
Hospital beds per 1,000 pop.	0.1	secondary	87
Improved-water source access,		tertiary	55
% of pop.	96		

Society

No. of households	21.9m	Cost of living, Dec. 2013	
Av. no. per household	3.5	New York = 100	79
Marriages per 1,000 pop.	11.6	Cars per 1,000 pop.	...
Divorces per 1,000 pop.	1.9	Colour TV households, % with:	
Religion, % of pop.		cable	...
Muslim	99.5	satellite	37.0
Christian	0.2	Telephone lines per 100 pop.	37.6
Other	0.2	Mobile telephone subscribers	
Non-religious	0.1	per 100 pop.	76.1
Hindu	<0.1	Broadband subs per 100 pop.	4.0
Jewish	<0.1	Internet hosts per 1,000 pop.	2.5

a Iranian year ending March 20 2012.

IRELAND

Area	70,282 sq km	Capital	Dublin
Arable as % of total land	15.4	Currency	Euro (€)

People

Population	4.6m	Life expectancy: men	78.4 yrs
Pop. per sq km	64.3	women	82.7 yrs
Average annual growth		Adult literacy	...
in pop. 2010–15	1.1%	Fertility rate (per woman)	2
Pop. under 15	21.6%	Urban population	63.4%
Pop. over 60	16.9%		per 1,000 pop.
No. of men per 100 women	100.1	Crude birth rate	15.5
Human Development Index	89.9	Crude death rate	6.4

The economy

GDP	€164bn	GDP per head	$45,950
GDP	$211bn	GDP per head in purchasing	
Av. ann. growth in real		power parity (USA=100)	84.7
GDP 2007–12	-1.2%	Economic freedom index	76.2

Origins of GDP		Components of GDP	
	% of total		% of total
Agriculture	2	Private consumption	54
Industry, of which:	28	Public consumption	25
manufacturing	23	Investment	15
Services	71	Exports	59
		Imports	-53

Structure of employment

	% of total		% of labour force
Agriculture	4.7	Unemployed 2012	14.7
Industry	18.3	Av. ann. rate 2000–12	7.4
Services	76.9		

Energy

	m TOE		
Total output	1.8	Net energy imports as %	
Total consumption	13.2	of energy use	86
Consumption per head			
kg oil equivalent	2,888		

Inflation and finance

Consumer price		*av. ann. increase 2008–13*	
inflation 2013[a]	0.5%	Euro area:	
Av. ann. inflation 2008–13[a]	0.1%	Narrow money (M1)	6.0%
Money market rate, Dec. 2013	0.21%	Broad money	0.8%
		H'hold saving rate, 2013	5.1%

Exchange rates

	end 2013		2013
€ per $	0.73	Effective rates	2005 = 100
€ per SDR	1.12	– nominal	104.08
		– real	98.35

Trade

Principal exports		Principal imports	
	$bn fob		$bn cif
Chemicals & related products	69.9	Machinery & transport equip.	15.8
Machinery & transport equip.	12.5	Chemicals & related products	13.0
Food, drink & tobacco	11.8	Mineral fuels & lubricants	9.1
Raw materials	2.3	Food, drink & tobacco	8.2
Total incl. others	**117.8**	Total incl. others	**63.3**

Main export destinations		Main origins of imports	
	% of total		% of total
United States	17.0	United Kingdom	38.6
United Kingdom	16.3	United States	12.8
Belgium	14.8	Germany	7.4
Germany	7.9	Netherlands	5.4
EU27	58.9	EU27	66.9

Balance of payments, reserves and aid, $bn

Visible exports fob	119.3	Overall balance	-8.5
Visible imports fob	-63.6	Change in reserves	0.0
Trade balance	55.7	Level of reserves	
Invisibles inflows	180.6	end Dec.	1.7
Invisibles outflows	-225.5	No. months of import cover	0.1
Net transfers	-1.5	Official gold holdings, m oz	0.2
Current account balance	9.2	Aid given	0.81
– as % of GDP	4.4	– as % of GDP	0.38
Capital balance	-10.0		

Health and education

Health spending, % of GDP	8.1	Education spending, % of GDP	6.4
Doctors per 1,000 pop.	2.7	Enrolment, %: primary	105
Hospital beds per 1,000 pop.	2.9	secondary	118
Improved-water source access,		tertiary	73
% of pop.	100		

Society

No. of households	1.7m	Cost of living, Dec. 2013	
Av. no. per household	2.3	New York = 100	101
Marriages per 1,000 pop.	4.6	Cars per 1,000 pop.	406
Divorces per 1,000 pop.	0.7	Colour TV households, % with:	
Religion, % of pop.		cable	31.7
Christian	92.0	satellite	47.6
Non-religious	6.2	Telephone lines per 100 pop.	43.9
Muslim	1.1	Mobile telephone subscribers	
Other	0.4	per 100 pop.	107.2
Hindu	0.2	Broadband subs per 100 pop.	22.7
Jewish	<0.1	Internet hosts per 1,000 pop.	333.0

a Estimate.

ISRAEL

Area	20,770 sq km	Capital	Jerusalem[a]
Arable as % of total land	14.0	Currency	New Shekel (NIS)

People

Population	7.6m	Life expectancy: men	79.8 yrs
Pop. per sq km	365.9	women	83.5 yrs
Average annual growth		Adult literacy	...
in pop. 2010–15	1.3%	Fertility rate (per woman)	2.9
Pop. under 15	27.7%	Urban population	92.1%
Pop. over 60	15.3%		per 1,000 pop.
No. of men per 100 women	97.4	Crude birth rate	20.5
Human Development Index	88.8	Crude death rate	5.5

The economy

GDP	NIS993bn	GDP per head	$32,570
GDP	$258bn	GDP per head in purchasing	
Av. ann. growth in real		power parity (USA=100)	60.6
GDP 2007–12	3.7%	Economic freedom index	68.4

Origins of GDP		Components of GDP	
	% of total		% of total
Agriculture	2	Private consumption	56
Industry, of which:	27	Public consumption	23
manufacturing	20	Investment	21
Services	69	Exports	36
		Imports	-36

Structure of employment

	% of total		% of labour force
Agriculture	1.7	Unemployed 2012	6.9
Industry	20.4	Av. ann. rate 2000–12	8.2
Services	77.1		

Energy

	m TOE		
Total output	4.7	Net energy imports as %	
Total consumption	23.3	of energy use	80
Consumption per head			
kg oil equivalent	2,994		

Inflation and finance

Consumer price		*av. ann. increase 2008–13*	
inflation 2013	1.5%	Narrow money (M1)	15.7%
Av. ann. inflation 2008–13	2.5%	Broad money	9.1%
Treasury bill rate, Dec. 2013	0.88%		

Exchange rates

	end 2013		2013
NIS per $	3.47	Effective rates	2005 = 100
NIS per SDR	5.35	– nominal	122.73
NIS per €	4.79	– real	121.00

Trade

Principal exports		Principal imports	
	$bn fob		*$bn cif*
Chemicals & chemical products	15.5	Fuel	16.1
Polished diamonds	8.4	Diamonds	7.6
Communications, medical &		Machinery & equipment	6.9
scientific equipment	7.7	Chemicals	5.4
Electronics	4.7		
Total incl. others	**54.0**	Total incl. others	**72.3**

Main export destinations		Main origins of imports	
	% of total		*% of total*
United States	32.6	United States	13.0
Hong Kong	9.0	China	7.4
United Kingdom	6.7	Germany	6.4
Belgium	5.4	Switzerland	6.2

Balance of payments, reserves and debt, $bn

Visible exports fob	62.3	Change in reserves	1.0
Visible imports fob	-71.7	Level of reserves	
Trade balance	-9.3	end Dec.	75.9
Invisibles inflows	38.1	No. months of import cover	8.4
Invisibles outflows	-36.3	Official gold holdings, m oz	0.0
Net transfers	8.4	Foreign debt	97
Current account balance	0.8	– as % of GDP	37.6
– as % of GDP	0.3	– as % of total exports	95.9
Capital balance	-5.6	Debt service ratio	17.8
Overall balance	-0.1	Aid given	0.17
		– as % of GDP	0.07

Health and education

Health spending, % of GDP	7.5	Education spending, % of GDP	5.6
Doctors per 1,000 pop.	3.3	Enrolment, %: primary	104
Hospital beds per 1,000 pop.	3.3	secondary	102
Improved-water source access,		tertiary	62
% of pop.	100		

Society

No. of households	2.2m	Cost of living, Dec. 2013	
Av. no. per household	3.5	New York = 100	103
Marriages per 1,000 pop.	6.3	Cars per 1,000 pop.	288
Divorces per 1,000 pop.	1.7	Colour TV households, % with:	
Religion, % of pop.		cable	77.8
Jewish	75.6	satellite	19.2
Muslim	18.6	Telephone lines per 100 pop.	47.0
Non-religious	3.1	Mobile telephone subscribers	
Christian	2.0	per 100 pop.	120.7
Other	0.6	Broadband subs per 100 pop.	25.3
Hindu	<0.1	Internet hosts per 1,000 pop.	339.0

a Sovereignty over the city is disputed.

ITALY

Area	301,245 sq km	Capital	Rome
Arable as % of total land	23.1	Currency	Euro (€)

People

Population	61.0m	Life expectancy: men	79.5 yrs
Pop. per sq km	202.0	women	84.9 yrs
Average annual growth		Adult literacy	99.0%
in pop. 2010–15	0.2%	Fertility rate (per woman)	1.5
Pop. under 15	14.1%	Urban population	69.1%
Pop. over 60	27.2%		per 1,000 pop.
No. of men per 100 women	95.7	Crude birth rate	9.2
Human Development Index	87.2	Crude death rate	10.1

The economy

GDP	€1,567bn	GDP per head	$33,840
GDP	$2,015bn	GDP per head in purchasing	
Av. ann. growth in real		power parity (USA=100)	67.5
GDP 2007–12	-1.4%	Economic freedom index	60.9

Origins of GDP

	% of total
Agriculture	2
Industry, of which:	24
manufacturing	16
Services	74

Components of GDP

	% of total
Private consumption	61
Public consumption	20
Investment	18
Exports	30
Imports	-29

Structure of employment

	% of total		% of labour force
Agriculture	3.7	Unemployed 2012	10.7
Industry	27.8	Av. ann. rate 2000–12	8.4
Services	68.5		

Energy

	m TOE		
Total output	31.6	Net energy imports as %	
Total consumption	167.4	of energy use	81
Consumption per head			
kg oil equivalent	2,757		

Inflation and finance

Consumer price		*av. ann. increase 2008–13*	
inflation 2013[a]	1.3%	Euro area:	
Av. ann. inflation 2008–13[a]	2.0%	Narrow money (M1)	6.0%
Treasury bill rate, Dec. 2013	0.78%	Broad money	0.8%
		H'hold saving rate, 2013	4.9%

Exchange rates

	end 2013		2013
€ per $	0.73	Effective rates	2005 = 100
€ per SDR	1.12	– nominal	102.70
		– real	100.00

Trade

Principal exports		Principal imports	
	$bn fob		$bn cif
Machinery & transport equip.	170.1	Machinery & transport equip.	110.0
Chemicals & related products	57.2	Mineral fuels & lubricants	108.0
Food, drink & tobacco	36.3	Chemicals & related products	71.4
Mineral fuels & lubricants	29.7	Food, drink & tobacco	41.9
Total incl. others	**501.5**	Total incl. others	**489.1**

Main export destinations		Main origins of imports	
	% of total		% of total
Germany	12.5	Germany	14.5
France	11.1	France	8.3
United States	6.4	China	6.5
Switzerland	5.7	Netherlands	5.4
EU27	53.8	EU27	53.0

Balance of payments, reserves and aid, $bn

Visible exports fob	479.8	Overall balance	1.9
Visible imports fob	-455.1	Change in reserves	11.3
Trade balance	24.7	Level of reserves	
Invisibles inflows	172.4	end Dec.	181.2
Invisibles outflows	-183.0	No. months of import cover	3.4
Net transfers	-19.6	Official gold holdings, m oz	78.8
Current account balance	-5.5	Aid given	2.74
– as % of GDP	-0.3	– as % of GDP	0.14
Capital balance	24.0		

Health and education

Health spending, % of GDP	9.2	Education spending, % of GDP	4.5
Doctors per 1,000 pop.	4.1	Enrolment, %: primary	100
Hospital beds per 1,000 pop.	3.4	secondary	101
Improved-water source access,		tertiary	64
% of pop.	100		

Society

No. of households	24.9m	Cost of living, Dec. 2013	
Av. no. per household	2.5	New York = 100	98
Marriages per 1,000 pop.	3.4	Cars per 1,000 pop.	617
Divorces per 1,000 pop.	1.0	Colour TV households, % with:	
Religion, % of pop.		cable	1.1
Christian	83.3	satellite	29.0
Non-religious	12.4	Telephone lines per 100 pop.	35.4
Muslim	3.7	Mobile telephone subscribers	
Other	0.4	per 100 pop.	159.8
Hindu	0.1	Broadband subs per 100 pop.	22.1
Jewish	<0.1	Internet hosts per 1,000 pop.	427.1

a Estimate.

JAPAN

Area	377,727 sq km	Capital	Tokyo
Arable as % of total land	11.7	Currency	Yen (¥)

People

Population	126.4m	Life expectancy: men	80.0 yrs
Pop. per sq km	334.7	women	86.9 yrs
Average annual growth		Adult literacy	...
in pop. 2010–15	-0.1%	Fertility rate (per woman)	1.4
Pop. under 15	13.1%	Urban population	93.5%
Pop. over 60	32.3%		per 1,000 pop.
No. of men per 100 women	95.0	Crude birth rate	8.4
Human Development Index	89.0	Crude death rate	9.8

The economy

GDP	¥476trn	GDP per head	$46,730
GDP	$5,961bn	GDP per head in purchasing	
Av. ann. growth in real		power parity (USA=100)	68.8
GDP 2007–12	-0.2%	Economic freedom index	72.4

Origins of GDP		Components of GDP	
	% of total		% of total
Agriculture	1	Private consumption	61
Industry, of which:	26	Public consumption	20
manufacturing	19	Investment	21
Services	73	Exports	15
		Imports	-17

Structure of employment

	% of total		% of labour force
Agriculture	3.7	Unemployed 2012	4.3
Industry	25.3	Av. ann. rate 2000–12	4.6
Services	69.7		

Energy

	m TOE		
Total output	51.7	Net energy imports as %	
Total consumption	461.5	of energy use	89
Consumption per head			
kg oil equivalent	3,610		

Inflation and finance

Consumer price		av. ann. increase 2008–13	
inflation 2013	0.4%	Narrow money (M1)	3.7%
Av. ann. inflation 2008–13	-0.4%	Broad money	2.4%
Money market rate, Dec. 2013	0.07%	H'hold saving rate, 2013	0.9%

Exchange rates

	end 2013		2013
¥ per $	105.30	Effective rates	2005 = 100
¥ per SDR	162.16	– nominal	95.60
¥ per €	145.22	– real	77.60

Trade

Principal exports		Principal imports	
	$bn fob		*$bn cif*
Capital equipment	425.3	Industrial supplies	489.3
Industrial supplies	199.2	Capital equipment	191.6
Consumer durable goods	121.0	Food & direct consumer goods	71.7
Consumer non-durable goods	5.1	Consumer durable goods	57.5
Total incl. others	**798.4**	**Total incl. others**	**885.8**

Main export destinations		Main origins of imports	
	% of total		*% of total*
China	18.1	China	21.3
United States	17.8	United States	8.8
South Korea	7.7	Australia	6.4
Thailand	5.5	Saudi Arabia	6.2
Hong Kong	5.1	United Arab Emirates	5.0

Balance of payments, reserves and aid, $bn

Visible exports fob	776.6	Overall balance	-38.3
Visible imports fob	-830.1	Change in reserves	-27.9
Trade balance	-53.5	Level of reserves	
Invisibles inflows	369.5	end Dec.	1,267.9
Invisibles outflows	-240.9	No. months of import cover	14.2
Net transfers	-14.3	Official gold holdings, m oz	24.6
Current account balance	60.9	Aid given	10.60
– as % of GDP	1.0	– as % of GDP	0.18
Capital balance	-103.2		

Health and education

Health spending, % of GDP	10.1	Education spending, % of GDP	3.8
Doctors per 1,000 pop.	2.3	Enrolment, %: primary	103
Hospital beds per 1,000 pop.	13.7	secondary	102
Improved-water source access,		tertiary	60
% of pop.	100		

Society

No. of households	52.5m	Cost of living, Dec. 2013	
Av. no. per household	2.4	New York = 100	118
Marriages per 1,000 pop.	5.2	Cars per 1,000 pop.	305
Divorces per 1,000 pop.	1.8	Colour TV households, % with:	
Religion, % of pop.		cable	52.7
Non-religious	57.0	satellite	42.3
Buddhist	36.2	Telephone lines per 100 pop.	50.5
Other	5.0	Mobile telephone subscribers	
Christian	1.6	per 100 pop.	11.9
Muslim	0.2	Broadband subs per 100 pop.	27.7
Jewish	<0.1	Internet hosts per 1,000 pop.	590.5

KENYA

Area	582,646 sq km	Capital	Nairobi
Arable as % of total land	9.7	Currency	Kenyan shilling (KSh)

People

Population	42.7m	Life expectancy: men	59.7 yrs
Pop. per sq km	71.7	women	63.5 yrs
Average annual growth		Adult literacy	...
in pop. 2010–15	2.7%	Fertility rate (per woman)	4.4
Pop. under 15	42.2%	Urban population	25.6%
Pop. over 60	4.3%		per 1,000 pop.
No. of men per 100 women	99.8	Crude birth rate	35.1
Human Development Index	53.5	Crude death rate	8.3

The economy

GDP	KSh3,440bn	GDP per head	$940
GDP	$40.7bn	GDP per head in purchasing	
Av. ann. growth in real		power parity (USA=100)	3.4
GDP 2007–12	3.8%	Economic freedom index	57.1

Origins of GDP		**Components of GDP**	
	% of total		% of total
Agriculture	30	Private consumption	80
Industry, of which:	17	Public consumption	17
manufacturing	10	Investment	20
Services	53	Exports	27
		Imports	-44

Structure of employment

	% of total		% of labour force
Agriculture	...	Unemployed 2012	9.2
Industry	...	Av. ann. rate 2000–12	9.5
Services	...		

Energy

	m TOE		
Total output	16.2	Net energy imports as %	
Total consumption	20.2	of energy use	20
Consumption per head			
kg oil equivalent	480		

Inflation and finance

			av. ann. increase 2008–13
Consumer price			
inflation 2013	5.7%	Narrow money (M1)	14.9%
Av. ann. inflation 2008–13	8.7%	Broad money	17.0%
Treasury bill rate, Dec. 2013	9.52%		

Exchange rates

	end 2013		2013
KSh per $	86.31	Effective rates	2005 = 100
KSh per SDR	132.92	– nominal	...
KSh per €	119.03	– real	...

Trade

Principal exports		Principal imports	
	$bn fob		$bn cif
Tea	1.2	Industrial supplies	4.3
Horticultural products	1.1	Machinery & other capital equip.	2.6
Coffee	0.3	Transport equipment	1.7
Fish products	0.1	Food & drink	1.0
Total incl. others	**5.8**	Total incl. others	**15.5**

Main export destinations		Main origins of imports	
	% of total		% of total
Uganda	13.5	India	14.2
Tanzania	9.3	China	12.2
United Kingdom	6.2	United Arab Emirates	10.9
Netherlands	5.3	Saudi Arabia	4.6

Balance of payments, reserves and debt, $bn

Visible exports fob	6.2	Change in reserves	1.4
Visible imports fob	-15.5	Level of reserves	
Trade balance	-9.3	end Dec.	5.7
Invisibles inflows	5.0	No. months of import cover	3.8
Invisibles outflows	-2.8	Official gold holdings, m oz	0.0
Net transfers	2.8	Foreign debt	11.6
Current account balance	-4.3	– as % of GDP	28.4
– as % of GDP	-10.4	– as % of total exports	93.2
Capital balance	5.0	Debt service ratio	4.6
Overall balance	1.2		

Health and education

Health spending, % of GDP	4.7	Education spending, % of GDP	6.7
Doctors per 1,000 pop.	0.2	Enrolment, %: primary	112
Hospital beds per 1,000 pop.	1.4	secondary	60
Improved-water source access,		tertiary	4
% of pop.	62		

Society

No. of households	9.9m	Cost of living, Dec. 2013	
Av. no. per household	4.4	New York = 100	77
Marriages per 1,000 pop.	...	Cars per 1,000 pop.	16
Divorces per 1,000 pop.	...	Colour TV households, % with:	
Religion, % of pop.		cable	2.4
Christian	84.8	satellite	3.4
Muslim	9.7	Telephone lines per 100 pop.	0.6
Other	3.0	Mobile telephone subscribers	
Non-religious	2.5	per 100 pop.	71.2
Hindu	0.1	Broadband subs per 100 pop.	0.1
Jewish	<0.1	Internet hosts per 1,000 pop.	2.8

LATVIA

Area	63,700 sq km	Capital	Riga
Arable as % of total land	18.6	Currency	Lats (LVL)

People

Population	2.2m	Life expectancy: men	66.6 yrs
Pop. per sq km	34.4	women	77.5 yrs
Average annual growth		Adult literacy	...
in pop. 2010–15	-0.6%	Fertility rate (per woman)	1.6
Pop. under 15	14.8%	Urban population	67.7%
Pop. over 60	24.3%		per 1,000 pop.
No. of men per 100 women	85.2	Crude birth rate	10.9
Human Development Index	81.0	Crude death rate	15.7

The economy

GDP	LVL15.5bn	GDP per head	$13,950
GDP	$28.4bn	GDP per head in purchasing	
Av. ann. growth in real		power parity (USA=100)	42.1
GDP 2007–12	-2.8%	Economic freedom index	68.7

Origins of GDP		Components of GDP	
	% of total		% of total
Agriculture	4	Private consumption	62
Industry, of which:	22	Public consumption	15
manufacturing	12	Investment	26
Services	74	Exports	59
		Imports	-63

Structure of employment

	% of total		% of labour force
Agriculture	8.4	Unemployed 2012	14.9
Industry	23.5	Av. ann. rate 2000–12	12.1
Services	68.1		

Energy

			m TOE
Total output	2.1	Net energy imports as %	
Total consumption	4.4	of energy use	53
Consumption per head			
kg oil equivalent	2,124		

Inflation and finance

Consumer price		av. ann. increase 2008–13	
inflation 2013	0.0%	Narrow money (M1)	17.3%
Av. ann. inflation 2008–13	1.7%	Broad money	10.6%
Money market rate, Dec. 2013	0.05%		

Exchange rates

	end 2013		2013
LVL per $	0.52	Effective rates	2005 = 100
LVL per SDR	0.79	– nominal	106
LVL per €	0.72	– real	121.3

Trade

Principal exports		Principal imports	
	$bn fob		$bn cif
Foodstuffs	2.6	Machinery & equipment	2.9
Wood & wood products	1.9	Mineral products	2.9
Metals	1.8	Foodstuffs	2.5
Machinery & equipment	1.7	Metals	1.7
Total incl. others	**12.7**	Total incl. others	**16.1**

Main export destinations		Main origins of imports	
	% of total		% of total
Russia	19.7	Lithuania	20.3
Lithuania	16.1	Germany	12.4
Estonia	13.2	Poland	8.7
Germany	8.1	Estonia	8.1
EU27	63.5	EU27	78.1

Balance of payments, reserves and debt, $bn

Visible exports fob	12.3	Change in reserves	1.1
Visible imports fob	-15.4	Level of reserves	
Trade balance	-3.1	end Dec.	7.5
Invisibles inflows	5.9	No. months of import cover	4.6
Invisibles outflows	-4.4	Official gold holdings, m oz	0.2
Net transfers	0.8	Foreign debt	37.1
Current account balance	-0.7	– as % of GDP	130.9
– as % of GDP	-2.5	– as % of total exports	185.4
Capital balance	3.2	Debt service ratio	31.9
Overall balance	2.5	Aid given	0.02
		– as % of GDP	0.07

Health and education

Health spending, % of GDP	6.0	Education spending, % of GDP	5.0
Doctors per 1,000 pop.	2.9	Enrolment, %: primary	105
Hospital beds per 1,000 pop.	5.9	secondary	99
Improved-water source access,		tertiary	67
% of pop.	98		

Society

No. of households	0.8m	Cost of living, Dec. 2013	
Av. no. per household	2.5	New York = 100	...
Marriages per 1,000 pop.	5.5	Cars per 1,000 pop.	289
Divorces per 1,000 pop.	3.6	Colour TV households, % with:	
Religion, % of pop.		cable	42.1
Christian	55.8	satellite	12.7
Non-religious	43.8	Telephone lines per 100 pop.	24.3
Other	0.2	Mobile telephone subscribers	
Muslim	0.1	per 100 pop.	112.1
Hindu	<0.1	Broadband subs per 100 pop.	23.4
Jewish	<0.1	Internet hosts per 1,000 pop.	190.2

LITHUANIA

Area	65,200 sq km	Capital	Vilnius
Arable as % of total land	34.9	Currency	Litas (LTL)

People

Population	3.3m	Life expectancy: men	66.0 yrs
Pop. per sq km	50.8	women	78.1 yrs
Average annual growth		Adult literacy	99.7%
in pop. 2010–15	-0.5%	Fertility rate (per woman)	1.5
Pop. under 15	15.2%	Urban population	67.6%
Pop. over 60	20.8%		per 1,000 pop.
No. of men per 100 women	86.8	Crude birth rate	11.2
Human Development Index	83.4	Crude death rate	13.9

The economy

GDP	LTL114bn	GDP per head	$14,170
GDP	$42.3bn	GDP per head in purchasing	
Av. ann. growth in real		power parity (USA=100)	47.1
GDP 2007–12	-0.5%	Economic freedom index	73.0

Origins of GDP		Components of GDP	
	% of total		% of total
Agriculture	4	Private consumption	64
Industry, of which:	28	Public consumption	19
manufacturing	...	Investment	19
Services	68	Exports	78
		Imports	-79

Structure of employment

	% of total		% of labour force
Agriculture	8.9	Unemployed 2012	13.2
Industry	24.8	Av. ann. rate 2000–12	11.8
Services	65.9		

Energy

		m TOE	
Total output	1.5	Net energy imports as %	
Total consumption	7.3	of energy use	79
Consumption per head			
kg oil equivalent	2,405		

Inflation and finance

		av. ann. increase 2008–13	
Consumer price			
inflation 2013	1.2%	Narrow money (M1)	11.3%
Av. ann. inflation 2008–13	2.8%	Broad money	5.1%
Money market rate, Dec. 2013	0.08%		

Exchange rates

	end 2013		2013
LTL per $	2.51	Effective rates	2005 = 100
LTL per SDR	3.67	– nominal	...
LTL per €	3.46	– real	...

Trade

Principal exports		Principal imports	
	$bn fob		*$bn cif*
Mineral products	7.1	Mineral products	7.4
Machinery & equipment	3.2	Machinery & equipment	5.6
Transport equipment	2.7	Transport equipment	4.5
Chemicals	2.5	Chemicals	2.9
Total incl. others	**29.9**	Total incl. others	**32.0**

Main export destinations		Main origins of imports	
	% of total		*% of total*
Russia	18.9	Russia	31.3
Latvia	10.9	Germany	9.9
Germany	7.8	Poland	9.8
Estonia	7.7	Latvia	6.1
EU27	60.5	EU27	57.6

Balance of payments, reserves and debt, $bn

Visible exports fob	28.8	Change in reserves	0.3
Visible imports fob	-30.2	Level of reserves	
Trade balance	-1.5	end Dec.	8.5
Invisibles inflows	7.3	No. months of import cover	2.7
Invisibles outflows	-7.2	Official gold holdings, m oz	0.2
Net transfers	1.3	Foreign debt	27.9
Current account balance	-0.1	– as % of GDP	65.9
– as % of GDP	-0.2	– as % of total exports	74.8
Capital balance	0.6	Debt service ratio	27.6
Overall balance	0.1	Aid given	0.05
		– as % of GDP	0.12

Health and education

Health spending, % of GDP	6.7	Education spending, % of GDP	5.4
Doctors per 1,000 pop.	4.1	Enrolment, %: primary	99
Hospital beds per 1,000 pop.	7.0	secondary	107
Improved-water source access,		tertiary	77
% of pop.	96		

Society

No. of households	1.4m	Cost of living, Dec. 2013	
Av. no. per household	2.2	New York = 100	...
Marriages per 1,000 pop.	6.5	Cars per 1,000 pop.	576
Divorces per 1,000 pop.	3.3	Colour TV households, % with:	
Religion, % of pop.		cable	53.0
Christian	89.8	satellite	12.0
Non-religious	10.0	Telephone lines per 100 pop.	22.3
Hindu	<0.1	Mobile telephone subscribers	
Jewish	<0.1	per 100 pop.	165.1
Muslim	<0.1	Broadband subs per 100 pop.	21.2
Other	<0.1	Internet hosts per 1,000 pop.	368.8

MALAYSIA

Area	332,665 sq km	Capital	Kuala Lumpur
Arable as % of total land	5.5	Currency	Malaysian dollar/ringgit (M$)

People

Population	29.3m	Life expectancy: men	72.7 yrs
Pop. per sq km	87.3	women	77.3 yrs
Average annual growth		Adult literacy	93.1%
in pop. 2010–15	1.6%	Fertility rate (per woman)	2
Pop. under 15	26.1%	Urban population	75.4%
Pop. over 60	8.5%		per 1,000 pop.
No. of men per 100 women	103.0	Crude birth rate	17.7
Human Development Index	77.3	Crude death rate	4.7

The economy

GDP	M$941bn	GDP per head	$10,430
GDP	$305bn	GDP per head in purchasing	
Av. ann. growth in real		power parity (USA=100)	32.7
GDP 2007–12	4.3%	Economic freedom index	69.6

Origins of GDP		Components of GDP	
	% of total		% of total
Agriculture	10	Private consumption	49
Industry, of which:	41	Public consumption	14
manufacturing	24	Investment	26
Services	49	Exports	87
		Imports	-75

Structure of employment

	% of total		% of labour force
Agriculture	12.6	Unemployed 2012	3.1
Industry	28.4	Av. ann. rate 2000–12	3.4
Services	59.0		

Energy

	m TOE		
Total output	84.3	Net energy imports as %	
Total consumption	75.9	of energy use	-11
Consumption per head			
kg oil equivalent	2,639		

Inflation and finance

Consumer price		av. ann. increase 2008–13	
inflation 2013	2.1%	Narrow money (M1)	11.2%
Av. ann. inflation 2008–13	1.8%	Broad money	8.8%
Money market rate, Nov. 2013	2.99%		

Exchange rates

	end 2013		2013
M$ per $	3.28	Effective rates	2005 = 100
M$ per SDR	5.05	– nominal	106.60
M$ per €	4.52	– real	106.90

Trade

Principal exports	$bn fob	Principal imports	$bn cif
Machinery & transport equip.	86.3	Machinery & transport equip.	86.5
Mineral fuels	46.2	Mineral fuels	27.9
Manufactured goods	20.6	Manufactured goods	24.4
Chemicals	14.9	Chemicals	17.7
Total incl. others	**227.5**	Total incl. others	**187.5**

Main export destinations	% of total	Main origins of imports	% of total
Singapore	13.6	China	15.2
China	12.6	Singapore	13.3
Japan	11.8	Japan	10.3
United States	8.7	United States	8.1

Balance of payments, reserves and debt, $bn

Visible exports fob	227.7	Change in reserves	6.2
Visible imports fob	-186.9	Level of reserves	
Trade balance	40.7	end Dec.	139.7
Invisibles inflows	51.6	No. months of import cover	6.6
Invisibles outflows	-67.8	Official gold holdings, m oz	1.2
Net transfers	-5.9	Foreign debt	104.0
Current account balance	18.6	– as % of GDP	34.1
– as % of GDP	6.1	– as % of total exports	37.1
Capital balance	-7.5	Debt service ratio	3.4
Overall balance	1.3		

Health and education

Health spending, % of GDP	3.9	Education spending, % of GDP	5.9
Doctors per 1,000 pop.	1.2	Enrolment, %: primary	...
Hospital beds per 1,000 pop.	1.9	secondary	...
Improved-water source access,		tertiary	36
% of pop.	100		

Society

No. of households	6.7m	Cost of living, Dec. 2013	
Av. no. per household	4.3	New York = 100	70
Marriages per 1,000 pop.	5.3	Cars per 1,000 pop.	360
Divorces per 1,000 pop.	...	Colour TV households, % with:	
Religion, % of pop.		cable	12.7
Muslim	63.7	satellite	56.2
Buddhist	17.7	Telephone lines per 100 pop.	15.7
Christian	9.4	Mobile telephone subscribers	
Hindu	6.0	per 100 pop.	141.3
Other	2.5	Broadband subs per 100 pop.	8.4
Non-religious	0.7	Internet hosts per 1,000 pop.	17.2

MEXICO

Area	1,972,545 sq km	Capital	Mexico city
Arable as % of total land	13.1	Currency	Mexican peso (PS)

People

Population	116.1m	Life expectancy: men	74.9 yrs
Pop. per sq km	58.5	women	79.7 yrs
Average annual growth		Adult literacy	93.5%
in pop. 2010–15	1.2%	Fertility rate (per woman)	2.2
Pop. under 15	28.5%	Urban population	79.2%
Pop. over 60	9.5%		per 1,000 pop.
No. of men per 100 women	97.3	Crude birth rate	18.6
Human Development Index	75.6	Crude death rate	4.5

The economy

GDP	PS15,506bn	GDP per head	$9,750
GDP	$1,178bn	GDP per head in purchasing	
Av. ann. growth in real		power parity (USA=100)	31.7
GDP 2007–12	1.8%	Economic freedom index	66.8

Origins of GDP		**Components of GDP**	
	% of total		% of total
Agriculture	4	Private consumption	67
Industry, of which:	36	Public consumption	12
manufacturing	17	Investment	23
Services	61	Exports	33
		Imports	-34

Structure of employment

	% of total		% of labour force
Agriculture	13.4	Unemployed 2012	4.9
Industry	24.1	Av. ann. rate 2000–12	3.8
Services	61.9		

Energy

	m TOE		
Total output	228.2	Net energy imports as %	
Total consumption	186.2	of energy use	-23
Consumption per head			
kg oil equivalent	1,560		

Inflation and finance

Consumer price		*av. ann. increase 2008–13*	
inflation 2013	3.8%	Narrow money (M1)	11.1%
Av. ann. inflation 2008–13	4.2%	Broad money	10.2%
Money market rate, Dec. 2013	3.79%		

Exchange rates

	end 2013		2013
PS per $	13.08	Effective rates	2005 = 100
PS per SDR	20.14	– nominal	80.57
PS per €	18.04	– real	95.01

Trade

Principal exports		Principal imports	
	$bn fob		*$bn cif*
Manufactured goods	302.0	Intermediate goods	277.9
Crude oil & products	53.1	Consumer goods	54.3
Agricultural products	11.0	Capital goods	38.6
Mining products	4.9		
Total	**370.7**	Total	**370.8**

Main export destinations		Main origins of imports	
	% of total		*% of total*
United States	77.6	United States	54.9
Canada	3.0	China	16.9
Spain	1.9	Japan	5.2
China	1.5	South Korea	4.0

Balance of payments, reserves and debt, $bn

Visible exports fob	371.4	Change in reserves	17.8
Visible imports fob	-371.2	Level of reserves	
Trade balance	0.2	end Dec.	167.0
Invisibles inflows	29.3	No. months of import cover	4.6
Invisibles outflows	-66.9	Official gold holdings, m oz	4.0
Net transfers	22.6	Foreign debt	354.9
Current account balance	-14.8	– as % of GDP	30.0
– as % of GDP	-1.3	– as % of total exports	84.3
Capital balance	51.0	Debt service ratio	16.8
Overall balance	17.5		

Health and education

Health spending, % of GDP	6.1	Education spending, % of GDP	5.2
Doctors per 1,000 pop.	2.1	Enrolment, %: primary	104
Hospital beds per 1,000 pop.	1.5	secondary	...
Improved-water source access,		tertiary	28
% of pop.	95		

Society

No. of households	29.4m	Cost of living, Dec. 2013	
Av. no. per household	4.0	New York = 100	83
Marriages per 1,000 pop.	5.1	Cars per 1,000 pop.	...
Divorces per 1,000 pop.	0.8	Colour TV households, % with:	
Religion, % of pop.		cable	21.4
Christian	95.1	satellite	23.5
Non-religious	4.7	Telephone lines per 100 pop.	16.7
Hindu	<0.1	Mobile telephone subscribers	
Jewish	<0.1	per 100 pop.	83.4
Muslim	<0.1	Broadband subs per 100 pop.	10.5
Other	<0.1	Internet hosts per 1,000 pop.	165.7

MOROCCO

Area	446,550 sq km	Capital	Rabat
Arable as % of total land	17.8	Currency	Dirham (Dh)

People

Population	32.6m	Life expectancy: men	69.0 yrs
Pop. per sq km	72.3	women	72.6 yrs
Average annual growth		Adult literacy	67.1%
in pop. 2010–15	1.4%	Fertility rate (per woman)	2.8
Pop. under 15	27.9%	Urban population	58.5%
Pop. over 60	7.8%		per 1,000 pop.
No. of men per 100 women	96.2	Crude birth rate	23.2
Human Development Index	61.7	Crude death rate	6.3

The economy

GDP	Dh828bn	GDP per head	$2,900
GDP	$96.0bn	GDP per head in purchasing	
Av. ann. growth in real		power parity (USA=100)	10.1
GDP 2007–12	4.8%	Economic freedom index	58.3

Origins of GDP		**Components of GDP**	
	% of total		% of total
Agriculture	15	Private consumption	60
Industry, of which:	30	Public consumption	19
manufacturing	15	Investment	35
Services	56	Exports	36
		Imports	-50

Structure of employment

	% of total		% of labour force
Agriculture	39.2	Unemployed 2012	9.0
Industry	21.4	Av. ann. rate 2000–12	10.5
Services	39.3		

Energy

	m TOE		
Total output	0.8	Net energy imports as %	
Total consumption	17.3	of energy use	96
Consumption per head			
kg oil equivalent	539		

Inflation and finance

Consumer price		av. ann. increase 2008–13	
inflation 2013	1.9%	Narrow money (M1)	4.9%
Av. ann. inflation 2008–13	1.2%	Broad money	4.8%
Money market rate, Dec. 2013	3.05%		

Exchange rates

	end 2013		2013
Dh per $	8.15	Effective rates	2005 = 100
Dh per SDR	12.55	– nominal	105.20
Dh per €	11.24	– real	95.80

Trade

Principal exports		Principal imports	
	$bn fob		$bn cif
Fertilizers & chemicals	2.4	Fuel & lubricants	12.4
Clothing & textiles	2.2	Semi-finished goods	9.0
Electric cables & wires	1.9	Capital goods	8.5
Phosphoric acid	1.7	Consumer goods	7.6
Phosphate rock	1.5	Food, drink & tobacco	4.9
Total incl. others	**21.5**	Total incl. others	**45.3**

Main export destinations		Main origins of imports	
	% of total		% of total
France	21.0	Spain	13.1
Spain	17.3	France	12.1
Brazil	5.4	China	6.9
United States	4.6	United States	6.8

Balance of payments, reserves and debt, $bn

Visible exports fob	17.0	Change in reserves	-3.1
Visible imports fob	-38.9	Level of reserves	
Trade balance	-21.9	end Dec.	17.5
Invisibles inflows	16.0	No. months of import cover	4.2
Invisibles outflows	-11.0	Official gold holdings, m oz	0.7
Net transfers	7.1	Foreign debt	33.8
Current account balance	-9.8	– as % of GDP	35.1
– as % of GDP	-10.3	– as % of total exports	85.7
Capital balance	1.9	Debt service ratio	9.3
Overall balance	-8.4		

Health and education

Health spending, % of GDP	6.3	Education spending, % of GDP	5.4
Doctors per 1,000 pop.	0.6	Enrolment, %: primary	117
Hospital beds per 1,000 pop.	0.9	secondary	69
Improved-water source access,		tertiary	16
% of pop.	84		

Society

No. of households	6.8m	Cost of living, Dec. 2013	
Av. no. per household	4.8	New York = 100	66
Marriages per 1,000 pop.	...	Cars per 1,000 pop.	...
Divorces per 1,000 pop.	...	Colour TV households, % with:	
Religion, % of pop.		cable	...
Muslim	99.9	satellite	92.0
Christian	<0.1	Telephone lines per 100 pop.	10.1
Hindu	<0.1	Mobile telephone subscribers	
Jewish	<0.1	per 100 pop.	120.0
Non-religious	<0.1	Broadband subs per 100 pop.	2.1
Other	<0.1	Internet hosts per 1,000 pop.	8.6

NETHERLANDS

Area[a]	41,526 sq km	Capital	Amsterdam
Arable as % of total land	30.9	Currency	Euro (€)

People

Population	16.7m	Life expectancy: men	78.9 yrs
Pop. per sq km	397.6	women	82.8 yrs
Average annual growth		Adult literacy	...
in pop. 2010–15	0.3%	Fertility rate (per woman)	1.8
Pop. under 15	17.1%	Urban population	84.7%
Pop. over 60	23.4%		per 1,000 pop.
No. of men per 100 women	98.5	Crude birth rate	10.7
Human Development Index	91.5	Crude death rate	8.6

The economy

GDP	€599bn	GDP per head	$45,990
GDP	$771bn	GDP per head in purchasing	
Av. ann. growth in real		power parity (USA=100)	83.7
GDP 2007–12	-0.1%	Economic freedom index	74.2

Origins of GDP		Components of GDP	
	% of total		% of total
Agriculture	2	Private consumption	46
Industry, of which:	24	Public consumption	28
manufacturing	13	Investment	18
Services	74	Exports	88
		Imports	-80

Structure of employment

	% of total		% of labour force
Agriculture	2.3	Unemployed 2012	5.3
Industry	18.8	Av. ann. rate 2000–12	3.7
Services	78.9		

Energy

	m TOE		
Total output	64.4	Net energy imports as %	
Total consumption	77.4	of energy use	17
Consumption per head			
kg oil equivalent	4,638		

Inflation and finance

Consumer price			av. ann. increase 2008–13
inflation 2013	2.6%	Euro area:	
Av. ann. inflation 2008–13	2.0%	Narrow money (M1)	6.0%
Deposit rate, h'holds, Dec. 2013	2.33%	Broad money	0.8%
		H'hold saving rate, 2013	5.1%

Exchange rates

	end 2013		2013
€ per $	0.73	Effective rates	2005 = 100
€ per SDR	1.12	– nominal	102.90
		– real	99.70

Trade

Principal exports		Principal imports	
	$bn fob		*$bn cif*
Machinery & transport equip.	183.6	Machinery & transport equip.	168.5
Mineral fuels & lubricants	133.0	Mineral fuels & lubricants	154.3
Chemicals & related products	101.4	Chemicals & related products	65.3
Food, drink & tobacco	75.8	Food, drink & tobacco	50.7
Total incl. others	**552.9**	**Total incl. others**	**500.9**

Main export destinations		Main origins of imports	
	% of total		*% of total*
Germany	30.8	Germany	16.1
Belgium	15.8	China	14.0
France	10.2	Belgium	9.8
United Kingdom	9.3	United Kingdom	7.8
EU27	75.8	EU27	45.2

Balance of payments, reserves and aid, $bn

Visible exports fob	533.0	Overall balance	2.8
Visible imports fob	-477.5	Change in reserves	4.3
Trade balance	55.5	Level of reserves	
Invisibles inflows	215.7	end Dec.	54.7
Invisibles outflows	-181.5	No. months of import cover	1.0
Net transfers	-16.2	Official gold holdings, m oz	19.7
Current account balance	73.6	Aid given	5.52
– as % of GDP	9.6	– as % of GDP	0.72
Capital balance	-71.2		

Health and education

Health spending, % of GDP	12.4	Education spending, % of GDP	5.9
Doctors per 1,000 pop.	2.9	Enrolment, %: primary	108
Hospital beds per 1,000 pop.	4.7	secondary	128
Improved-water source access,		tertiary	76
% of pop.	100		

Society

No. of households	7.4m	Cost of living, Dec. 2013	
Av. no. per household	2.3	New York = 100	90
Marriages per 1,000 pop.	4.2	Cars per 1,000 pop.	475
Divorces per 1,000 pop.	2.1	Colour TV households, % with:	
Religion, % of pop.		cable	69.3
Christian	50.6	satellite	7.2
Non-religious	42.1	Telephone lines per 100 pop.	43.0
Muslim	6.0	Mobile telephone subscribers	
Other	0.6	per 100 pop.	118.0
Hindu	0.5	Broadband subs per 100 pop.	39.8
Jewish	0.2	Internet hosts per 1,000 pop.	857.2

a Includes water.

NEW ZEALAND

Area	270,534 sq km	Capital	Wellington
Arable as % of total land	1.8	Currency	New Zealand dollar (NZ$)

People

Population	4.5m	Life expectancy: men		79.1 yrs
Pop. per sq km	16.4	women		82.9 yrs
Average annual growth		Adult literacy		...
in pop. 2010–15	1.0%	Fertility rate (per woman)		2.1
Pop. under 15	20.2%	Urban population		86.4%
Pop. over 60	19.3%			per 1,000 pop.
No. of men per 100 women	96.5	Crude birth rate		14.3
Human Development Index	91.0	Crude death rate		7.0

The economy

GDP	NZ$211bn	GDP per head	$38,640
GDP	$171bn	GDP per head in purchasing	
Av. ann. growth in real		power parity (USA=100)	63.6
GDP 2007–12	0.7%	Economic freedom index	81.2

Origins of GDP		**Components of GDP**	
	% of total		% of total
Agriculture	4	Private consumption	61
Industry, of which:	26	Public consumption	20
manufacturing	...	Investment	20
Services	70	Exports	29
		Imports	-29

Structure of employment

	% of total		% of labour force
Agriculture	6.6	Unemployed 2012	6.9
Industry	20.9	Av. ann. rate 2000–12	5.2
Services	72.5		

Energy

	m TOE		
Total output	16.1	Net energy imports as %	
Total consumption	18.2	of energy use	11
Consumption per head			
kg oil equivalent	4,124		

Inflation and finance

		av. ann. increase 2008–13	
Consumer price			
inflation 2013	1.1%	Narrow money (M1)	10.5%
Av. ann. inflation 2008–13	2.1%	Broad money	4.8%
Money market rate, Dec. 2013	2.50%	H'hold saving rate, 2013	-0.2%

Exchange rates

	end 2013		2013
NZ$ per $	1.22	Effective rates	2005 = 100
NZ$ per SDR	1.88	– nominal	105.40
NZ$ per €	1.68	– real	107.70

Trade

Principal exports		Principal imports	
	$bn fob		$bn cif
Dairy produce	9.3	Machinery & electrical equip.	7.7
Meat	4.2	Mineral fuels	6.8
Forestry products	3.5	Transport equipment	4.7
Wool	0.6		
Total incl. others	**37.3**	Total incl. others	**38.3**

Main export destinations		Main origins of imports	
	% of total		% of total
Australia	21.0	China	16.4
China	15.0	Australia	15.2
United States	9.2	United States	9.3
Japan	7.0	Japan	6.5

Balance of payments, reserves and aid, $bn

Visible exports fob	37.9	Overall balance	0.5
Visible imports fob	-37.8	Change in reserves	0.6
Trade balance	0.1	Level of reserves	
Invisibles inflows	18.2	end Dec.	17.6
Invisibles outflows	-24.8	No. months of import cover	3.4
Net transfers	-0.4	Official gold holdings, m oz	0.0
Current account balance	-7.0	Aid given	0.45
– as % of GDP	-4.1	– as % of GDP	0.26
Capital balance	4.3		

Health and education

Health spending, % of GDP	10.3	Education spending, % of GDP	7.4
Doctors per 1,000 pop.	2.7	Enrolment, %: primary	100
Hospital beds per 1,000 pop.	2.3	secondary	120
Improved-water source access,		tertiary	81
% of pop.	100		

Society

No. of households	1.6m	Cost of living, Dec. 2013	
Av. no. per household	2.9	New York = 100	104
Marriages per 1,000 pop.	4.6	Cars per 1,000 pop.	641
Divorces per 1,000 pop.	1.9	Colour TV households, % with:	
Religion, % of pop.		cable	5.9
Christian	57.0	satellite	40.7
Non-religious	36.6	Telephone lines per 100 pop.	42.2
Other	2.8	Mobile telephone subscribers	
Hindu	2.1	per 100 pop.	110.4
Muslim	1.2	Broadband subs per 100 pop.	27.8
Jewish	0.2	Internet hosts per 1,000 pop.	702.4

NIGERIA

Area	923,768 sq km	Capital	Abuja
Arable as % of total land	39.5	Currency	Naira (N)

People

Population	166.6m	Life expectancy: men	52.0 yrs
Pop. per sq km	175.9	women	52.6 yrs
Average annual growth		Adult literacy	51.1%
in pop. 2010–15	2.3%	Fertility rate (per woman)	6
Pop. under 15	44.4%	Urban population	52.1%
Pop. over 60	4.5%		per 1,000 pop.
No. of men per 100 women	102.5	Crude birth rate	41.5
Human Development Index	50.4	Crude death rate	13.4

The economy

GDP	N41,178bn	GDP per head	$1,560
GDP	$263bn	GDP per head in purchasing	
Av. ann. growth in real		power parity (USA=100)	5.1
GDP 2007–12	6.9%	Economic freedom index	54.3

Origins of GDP		Components of GDP	
	% of total		% of total
Agriculture	22	Private consumption	59
Industry, of which:	27	Public consumption	9
manufacturing	7	Investment	13
Services	51	Exports	32
		Imports	-13

Structure of employment

	% of total		% of labour force
Agriculture	...	Unemployed 2012	7.5
Industry	...	Av. ann. rate 2000–12	7.6
Services	...		

Energy

	m TOE		
Total output	256.9	Net energy imports as %	
Total consumption	118.3	of energy use	-117
Consumption per head			
kg oil equivalent	721		

Inflation and finance

		av. ann. increase 2008–13	
Consumer price			
inflation 2013	8.5%	Narrow money (M1)	8.0%
Av. ann. inflation 2008–13	11.5%	Broad money	12.6%
Treasury bill rate, Dec. 2013	10.92%		

Exchange rates

	end 2013		2013
N per $	155.20	Effective rates	2005 = 100
N per SDR	239.01	– nominal	82.30
N per €	214.04	– real	158.30

Trade

Principal exports		**Principal imports**	
	$bn fob		*$bn cif*
Crude oil	80.4	Machinery & transport equip.	14.1
Gas	10.9	Food & live animals	8.2
Cocoa & cocoa butter	0.1	Manufactured goods	7.4
Rubber	0.1	Chemicals	5.9
Total incl. others	**96.0**	**Total incl. others**	**58.3**

Main export destinations		**Main origins of imports**	
	% of total		*% of total*
United States	18.5	China	18.2
India	12.7	United States	10.0
Netherlands	9.5	India	5.5
Spain	8.6	United Kingdom	3.5

Balance of payments, reserves and debt, $bn

Visible exports fob	95.7	Change in reserves	11.3
Visible imports fob	-53.4	Level of reserves	
Trade balance	42.3	end Dec.	47.5
Invisibles inflows	3.4	No. months of import cover	5.7
Invisibles outflows	-47.2	Official gold holdings, m oz	0.7
Net transfers	21.9	Foreign debt	10.1
Current account balance	20.4	– as % of GDP	3.1
– as % of GDP	7.8	– as % of total exports	11.8
Capital balance	-1.3	Debt service ratio	0.3
Overall balance	11.1		

Health and education

Health spending, % of GDP	6.1	Education spending, % of GDP	...
Doctors per 1,000 pop.	0.4	Enrolment, %: primary	85
Hospital beds per 1,000 pop.	...	secondary	44
Improved-water source access,		tertiary	...
% of pop.	64		

Society

No. of households	35.7m	Cost of living, Dec. 2013	
Av. no. per household	4.8	New York = 100	62
Marriages per 1,000 pop.	...	Cars per 1,000 pop.	...
Divorces per 1,000 pop.	...	Colour TV households, % with:	
Religion, % of pop.		cable	1.9
Christian	49.3	satellite	...
Muslim	48.8	Telephone lines per 100 pop.	0.3
Other	1.4	Mobile telephone subscribers	
Non-religious	0.4	per 100 pop.	66.8
Hindu	<0.1	Broadband subs per 100 pop.	0.0
Jewish	<0.1	Internet hosts per 1,000 pop.	0.0

NORWAY

Area	323,878 sq km	Capital	Oslo
Arable as % of total land	2.7	Currency	Norwegian krone (Nkr)

People

Population	5.0m	Life expectancy: men	79.3 yrs
Pop. per sq km	15.1	women	83.5 yrs
Average annual growth		Adult literacy	...
in pop. 2010–15	1.0%	Fertility rate (per woman)	1.9
Pop. under 15	18.6%	Urban population	80.5%
Pop. over 60	21.6%		per 1,000 pop.
No. of men per 100 women	100.1	Crude birth rate	12.4
Human Development Index	94.4	Crude death rate	8.4

The economy

GDP	NKr2,909bn	GDP per head	$99,640
GDP	$500bn	GDP per head in purchasing	
Av. ann. growth in real		power parity (USA=100)	127.8
GDP 2007–12	0.6%	Economic freedom index	70.9

Origins of GDP		Components of GDP	
	% of total		% of total
Agriculture	1	Private consumption	40
Industry, of which:	42	Public consumption	21
manufacturing	7	Investment	25
Services	57	Exports	41
		Imports	-28

Structure of employment

	% of total		% of labour force
Agriculture	2.2	Unemployed 2012	3.2
Industry	20.2	Av. ann. rate 2000–12	3.5
Services	77.4		

Energy

	m TOE		
Total output	195.4	Net energy imports as %	
Total consumption	28.1	of energy use	-594
Consumption per head			
kg oil equivalent	5,681		

Inflation and finance

Consumer price		av. ann. increase 2008–13	
inflation 2013	2.1%	Narrow money (M1)	...
Av. ann. inflation 2008–13	1.7%	Broad money	...
Interbank rate, Dec. 2013	1.66%	H'hold saving rate, 2013	9.0%

Exchange rates

	end 2013		2013
Nkr per $	6.08	Effective rates	2005 = 100
Nkr per SDR	9.36	– nominal	96.6
Nkr per €	8.38	– real	95.7

Trade

Principal exports		Principal imports	
	$bn fob		*$bn cif*
Mineral fuels & lubricants	112.5	Machinery & transport equip.	22.4
Machinery & transport equip.	12.8	Manufactured goods	13.3
Manufactured goods	11.9	Miscellaneous manufactured	
Food & beverages	9.3	articles	13.0
		Chemicals & mineral products	8.5
Total incl. others	**161.0**	Total incl. others	**87.3**

Main export destinations		Main origins of imports	
	% of total		*% of total*
United Kingdom	26.5	Sweden	13.5
Netherlands	12.3	Germany	12.4
Germany	12.0	China	9.2
Sweden	6.3	Denmark	6.2
EU27	81.2	EU27	64.3

Balance of payments, reserves and aid, $bn

Visible exports fob	166.0	Overall balance	1.4
Visible imports fob	-89.1	Change in reserves	2.5
Trade balance	76.9	Level of reserves	
Invisibles inflows	85.6	end Dec.	51.9
Invisibles outflows	-84.4	No. months of import cover	3.6
Net transfers	-5.6	Official gold holdings, m oz	0.0
Current account balance	72.6	Aid given	4.75
– as % of GDP	14.5	– as % of GDP	0.95
Capital balance	-51.3		

Health and education

Health spending, % of GDP	9.0	Education spending, % of GDP	6.9
Doctors per 1,000 pop.	3.7	Enrolment, %: primary	109
Hospital beds per 1,000 pop.	3.3	secondary	113
Improved-water source access,		tertiary	73
% of pop.	100		

Society

No. of households	2.2m	Cost of living, Dec. 2013	
Av. no. per household	2.2	New York = 100	128
Marriages per 1,000 pop.	4.9	Cars per 1,000 pop.	492
Divorces per 1,000 pop.	2.0	Colour TV households, % with:	
Religion, % of pop.		cable	44.5
Christian	84.7	satellite	38.5
Non-religious	10.1	Telephone lines per 100 pop.	28.0
Muslim	3.7	Mobile telephone subscribers	
Other	0.9	per 100 pop.	116.7
Hindu	0.5	Broadband subs per 100 pop.	36.3
Jewish	<0.1	Internet hosts per 1,000 pop.	675.3

PAKISTAN

Area	803,940 sq km	Capital	Islamabad
Arable as % of total land	26.9	Currency	Pakistan rupee (PRs)

People

Population	180.0m	Life expectancy: men	65.6 yrs
Pop. per sq km	222.0	women	67.4 yrs
Average annual growth		Adult literacy	54.9%
in pop. 2010–15	1.7%	Fertility rate (per woman)	3.2
Pop. under 15	33.8%	Urban population	37.6%
Pop. over 60	6.5%		per 1,000 pop..
No. of men per 100 women	103.4	Crude birth rate	25.4
Human Development Index	53.7	Crude death rate	7.0

The economy

GDP	PRs20,091bn	GDP per head	$1,260
GDP	$225bn	GDP per head in purchasing	
Av. ann. growth in real		power parity (USA=100)	5.3
GDP 2007–12	2.6%	Economic freedom index	55.2

Origins of GDP		**Components of GDP**	
	% of total		% of total
Agriculture	24	Private consumption	83
Industry, of which:	22	Public consumption	10
manufacturing	14	Investment	15
Services	54	Exports	12
		Imports	-20

Structure of employment

	% of total		% of labour force
Agriculture	43.7	Unemployed 2012	5.1
Industry	21.5	Av. ann. rate 2000–12	6.2
Services	33.2		

Energy

	m TOE		
Total output	65.1	Net energy imports as %	
Total consumption	84.8	of energy use	23
Consumption per head			
kg oil equivalent	482		

Inflation and finance

			av. ann. increase 2008–13
Consumer price			
inflation 2013	7.4%	Narrow money (M1)	16.4%
Av. ann. inflation 2008–13	11.9%	Broad money	15.0%
Money market rate, Dec. 2013	9.88%		

Exchange rates

	end 2013		2013
PRs per $	105.68	Effective rates	2005 = 100
PRs per SDR	162.74	– nominal	52.10
PRs per €	145.74	– real	103.80

Trade

Principal exports		Principal imports	
	$bn fob		*$bn cif*
Cotton fabrics	2.6	Petroleum products	10.7
Knitwear	2.1	Crude oil	5.5
Cotton yarn & thread	2.0	Palm oil	2.4
Rice	2.0	Telecoms equipment	1.0
Total incl. others	**25.1**	Total incl. others	**44.2**

Main export destinations		Main origins of imports	
	% of total		*% of total*
United States	14.2	China	23.1
China	11.7	Saudi Arabia	14.4
United Arab Emirates	8.9	United Arab Emirates	14.2
Afghanistan	8.2	Kuwait	7.4

Balance of payments, reserves and debt, $bn

Visible exports fob	24.8	Change in reserves	-4.0
Visible imports fob	-40.4	Level of reserves	
Trade balance	-15.6	end Dec.	13.7
Invisibles inflows	7.2	No. months of import cover	3.1
Invisibles outflows	-12.5	Official gold holdings, m oz	2.1
Net transfers	18.6	Foreign debt	61.9
Current account balance	-2.3	– as % of GDP	27.5
– as % of GDP	-1.0	– as % of total exports	134.6
Capital balance	0.5	Debt service ratio	9.8
Overall balance	-2.3		

Health and education

Health spending, % of GDP	3.1	Education spending, % of GDP	2.1
Doctors per 1,000 pop.	0.8	Enrolment, %: primary	...
Hospital beds per 1,000 pop.	0.6	secondary	37
Improved-water source access,		tertiary	10
% of pop.	91		

Society

No. of households	30.1m	Cost of living, Dec. 2013	
Av. no. per household	6.8	New York = 100	40
Marriages per 1,000 pop.	...	Cars per 1,000 pop.	10
Divorces per 1,000 pop.	...	Colour TV households, % with:	
Religion, % of pop.		cable	1.3
Muslim	96.4	satellite	15.4
Hindu	1.9	Telephone lines per 100 pop.	3.2
Christian	1.6	Mobile telephone subscribers	
Jewish	<0.1	per 100 pop.	67.1
Non-religious	<0.1	Broadband subs per 100 pop.	0.5
Other	<0.1	Internet hosts per 1,000 pop.	3.1

PERU

Area	1,285,216 sq km	Capital	Lima
Arable as % of total land	2.9	Currency	Nuevo Sol (New Sol)

People

Population	29.7m	Life expectancy: men		72.0 yrs
Pop. per sq km	23.0	women		77.4 yrs
Average annual growth		Adult literacy		...
in pop. 2010–15	1.3%	Fertility rate (per woman)		2.4
Pop. under 15	28.8%	Urban population		78.6%
Pop. over 60	9.3%			per 1,000 pop.
No. of men per 100 women	100.4	Crude birth rate		19.8
Human Development Index	73.7	Crude death rate		5.3

The economy

GDP	New Soles 538bn	GDP per head	$6,800
GDP	$204bn	GDP per head in purchasing	
Av. ann. growth in real		power parity (USA=100)	20.8
GDP 2007–12	6.5%	Economic freedom index	67.4

Origins of GDP		**Components of GDP**	
	% of total		% of total
Agriculture	7	Private consumption	60
Industry, of which:	35	Public consumption	10
manufacturing	14	Investment	28
Services	58	Exports	26
		Imports	-24

Structure of employment

	% of total		% of labour force
Agriculture	25.8	Unemployed 2012	4.0
Industry	17.4	Av. ann. rate 2000–12	4.8
Services	56.8		

Energy

	m TOE		
Total output	23.4	Net energy imports as %	
Total consumption	20.6	of energy use	-14
Consumption per head			
kg oil equivalent	695		

Inflation and finance

Consumer price		*av. ann. increase 2008–13*	
inflation 2013	2.8%	Narrow money (M1)	24.6%
Av. ann. inflation 2008–13	2.9%	Broad money	14.4%
Money market rate, Dec. 2013	4.09%		

Exchange rates

	end 2013		2013
New Soles per $	2.80	Effective rates	2005 = 100
New Soles per SDR	4.30	– nominal	...
New Soles per €	3.86	– real	...

Trade

Principal exports	$bn fob	Principal imports	$bn cif
Copper	10.5	Intermediate goods	19.3
Gold	9.6	Capital goods	13.3
Fishmeal	2.3	Consumer goods	8.3
Zinc	1.3	Other goods	0.3
Total incl. others	**46.2**	Total incl. others	**42.2**

Main export destinations	% of total	Main origins of imports	% of total
China	16.8	United States	25.0
United States	13.8	China	14.3
Canada	7.4	Brazil	6.5
Japan	5.6	Argentina	4.9

Balance of payments, reserves and debt, $bn

Visible exports fob	45.9	Change in reserves	15.2
Visible imports fob	-40.4	Level of reserves	
Trade balance	5.6	end Dec.	64.1
Invisibles inflows	5.6	No. months of import cover	12.5
Invisibles outflows	-21.3	Official gold holdings, m oz	1.1
Net transfers	3.3	Foreign debt	54.1
Current account balance	-6.8	– as % of GDP	27.1
– as % of GDP	-3.4	– as % of total exports	98.5
Capital balance	20.0	Debt service ratio	11.7
Overall balance	15.2		

Health and education

Health spending, % of GDP	5.1	Education spending, % of GDP	2.8
Doctors per 1,000 pop.	1.1	Enrolment, %: primary	100
Hospital beds per 1,000 pop.	1.5	secondary	86
Improved-water source access, % of pop.	87	tertiary	43

Society

No. of households	7.6m	Cost of living, Dec. 2013	
Av. no. per household	3.9	New York = 100	69
Marriages per 1,000 pop.	3.3	Cars per 1,000 pop.	...
Divorces per 1,000 pop.	...	Colour TV households, % with:	
Religion, % of pop.		cable	32.5
Christian	95.5	satellite	0.2
Non-religious	3.0	Telephone lines per 100 pop.	11.4
Other	1.5	Mobile telephone subscribers	
Hindu	<0.1	per 100 pop.	98.0
Jewish	<0.1	Broadband subs per 100 pop.	4.7
Muslim	<0.1	Internet hosts per 1,000 pop.	16.8

PHILIPPINES

Area	300,000 sq km	Capital	Manila
Arable as % of total land	18.1	Currency	Philippine peso (P)

People

Population	96.5m	Life expectancy: men	63.5 yrs
Pop. per sq km	316.0	women	72.2 yrs
Average annual growth		Adult literacy	...
in pop. 2010–15	1.7%	Fertility rate (per woman)	3.1
Pop. under 15	34.1%	Urban population	49.8%
Pop. over 60	6.4%		per 1,000 pop.
No. of men per 100 women	100.7	Crude birth rate	17.7
Human Development Index	66.0	Crude death rate	6.0

The economy

GDP	P10,565bn	GDP per head	$2,590
GDP	$250bn	GDP per head in purchasing	
Av. ann. growth in real		power parity (USA=100)	8.4
GDP 2007–12	4.7%	Economic freedom index	60.1

Origins of GDP		Components of GDP	
	% of total		% of total
Agriculture	12	Private consumption	74
Industry, of which:	31	Public consumption	11
manufacturing	21	Investment	18
Services	57	Exports	31
		Imports	-34

Structure of employment

	% of total		% of labour force
Agriculture	32.2	Unemployed 2012	7.0
Industry	15.4	Av. ann. rate 2000–12	8.9
Services	52.5		

Energy

	m TOE		
Total output	23.9	Net energy imports as %	
Total consumption	40.5	of energy use	41
Consumption per head			
kg oil equivalent	426		

Inflation and finance

Consumer price		av. ann. increase 2008–13	
inflation 2013	2.9%	Narrow money (M1)	14.0%
Av. ann. inflation 2008–13	3.8%	Broad money	13.6%
Money market rate, Dec. 2013	2.01%		

Exchange rates

	end 2013		2013
P per $	44.41	Effective rates	2005 = 100
P per SDR	68.40	– nominal	111.90
P per €	61.25	– real	136.00

Trade

Principal exports		Principal imports	
	$bn fob		*$bn cif*
Electrical & electronic equip.	22.8	Capital goods	17.5
Clothing	1.6	Mineral fuels	13.8
Coconut oil	1.0	Chemicals	6.3
Petroleum products	0.5	Manufactured goods	5.2
Total incl. others	**52.1**	Total incl. others	**65.8**

Main export destinations		Main origins of imports	
	% of total		*% of total*
Japan	19.0	United States	11.9
United States	14.2	China	11.1
China	11.8	Japan	10.8
Hong Kong	9.2	South Korea	7.5

Balance of payments, reserves and debt, $bn

Visible exports fob	46.4	Change in reserves	8.6
Visible imports fob	-65.3	Level of reserves	
Trade balance	-18.9	end Dec.	83.7
Invisibles inflows	28.7	No. months of import cover	11.5
Invisibles outflows	-22.3	Official gold holdings, m oz	6.2
Net transfers	19.5	Foreign debt	61.4
Current account balance	6.9	– as % of GDP	24.6
– as % of GDP	2.8	– as % of total exports	63.1
Capital balance	6.8	Debt service ratio	6.0
Overall balance	9.2		

Health and education

Health spending, % of GDP	4.6	Education spending, % of GDP	2.7
Doctors per 1,000 pop.	...	Enrolment, %: primary	106
Hospital beds per 1,000 pop.	1.0	secondary	85
Improved-water source access,		tertiary	28
% of pop.	92		

Society

No. of households	21.3m	Cost of living, Dec. 2013	
Av. no. per household	4.6	New York = 100	62
Marriages per 1,000 pop.	5.6	Cars per 1,000 pop.	9
Divorces per 1,000 pop.	...	Colour TV households, % with:	
Religion, % of pop.		cable	52.5
Christian	92.6	satellite	0.6
Muslim	5.5	Telephone lines per 100 pop.	4.1
Other	1.7	Mobile telephone subscribers	
Non-religious	0.1	per 100 pop.	106.5
Hindu	<0.1	Broadband subs per 100 pop.	2.2
Jewish	<0.1	Internet hosts per 1,000 pop.	5.1

POLAND

Area	312,683 sq km	Capital	Warsaw
Arable as % of total land	36.5	Currency	Zloty (Zl)

People

Population	38.3m	Life expectancy: men	72.2 yrs
Pop. per sq km	122.0	women	80.5 yrs
Average annual growth		Adult literacy	...
in pop. 2010–15	0.0%	Fertility rate (per woman)	1.4
Pop. under 15	15.0%	Urban population	60.7%
Pop. over 60	21.1%		per 1,000 pop.
No. of men per 100 women	93.2	Crude birth rate	10.8
Human Development Index	83.4	Crude death rate	10.5

The economy

GDP	Zl1,595bn	GDP per head	$12,710
GDP	$490bn	GDP per head in purchasing	
Av. ann. growth in real		power parity (USA=100)	44.0
GDP 2007–12	3.4%	Economic freedom index	67.0

Origins of GDP		Components of GDP	
	% of total		% of total
Agriculture	4	Private consumption	61
Industry, of which:	32	Public consumption	18
manufacturing	18	Investment	21
Services	65	Exports	46
		Imports	-46

Structure of employment

	% of total		% of labour force
Agriculture	12.6	Unemployed 2012	10.1
Industry	30.4	Av. ann. rate 2000–12	13.7
Services	57.0		

Energy

	m TOE		
Total output	68.5	Net energy imports as %	
Total consumption	101.3	of energy use	32
Consumption per head			
kg oil equivalent	2,629		

Inflation and finance

Consumer price		av. ann. increase 2008–13	
inflation 2013	0.9%	Narrow money (M1)	9.7%
Av. ann. inflation 2008–13	3.0%	Broad money	8.0%
Money market rate, Dec. 2013	2.52%	H'hold saving rate, 2013	-0.5%

Exchange rates

	end 2013		2013
Zl per $	3.01	Effective rates	2005 = 100
Zl per SDR	4.64	– nominal	99.4
Zl per €	4.15	– real	102.3

Trade

Principal exports		Principal imports	
	$bn fob		*$bn cif*
Machinery & transport equip.	69.1	Machinery & transport equip.	63.7
Manufactured goods	39.0	Manufactured goods	34.4
Foodstuffs & live animals	19.3	Chemicals & chemical products	27.6
Total incl. others	**184.7**	Total incl. others	**198.5**

Main export destinations		Main origins of imports	
	% of total		*% of total*
Germany	25.2	Germany	26.2
United Kingdom	6.8	Russia	11.5
Czech Republic	6.3	Netherlands	5.7
France	5.9	Italy	5.1
EU27	76.0	EU27	67.7

Balance of payments, reserves and debt, $bn

Visible exports fob	190.8	Change in reserves	11.2
Visible imports fob	-197.5	Level of reserves	
Trade balance	-6.7	end Dec.	108.9
Invisibles inflows	46.2	No. months of import cover	5.0
Invisibles outflows	-62.9	Official gold holdings, m oz	3.3
Net transfers	5.1	Foreign debt	365.1
Current account balance	-18.3	– as % of GDP	74.6
– as % of GDP	-3.7	– as % of total exports	150.2
Capital balance	33.5	Debt service ratio	21.7
Overall balance	11.2	Aid given	0.42
		– as % of GDP	0.09

Health and education

Health spending, % of GDP	6.7	Education spending, % of GDP	5.2
Doctors per 1,000 pop.	2.2	Enrolment, %: primary	101
Hospital beds per 1,000 pop.	6.5	secondary	98
Improved-water source access,		tertiary	73
% of pop.	100		

Society

No. of households	14.8m	Cost of living, Dec. 2013	
Av. no. per household	2.6	New York = 100	69
Marriages per 1,000 pop.	5.3	Cars per 1,000 pop.	507
Divorces per 1,000 pop.	1.7	Colour TV households, % with:	
Religion, % of pop.		cable	33.8
Christian	94.3	satellite	62.8
Non-religious	5.6	Telephone lines per 100 pop.	15.6
Hindu	<0.1	Mobile telephone subscribers	
Jewish	<0.1	per 100 pop.	140.3
Muslim	<0.1	Broadband subs per 100 pop.	15.5
Other	<0.1	Internet hosts per 1,000 pop.	349.3

PORTUGAL

Area	88,940 sq km	Capital	Lisbon
Arable as % of total land	12.0	Currency	Euro (€)

People

Population	10.7m	Life expectancy: men	76.8 yrs
Pop. per sq km	116.0	women	82.8 yrs
Average annual growth		Adult literacy	...
in pop. 2010–15	0.0%	Fertility rate (per woman)	1.3
Pop. under 15	14.8%	Urban population	63.2%
Pop. over 60	24.7%		per 1,000 pop.
No. of men per 100 women	94.0	Crude birth rate	8.8
Human Development Index	82.2	Crude death rate	10.3

The economy

GDP	€165bn	GDP per head	$20,190
GDP	$212bn	GDP per head in purchasing	
Av. ann. growth in real		power parity (USA=100)	50.2
GDP 2007–12	-1.1%	Economic freedom index	63.5

Origins of GDP		Components of GDP	
	% of total		% of total
Agriculture	2	Private consumption	66
Industry, of which:	24	Public consumption	18
manufacturing	14	Investment	17
Services	74	Exports	39
		Imports	-39

Structure of employment

	% of total		% of labour force
Agriculture	10.5	Unemployed 2012	15.6
Industry	25.6	Av. ann. rate 2000–12	8.1
Services	63.8		

Energy

	m TOE		
Total output	5.3	Net energy imports as %	
Total consumption	23.1	of energy use	77
Consumption per head			
kg oil equivalent	2,187		

Inflation and finance

Consumer price		*av. ann. increase 2008–13*	
inflation 2013[a]	0.4%	Euro area:	
Av. ann. inflation 2008–13[a]	1.4%	Narrow money (M1)	6.0%
Deposit rate, h'holds Dec. 2013	2.24%	Broad money	0.8%
		H'hold saving rate[b], 2013	12.6%

Exchange rates

	end 2013		2013
€ per $	0.73	Effective rates	2005 = 100
€ per SDR	1.12	– nominal	102.00
		– real	100.10

Trade

Principal exports		Principal imports	
	$bn fob		*$bn cif*
Machinery & transport equip.	15.4	Chemicals & related products	20.2
Food, drink & tobacco	5.9	Machinery & transport equip.	16.4
Chemicals & related products	5.1	Mineral fuels & lubricants	14.8
Mineral fuels & lubricants	4.8	Food, drink & tobacco	9.5
Total incl. others	**58.2**	Total incl. others	**72.2**

Main export destinations		Main origins of imports	
	% of total		*% of total*
Spain	22.6	Spain	31.5
Germany	12.3	Germany	11.5
France	11.8	France	6.6
Angola	6.5	Italy	5.3
EU27	71.0	EU27	71.8

Balance of payments, reserves and debt, $bn

Visible exports fob	58.1	Overall balance	-10.4
Visible imports fob	-69.7	Change in reserves	1.8
Trade balance	-11.6	Level of reserves	
Invisibles inflows	33.8	end Dec.	22.6
Invisibles outflows	-31.4	No. months of import cover	2.7
Net transfers	4.8	Official gold holdings, m oz	12.3
Current account balance	-4.4	Aid given	0.58
– as % of GDP	-2.1	– as % of GDP	0.27
Capital balance	-5.3		

Health and education

Health spending, % of GDP	9.4	Education spending, % of GDP	5.6
Doctors per 1,000 pop.	3.9	Enrolment, %: primary	112
Hospital beds per 1,000 pop.	3.4	secondary	110
Improved-water source access,		tertiary	66
% of pop.	100		

Society

No. of households	4.2m	Cost of living, Dec. 2013	
Av. no. per household	2.5	New York = 100	77
Marriages per 1,000 pop.	3.3	Cars per 1,000 pop.	428
Divorces per 1,000 pop.	2.5	Colour TV households, % with:	
Religion, % of pop.		cable	56.1
Christian	93.8	satellite	20.1
Non-religious	4.4	Telephone lines per 100 pop.	43.0
Other	1.0	Mobile telephone subscribers	
Muslim	0.6	per 100 pop.	116.1
Hindu	0.1	Broadband subs per 100 pop.	22.6
Jewish	<0.1	Internet hosts per 1,000 pop.	364.7

a Estimate.
b Gross.

ROMANIA

Area	237,500 sq km	Capital	Bucharest
Arable as % of total land	39.1	Currency	Leu (RON)

People

Population	21.4m	Life expectancy: men		70.2 yrs
Pop. per sq km	90.0	women		77.4 yrs
Average annual growth		Adult literacy		...
in pop. 2010–15	-0.3%	Fertility rate (per woman)		1.4
Pop. under 15	15.1%	Urban population		52.9%
Pop. over 60	21.0%			per 1,000 pop.
No. of men per 100 women	94.3	Crude birth rate		10.3
Human Development Index	78.5	Crude death rate		12.5

The economy

GDP	RON587bn	GDP per head	$8,440
GDP	$169bn	GDP per head in purchasing	
Av. ann. growth in real		power parity (USA=100)	34.9
GDP 2007–12	1.0%	Economic freedom index	65.5

Origins of GDP		Components of GDP	
	% of total		% of total
Agriculture	6	Private consumption	72
Industry, of which:	42	Public consumption	7
manufacturing	...	Investment	27
Services	52	Exports	40
		Imports	-45

Structure of employment

	% of total		% of labour force
Agriculture	29.0	Unemployed 2012	7.0
Industry	28.6	Av. ann. rate 2000–12	7.1
Services	42.4		

Energy

	m TOE		
Total output	27.6	Net energy imports as %	
Total consumption	35.8	of energy use	23
Consumption per head			
kg oil equivalent	1,676		

Inflation and finance

Consumer price		av. ann. increase 2008–13	
inflation 2013	4.0%	Narrow money (M1)	1.6%
Av. ann. inflation 2008–13	5.0%	Broad money	6.8%
Money market rate, Dec. 2013	1.80%		

Exchange rates

	end 2013		2013
RON per $	3.26	Effective rates	2005 = 100
RON per SDR	5.01	– nominal	84.60
RON per €	4.50	– real	104.70

Trade

Principal exports		Principal imports	
	$bn fob		$bn cif
Machinery & equipment,		Machinery & equipment,	
incl. transport	23.1	incl. transport	23.1
Textiles & apparel	4.5	Chemical products	9.5
Basic metals & products	3.2	Minerals, fuels & lubricants	8.5
Minerals, fuels & lubricants	3.2	Textiles & products	4.4
Total incl. others	**57.9**	Total incl. others	**70.3**

Main export destinations		Main origins of imports	
	% of total		% of total
Germany	18.7	Germany	17.4
Italy	12.1	Italy	10.9
France	7.0	Hungary	9.0
Turkey	5.4	France	5.7
EU27	70.2	EU27	73.5

Balance of payments, reserves and debt, $bn

Visible exports fob	51.3	Change in reserves	-1.4
Visible imports fob	-62.7	Level of reserves	
Trade balance	-11.5	end Dec.	46.7
Invisibles inflows	14.5	No. months of import cover	7.2
Invisibles outflows	-14.9	Official gold holdings, m oz	3.3
Net transfers	4.4	Foreign debt	131.9
Current account balance	-7.5	– as % of GDP	78.9
– as % of GDP	-4.4	– as % of total exports	182.5
Capital balance	6.6	Debt service ratio	30.6
Overall balance	0.3	Aid given	0.14
		– as % of GDP	0.08

Health and education

Health spending, % of GDP	5.1	Education spending, % of GDP	4.2
Doctors per 1,000 pop.	2.4	Enrolment, %: primary	99
Hospital beds per 1,000 pop.	6.1	secondary	96
Improved-water source access,		tertiary	52
% of pop.	...		

Society

No. of households	7.5m	Cost of living, Dec. 2013	
Av. no. per household	2.9	New York = 100	55
Marriages per 1,000 pop.	5.0	Cars per 1,000 pop.	...
Divorces per 1,000 pop.	1.5	Colour TV households, % with:	
Religion, % of pop.		cable	45.9
Christian	99.5	satellite	37.4
Muslim	0.3	Telephone lines per 100 pop.	21.4
Non-religious	0.1	Mobile telephone subscribers	
Hindu	<0.1	per 100 pop.	105.0
Jewish	<0.1	Broadband subs per 100 pop.	16.2
Other	<0.1	Internet hosts per 1,000 pop.	142.8

RUSSIA

Area	17,075,400 sq km	Capital	Moscow
Arable as % of total land	7.4	Currency	Rouble (Rb)

People

Population	142.7m	Life expectancy: men		61.7 yrs
Pop. per sq km	8.0		women	74.3 yrs
Average annual growth		Adult literacy		...
in pop. 2010–15	-0.2%	Fertility rate (per woman)		1.5
Pop. under 15	15.8%	Urban population		74.5%
Pop. over 60	19.0%			per 1,000 pop.
No. of men per 100 women	86.1	Crude birth rate		11.8
Human Development Index	77.8	Crude death rate		15.5

The economy

GDP	Rb62,599bn	GDP per head	$14,040
GDP	$2,015bn	GDP per head in purchasing	
Av. ann. growth in real		power parity (USA=100)	45.6
GDP 2007–12	1.8%	Economic freedom index	51.9

Origins of GDP		**Components of GDP**	
	% of total		% of total
Agriculture	4	Private consumption	48
Industry, of which:	36	Public consumption	19
manufacturing	15	Investment	26
Services	60	Exports	29
		Imports	-22

Structure of employment

	% of total		% of labour force
Agriculture	9.7	Unemployed 2012	5.5
Industry	27.9	Av. ann. rate 2000–12	7.5
Services	62.3		

Energy

	m TOE		
Total output	1,314.9	Net energy imports as %	
Total consumption	731.0	of energy use	-80
Consumption per head			
kg oil equivalent	5,113		

Inflation and finance

Consumer price		av. ann. increase 2008–13	
inflation 2013	6.8%	Narrow money (M1)	13.0%
Av. ann. inflation 2008–13	7.7%	Broad money	18.0%
Money market rate, Dec. 2013	6.40%		

Exchange rates

	end 2013		2013
Rb per $	32.73	Effective rates	2005 = 100
Rb per SDR	50.40	– nominal	88.70
Rb per €	45.14	– real	132.80

Trade

Principal exports		**Principal imports**	
	$bn fob		*$bn cif*
Fuels	374.5	Manufactures	278.7
Manufactures	84.4	Food	40.3
Ores & metals	26.4	Ores & metals	6.7
Food	15.8	Agricultural raw materials	3.4
Agricultural raw materials	10.5	Fuels	3.4
Total	**527.4**	Total	**335.8**

Main export destinations		**Main origins of imports**	
	% of total		*% of total*
Netherlands	14.4	China	15.4
China	6.4	Germany	9.4
Italy	5.3	Ukraine	5.5
Germany	4.5	Italy	3.9

Balance of payments, reserves and debt, $bn

Visible exports fob	527.4	Change in reserves	40.2
Visible imports fob	-335.8	Level of reserves	
Trade balance	191.7	end Dec.	537.6
Invisibles inflows	110.1	No. months of import cover	11.5
Invisibles outflows	-224.3	Official gold holdings, m oz	30.8
Net transfers	-6.1	Foreign debt	539.5
Current account balance	71.3	– as % of GDP	26.8
– as % of GDP	3.5	– as % of total exports	84.0
Capital balance	-30.9	Debt service ratio	9.7
Overall balance	30.0	Aid given	0.47
		– as % of GDP	0.02

Health and education

Health spending, % of GDP	6.3	Education spending, % of GDP	4.1
Doctors per 1,000 pop.	4.3	Enrolment, %: primary	134
Hospital beds per 1,000 pop.	...	secondary	85
Improved-water source access,		tertiary	75
% of pop.	97		

Society

No. of households	56.3m	Cost of living, Dec. 2013	
Av. no. per household	2.5	New York = 100	88
Marriages per 1,000 pop.	9.2	Cars per 1,000 pop.	277
Divorces per 1,000 pop.	4.7	Colour TV households, % with:	
Religion, % of pop.		cable	32.9
Christian	73.3	satellite	24.7
Non-religious	16.2	Telephone lines per 100 pop.	30.1
Muslim	10.0	Mobile telephone subscribers	
Jewish	0.2	per 100 pop.	182.9
Hindu	<0.1	Broadband subs per 100 pop.	14.5
Other	<0.1	Internet hosts per 1,000 pop.	107.8

SAUDI ARABIA

Area	2,200,000 sq km	Capital	Riyadh
Arable as % of total land	1.4	Currency	Riyal (SR)

People

Population	28.7m	Life expectancy: men	73.8 yrs
Pop. per sq km	13.0	women	77.5 yrs
Average annual growth		Adult literacy	...
in pop. 2010–15	1.9%	Fertility rate (per woman)	2.7
Pop. under 15	29.0%	Urban population	83.1%
Pop. over 60	4.9%		per 1,000 pop.
No. of men per 100 women	124.0	Crude birth rate	19.6
Human Development Index	83.6	Crude death rate	3.3

The economy

GDP	SR2,666bn	GDP per head	$25,140
GDP	$711bn	GDP per head in purchasing	
Av. ann. growth in real		power parity (USA=100)	60.3
GDP 2007–12	6.2%	Economic freedom index	62.2

Origins of GDP		Components of GDP	
	% of total		% of total
Agriculture	2	Private consumption	28
Industry, of which:	63	Public consumption	20
manufacturing	10	Investment	26
Services	35	Exports	56
		Imports	-30

Structure of employment

	% of total		% of labour force
Agriculture	4.7	Unemployed 2012	5.6
Industry	24.7	Av. ann. rate 2000–12	5.3
Services	70.7		

Energy

	m TOE		
Total output	601.7	Net energy imports as %	
Total consumption	187.1	of energy use	-222
Consumption per head			
kg oil equivalent	6,738		

Inflation and finance

			av. ann. increase 2008–13
Consumer price			
inflation 2013	3.5%	Narrow money (M1)	18.6%
Av. ann. inflation 2008–13	3.6%	Broad money	10.7%
Money market rate, Dec. 2013	0.85%		

Exchange rates

	end 2013		2013
SR per $	3.75	Effective rates	2005 = 100
SR per SDR	5.78	– nominal	94.5
SR per €	5.17	– real	100.1

Trade

Principal exports		Principal imports	
	$bn fob		*$bn cif*
Crude oil	303.2	Machinery & transport equip.	68.7
Refined petroleum products	40.3	Foodstuffs	21.7
		Chemical & metal products	12.9
Total incl. others	**388.4**	Total incl. others	**155.6**

Main export destinations		Main origins of imports	
	% of total		*% of total*
Japan	14.2	China	13.4
China	13.6	United States	13.2
United States	13.6	Germany	6.5
South Korea	9.9	South Korea	6.3

Balance of payments, reserves and aid, $bn

Visible exports fob	388.4	Overall balance	115.8
Visible imports fob	-141.8	Change in reserves	117.1
Trade balance	246.6	Level of reserves	
Invisibles inflows	34.7	end Dec.	673.7
Invisibles outflows	-86.1	No. months of import cover	35.5
Net transfers	-30.4	Official gold holdings, m oz	10.4
Current account balance	164.8	Aid given	1.30
– as % of GDP	23.2	– as % of GDP	0.18
Capital balance	-6.6		

Health and education

Health spending, % of GDP	3.2	Education spending, % of GDP	5.1
Doctors per 1,000 pop.	0.9	Enrolment, %: primary	84
Hospital beds per 1,000 pop.	2.1	secondary	114
Improved-water source access,		tertiary	51
% of pop.	97		

Society

No. of households	5.2m	Cost of living, Dec. 2013	
Av. no. per household	5.6	New York = 100	57
Marriages per 1,000 pop.	4.5	Cars per 1,000 pop.	353
Divorces per 1,000 pop.	0.9	Colour TV households, % with:	
Religion, % of pop.		cable	0.3
Muslim	93.0	satellite	99.5
Christian	4.4	Telephone lines per 100 pop.	17.0
Hindu	1.1	Mobile telephone subscribers	
Other	0.9	per 100 pop.	187.4
Non-religious	0.7	Broadband subs per 100 pop.	7.0
Jewish	<0.1	Internet hosts per 1,000 pop.	10.3

SINGAPORE

Area	639 sq km	Capital	Singapore
Arable as % of total land	0.9	Currency	Singapore dollar (S$)

People

Population	5.3m	Life expectancy:	men	79.7 yrs
Pop. per sq km	7,427.0		women	84.6 yrs
Average annual growth		Adult literacy		...
in pop. 2010–15	2.2%	Fertility rate (per woman)		1.3
Pop. under 15	16.1%	Urban population		100.0%
Pop. over 60	15.8%			per 1,000 pop.
No. of men per 100 women	101.7	Crude birth rate		9.9
Human Development Index	90.1	Crude death rate		4.7

The economy

GDP	S$346bn	GDP per head	$51,710
GDP	$275bn	GDP per head in purchasing	
Av. ann. growth in real		power parity (USA=100)	117.5
GDP 2007–12	4.3%	Economic freedom index	89.4

Origins of GDP		**Components of GDP**	
	% of total		% of total
Agriculture	0	Private consumption	41
Industry, of which:	27	Public consumption	10
manufacturing	21	Investment	27
Services	73	Exports	201
		Imports	-178

Structure of employment

	% of total		% of labour force
Agriculture	1.1	Unemployed 2012	2.8
Industry	21.8	Av. ann. rate 2000–12	3.8
Services	77.1		

Energy

	m TOE		
Total output	0.9	Net energy imports as %	
Total consumption	33.4	of energy use	97
Consumption per head			
kg oil equivalent	6,452		

Inflation and finance

Consumer price		av. ann. increase 2008–13	
inflation 2013	2.4%	Narrow money (M1)	15.4%
Av. ann. inflation 2008–13	3.1%	Broad money	8.3%
Money market rate, Dec. 2013	0.40%		

Exchange rates

	end 2013		2013
S$ per $	1.27	Effective rates	2005 = 100
S$ per SDR	1.95	– nominal	123.00
S$ per €	1.75	– real	127.20

Trade

Principal exports		**Principal imports**	
	$bn fob		*$bn cif*
Mineral fuels	104.8	Machinery & transport equip.	157.0
Electronic components & parts	95.8	Mineral fuels	123.9
Chemicals & products	54.0	Misc. manufactured articles	27.2
Manufactured products	32.0	Manufactured products	23.7
Total incl. others	**409.2**	Total incl. others	**380.3**

Main export destinations		**Main origins of imports**	
	% of total		*% of total*
Malaysia	12.3	Malaysia	10.6
China	10.9	China	10.3
Hong Kong	10.7	United States	10.1
Indonesia	10.6	South Korea	6.7
United States	5.4	Japan	6.2

Balance of payments, reserves and debt, $bn

Visible exports fob	434.4	Change in reserves	22.1
Visible imports fob	-371.5	Level of reserves	
Trade balance	62.9	end Dec.	265.9
Invisibles inflows	189.2	No. months of import cover	5.6
Invisibles outflows	-195.3	Official gold holdings, m oz	4.1
Net transfers	-7.4	Foreign debt	24.7
Current account balance	49.4	– as % of GDP	8.5
– as % of GDP	18.0	– as % of total exports	4.0
Capital balance	-21.7	Debt service ratio	0.7
Overall balance	26.2		

Health and education

Health spending, % of GDP	4.7	Education spending, % of GDP	3.0
Doctors per 1,000 pop.	1.9	Enrolment, %: primary	...
Hospital beds per 1,000 pop.	2.0	secondary	...
Improved-water source access,		tertiary	...
% of pop.	100		

Society

No. of households	1.5m	Cost of living, Dec. 2013	
Av. no. per household	3.5	New York = 100	130
Marriages per 1,000 pop.	7.3	Cars per 1,000 pop.	...
Divorces per 1,000 pop.	1.8	Colour TV households, % with:	
Religion, % of pop.		cable	55.8
Buddhist	33.9	satellite	...
Christian	18.2	Telephone lines per 100 pop.	37.5
Non-religious	16.4	Mobile telephone subscribers	
Muslim	14.3	per 100 pop.	152.1
Other	12.0	Broadband subs per 100 pop.	25.4
Hindu	5.2	Internet hosts per 1,000 pop.	397.9

SLOVAKIA

Area	49,035 sq km	Capital	Bratislava
Arable as % of total land	28.9	Currency	Euro (€)

People

Population	5.5m	Life expectancy: men	71.5 yrs
Pop. per sq km	112.0	women	79.2 yrs
Average annual growth		Adult literacy	...
in pop. 2010–15	0.1%	Fertility rate (per woman)	1.4
Pop. under 15	15.1%	Urban population	54.6%
Pop. over 60	19.2%		per 1,000 pop.
No. of men per 100 women	94.6	Crude birth rate	10.7
Human Development Index	83.0	Crude death rate	10.3

The economy

GDP	€71.1bn	GDP per head	$16,860
GDP	$91.1bn	GDP per head in purchasing	
Av. ann. growth in real		power parity (USA=100)	49.9
GDP 2007–12	1.9%	Economic freedom index	66.4

Origins of GDP		**Components of GDP**	
	% of total		% of total
Agriculture	4	Private consumption	57
Industry, of which:	35	Public consumption	18
manufacturing	21	Investment	22
Services	61	Exports	89
		Imports	-87

Structure of employment

	% of total		% of labour force
Agriculture	3.2	Unemployed 2012	13.9
Industry	37.5	Av. ann. rate 2000–12	15.1
Services	59.2		

Energy

	m TOE		
Total output	6.4	Net energy imports as %	
Total consumption	17.3	of energy use	63
Consumption per head			
kg oil equivalent	3,214		

Inflation and finance

Consumer price		av. ann. increase 2008–13	
inflation 2013	1.5%	Euro area:	
Av. ann. inflation 2008–13	2.2%	Narrow money (M1)	6.0%
Deposit rate, h'holds Dec. 2013	1.64%	Broad money	0.8%
		H'hold saving rate, 2013	3.0%

Exchange rates

	end 2013		2013
€ per $	0.73	Effective rates	2005 = 100
€ per SDR	1.12	– nominal	131.06
		– real	136.80

Trade

Principal exports	$bn fob	Principal imports	$bn cif
Machinery & transport equip.	45.9	Machinery & transport equip.	21.2
Intermediate & manuf. products	18.9	Intermediate & manuf. products	11.5
Chemicals	2.3	Fuels	10.0
Miscellaneous manuf. products	2.2	Chemicals	4.7
Total incl. others	**80.0**	Total incl. others	**79.1**

Main export destinations	% of total	Main origins of imports	% of total
Germany	21.4	Germany	17.8
Czech Republic	14.1	Czech Republic	17.1
Poland	8.4	Russia	9.7
Hungary	7.3	Hungary	7.6
EU27	83.8	EU27	73.6

Balance of payments, reserves and debt, $bn

Visible exports fob	80.8	Change in reserves	0.1
Visible imports fob	-76.1	Level of reserves	
Trade balance	4.6	end Dec.	2.5
Invisibles inflows	10.4	No. months of import cover	0.3
Invisibles outflows	-12.2	Official gold holdings, m oz	1.0
Net transfers	-0.8	Foreign debt	...
Current account balance	2.0	– as % of GDP	...
– as % of GDP	2.2	– as % of total exports	...
Capital balance	1.3	Debt service ratio	...
Overall balance	0.0	Aid given	0.08
		– as % of GDP	0.09

Health and education

Health spending, % of GDP	7.8	Education spending, % of GDP	4.2
Doctors per 1,000 pop.	3.0	Enrolment, %: primary	102
Hospital beds per 1,000 pop.	6.0	secondary	94
Improved-water source access,		tertiary	55
% of pop.	100		

Society

No. of households	2.3m	Cost of living, Dec. 2013	
Av. no. per household	2.3	New York = 100	...
Marriages per 1,000 pop.	4.8	Cars per 1,000 pop.	337
Divorces per 1,000 pop.	2.0	Colour TV households, % with:	
Religion, % of pop.		cable	43.0
Christian	85.3	satellite	49.6
Non-religious	14.3	Telephone lines per 100 pop.	17.9
Muslim	0.2	Mobile telephone subscribers	
Other	0.1	per 100 pop.	111.9
Hindu	<0.1	Broadband subs per 100 pop.	14.7
Jewish	<0.1	Internet hosts per 1,000 pop.	242.0

SLOVENIA

Area	20,253 sq km	Capital	Ljubljana
Arable as % of total land	8.4	Currency	Euro (€)

People

Population	2.0m	Life expectancy: men	76.2 yrs
Pop. per sq km	100.0	women	82.7 yrs
Average annual growth		Adult literacy	99.7%
in pop. 2010–15	0.2%	Fertility rate (per woman)	1.5
Pop. under 15	14.3%	Urban population	49.8%
Pop. over 60	23.8%		per 1,000 pop.
No. of men per 100 women	95.7	Crude birth rate	10.0
Human Development Index	87.4	Crude death rate	9.8

The economy

GDP	€35.3bn	GDP per head	$22,010
GDP	$45.3bn	GDP per head in purchasing	
Av. ann. growth in real		power parity (USA=100)	55.0
GDP 2007–12	-1.1%	Economic freedom index	62.7

Origins of GDP		**Components of GDP**	
	% of total		% of total
Agriculture	2	Private consumption	57
Industry, of which:	32	Public consumption	20
manufacturing	21	Investment	21
Services	66	Exports	71
		Imports	-70

Structure of employment

	% of total		% of labour force
Agriculture	8.3	Unemployed 2012	8.8
Industry	30.8	Av. ann. rate 2000–12	6.4
Services	60.3		

Energy

	m TOE		
Total output	3.8	Net energy imports as %	
Total consumption	7.2	of energy use	48
Consumption per head			
kg oil equivalent	3,531		

Inflation and finance

Consumer price		*av. ann. increase 2008–13*	
inflation 2013	1.6%	Euro area:	
Av. ann. inflation 2008–13	1.7%	Narrow money (M1)	6.0%
Money market rate, Dec. 2013	0.21%	Broad money	0.8%
		H'hold saving rate, 2013	7.2%

Exchange rates

	end 2013		2013
€ per $	0.73	Effective rates	2005 = 100
€ per SDR	1.12	– nominal	...
		– real	...

Trade

Principal exports	$bn fob	Principal imports	$bn cif
Machinery & transport equip.	9.7	Machinery & transport equip.	7.7
Manufactures	5.9	Manufactures	5.2
Chemicals	4.8	Chemicals	4.1
Miscellaneous manufactures	2.8	Miscellaneous manufactures	2.5
Total incl. others	**27.3**	Total incl. others	**28.3**

Main export destinations	% of total	Main origins of imports	% of total
Germany	23.5	Italy	18.7
Italy	14.1	Germany	18.5
Austria	9.2	Austria	11.8
Croatia	7.2	Croatia	5.4
EU27	68.8	EU27	67.2

Balance of payments, reserves and debt, $bn

Visible exports fob	27.8	Change in reserves	0.0
Visible imports fob	-27.6	Level of reserves	
Trade balance	0.3	end Dec.	1.0
Invisibles inflows	7.3	No. months of import cover	0.3
Invisibles outflows	-6.1	Official gold holdings, m oz	0.1
Net transfers	0.0	Foreign debt	...
Current account balance	1.5	– as % of GDP	...
– as % of GDP	3.3	– as % of total exports	...
Capital balance	-1.6	Debt service ratio	...
Overall balance	0.0	Aid given	0.06
		– as % of GDP	0.13

Health and education

Health spending, % of GDP	8.8	Education spending, % of GDP	5.7
Doctors per 1,000 pop.	2.5	Enrolment, %: primary	99
Hospital beds per 1,000 pop.	4.6	secondary	98
Improved-water source access,		tertiary	86
% of pop.	100		

Society

No. of households	0.8m	Cost of living, Dec. 2013	
Av. no. per household	2.7	New York = 100	...
Marriages per 1,000 pop.	3.4	Cars per 1,000 pop.	521
Divorces per 1,000 pop.	1.2	Colour TV households, % with:	
Religion, % of pop.		cable	70.7
Christian	78.4	satellite	9.1
Non-religious	18.0	Telephone lines per 100 pop.	39.9
Muslim	3.6	Mobile telephone subscribers	
Hindu	<0.1	per 100 pop.	108.6
Jewish	<0.1	Broadband subs per 100 pop.	24.3
Other	<0.1	Internet hosts per 1,000 pop.	223.2

SOUTH AFRICA

Area	1,225,815 sq km	Capital	Pretoria
Arable as % of total land	9.9	Currency	Rand (R)

People

Population	50.7m	Life expectancy: men	54.9 yrs
Pop. per sq km	41.0	women	59.1 yrs
Average annual growth		Adult literacy	93.0%
in pop. 2010–15	0.8%	Fertility rate (per woman)	2.4
Pop. under 15	29.5%	Urban population	63.8%
Pop. over 60	8.6%		per 1,000 pop.
No. of men per 100 women	98.1	Crude birth rate	21.0
Human Development Index	65.8	Crude death rate	12.9

The economy

GDP	R3,155bn	GDP per head	$7,350
GDP	$384bn	GDP per head in purchasing	
Av. ann. growth in real		power parity (USA=100)	21.3
GDP 2007–12	2.2%	Economic freedom index	62.5

Origins of GDP		Components of GDP	
	% of total		% of total
Agriculture	3	Private consumption	61
Industry, of which:	28	Public consumption	22
manufacturing	12	Investment	19
Services	69	Exports	28
		Imports	-31

Structure of employment

	% of total		% of labour force
Agriculture	4.6	Unemployed 2012	25.0
Industry	24.3	Av. ann. rate 2000–12	24.7
Services	62.7		

Energy

	m TOE		
Total output	162.6	Net energy imports as %	
Total consumption	141.4	of energy use	-15
Consumption per head			
kg oil equivalent	2,795		

Inflation and finance

Consumer price		av. ann. increase 2008–13	
inflation 2013	5.8%	Narrow money (M1)	8.5%
Av. ann. inflation 2008–13	5.6%	Broad money	5.6%
Money market rate, Dec. 2013	4.86%		

Exchange rates

	end 2013		2013
R per $	10.49	Effective rates	2005 = 100
R per SDR	16.15	– nominal	57.30
R per €	14.47	– real	75.60

Trade

Principal exports		Principal imports	
	$bn fob		*$bn cif*
Gold	8.7	Petrochemicals	15.8
Coal	6.5	Petroleum oils & other	4.8
Platinum	6.0	Car & other components	4.7
Car & other components	2.7	Equipment components for cars	3.1
Total incl. others	**99.6**	Total incl. others	**103.9**

Main export destinations		Main origins of imports	
	% of total		*% of total*
China	10.4	China	15.4
United States	7.4	Germany	10.8
Japan	5.3	Saudi Arabia	8.3
India	3.7	United States	7.9

Balance of payments, reserves and debt, $bn

Visible exports fob	99.3	Change in reserves	1.9
Visible imports fob	-104.0	Level of reserves	
Trade balance	-4.8	end Dec.	50.7
Invisibles inflows	21.1	No. months of import cover	4.5
Invisibles outflows	-32.5	Official gold holdings, m oz	4.0
Net transfers	-3.8	Foreign debt	137.5
Current account balance	-20.0	– as % of GDP	35.9
– as % of GDP	-5.2	– as % of total exports	113.2
Capital balance	21.4	Debt service ratio	7.4
Overall balance	1.2		

Health and education

Health spending, % of GDP	8.8	Education spending, % of GDP	6.0
Doctors per 1,000 pop.	0.8	Enrolment, %: primary	102
Hospital beds per 1,000 pop.	10.3	secondary	102
Improved-water source access,		tertiary	...
% of pop.	95		

Society

No. of households	14.7m	Cost of living, Dec. 2013	
Av. no. per household	3.6	New York = 100	61
Marriages per 1,000 pop.	3.5	Cars per 1,000 pop.	...
Divorces per 1,000 pop.	0.6	Colour TV households, % with:	
Religion, % of pop.		cable	...
Christian	81.2	satellite	8.9
Non-religious	14.9	Telephone lines per 100 pop.	7.7
Muslim	1.7	Mobile telephone subscribers	
Hindu	1.1	per 100 pop.	130.6
Other	0.9	Broadband subs per 100 pop.	2.1
Jewish	0.1	Internet hosts per 1,000 pop.	70.9

SOUTH KOREA

Area	99,274 sq km	Capital	Seoul
Arable as % of total land	15.4	Currency	Won (W)

People

Population	48.6m	Life expectancy: men	77.9 yrs
Pop. per sq km	484.0	women	84.6 yrs
Average annual growth		Adult literacy	...
in pop. 2010–15	0.5%	Fertility rate (per woman)	1.3
Pop. under 15	14.9%	Urban population	84.3%
Pop. over 60	17.1%		per 1,000 pop.
No. of men per 100 women	99.4	Crude birth rate	9.6
Human Development Index	89.1	Crude death rate	5.6

The economy

GDP	W1,272trn	GDP per head	$22,590
GDP	$1,130bn	GDP per head in purchasing	
Av. ann. growth in real		power parity (USA=100)	58.0
GDP 2007–12	2.9%	Economic freedom index	71.2

Origins of GDP		**Components of GDP**	
	% of total		% of total
Agriculture	3	Private consumption	54
Industry, of which:	39	Public consumption	16
manufacturing	31	Investment	28
Services	58	Exports	57
		Imports	-53

Structure of employment

	% of total		% of labour force
Agriculture	6.6	Unemployed 2012	3.2
Industry	17.0	Av. ann. rate 2000–12	3.6
Services	76.4		

Energy

	m TOE		
Total output	47.0	Net energy imports as %	
Total consumption	260.4	of energy use	82
Consumption per head			
kg oil equivalent	5,232		

Inflation and finance

Consumer price		av. ann. increase 2008–13	
inflation 2013	1.3%	Narrow money (M1)	9.3%
Av. ann. inflation 2008–13	2.6%	Broad money	6.1%
Money market rate, Dec. 2013	2.50%	H'hold saving rate, 2013	5.1%

Exchange rates

	end 2013		2013
W per $	1,055.40	Effective rates	2005 = 100
W per SDR	1,625.30	– nominal	...
W per €	1,455.50	– real	85.84

Trade

Principal exports		Principal imports	
	$bn fob		*$bn cif*
Machinery & transport equip.	287.8	Mineral fuels & lubricants	186.2
Manufactured goods	75.8	Machinery & transport equip.	127.8
Chemicals & related products	61.3	Manufactured goods	56.8
Mineral fuels & lubricants	57.5	Chemicals & related products	47.4
Total incl. others	**547.9**	Total incl. others	**519.6**

Main export destinations		Main origins of imports	
	% of total		*% of total*
China	24.5	China	15.5
United States	10.7	Japan	12.4
Japan	7.1	United States	8.4
Hong Kong	6.0	Saudi Arabia	7.6

Balance of payments, reserves and debt, $bn

Visible exports fob	552.7	Change in reserves	20.8
Visible imports fob	-514.2	Level of reserves	
Trade balance	38.5	end Dec.	327.7
Invisibles inflows	130.4	No. months of import cover	6.2
Invisibles outflows	-122.8	Official gold holdings, m oz	2.7
Net transfers	-2.8	Foreign debt	425.1
Current account balance	43.3	– as % of GDP	37.6
– as % of GDP	3.8	– as % of total exports	62.2
Capital balance	-31.8	Debt service ratio	7.8
Overall balance	11.9	Aid given	1.60
		– as % of GDP	0.14

Health and education

Health spending, % of GDP	7.5	Education spending, % of GDP	5
Doctors per 1,000 pop.	2.1	Enrolment, %: primary	104
Hospital beds per 1,000 pop.	...	secondary	97
Improved-water source access,		tertiary	98
% of pop.	98		

Society

No. of households	17.9m	Cost of living, Dec. 2013	
Av. no. per household	2.7	New York = 100	108
Marriages per 1,000 pop.	6.6	Cars per 1,000 pop.	296
Divorces per 1,000 pop.	2.3	Colour TV households, % with:	
Religion, % of pop.		cable	81.8
Non-religious	46.4	satellite	13.5
Christian	29.4	Telephone lines per 100 pop.	61.4
Buddhist	22.9	Mobile telephone subscribers	
Other	1.0	per 100 pop.	109.4
Muslim	0.2	Broadband subs per 100 pop.	37.3
Jewish	<0.1	Internet hosts per 1,000 pop.	6.7

SPAIN

Area	504,782 sq km	Capital	Madrid
Arable as % of total land	25.1	Currency	Euro (€)

People

Population	46.8m	Life expectancy: men	78.8 yrs
Pop. per sq km	92.0	women	85.2 yrs
Average annual growth		Adult literacy	97.7%
in pop. 2010–15	0.4%	Fertility rate (per woman)	1.5
Pop. under 15	15.4%	Urban population	78.0%
Pop. over 60	23.1%		per 1,000 pop.
No. of men per 100 women	97.5	Crude birth rate	10.5
Human Development Index	86.9	Crude death rate	8.7

The economy

GDP	€1,029bn	GDP per head	$28,290
GDP	$1,323bn	GDP per head in purchasing	
Av. ann. growth in real		power parity (USA=100)	62.1
GDP 2007–12	-1.0%	Economic freedom index	67.2

Origins of GDP

	% of total
Agriculture	2
Industry, of which:	26
manufacturing	13
Services	72

Components of GDP

	% of total
Private consumption	59
Public consumption	20
Investment	20
Exports	33
Imports	-32

Structure of employment

	% of total		% of labour force
Agriculture	4.4	Unemployed 2012	25.2
Industry	20.7	Av. ann. rate 2000–12	14.0
Services	74.9		

Energy

	m TOE		
Total output	31.8	Net energy imports as %	
Total consumption	125.6	of energy use	75
Consumption per head			
kg oil equivalent	2,719		

Inflation and finance

Consumer price		av. ann. increase 2008–13	
inflation 2013	1.5%	Euro area:	
Av. ann. inflation 2008–13	1.8%	Narrow money (M1)	6.0%
Money market rate, Dec. 2013	0.13%	Broad money	0.8%
		H'hold saving rate[a], 2013	10.4%

Exchange rates

	end 2013		2013
€ per $	0.73	Effective rates	2005 = 100
€ per SDR	1.12	– nominal	103.80
		– real	95.20

Trade

Principal exports		Principal imports	
	$bn fob		$bn cif
Machinery & transport equip.	89.4	Machinery & transport equip.	81.8
Food, drink & tobacco	40.8	Mineral fuels & lubricants	79.1
Chemicals & related products	39.6	Chemicals & related products	48.3
Mineral fuels & lubricants	29.3	Food, drink & tobacco	32.3
Total incl. others	**286.4**	**Total incl. others**	**326.0**

Main export destinations		Main origins of imports	
	% of total		% of total
France	16.8	Germany	12.2
Germany	11.0	France	11.8
Italy	7.7	Italy	6.9
Portugal	7.3	China	5.8
EU27	63.6	EU27	54.2

Balance of payments, reserves and aid, $bn

Visible exports fob	292.1	Overall balance	2.9
Visible imports fob	-325.6	Change in reserves	3.8
Trade balance	-33.5	Level of reserves	
Invisibles inflows	185.8	end Dec.	50.5
Invisibles outflows	-163.2	No. months of import cover	1.2
Net transfers	-5.5	Official gold holdings, m oz	9.1
Current account balance	-16.3	Aid given	2.04
– as % of GDP	-1.2	– as % of GDP	0.15
Capital balance	11.9		

Health and education

Health spending, % of GDP	9.6	Education spending, % of GDP	5.0
Doctors per 1,000 pop.	3.7	Enrolment, %: primary	103
Hospital beds per 1,000 pop.	3.1	secondary	131
Improved-water source access,		tertiary	83
% of pop.	100		

Society

No. of households	18.1m	Cost of living, Dec. 2013	
Av. no. per household	2.6	New York = 100	99
Marriages per 1,000 pop.	3.5	Cars per 1,000 pop.	483
Divorces per 1,000 pop.	2.2	Colour TV households, % with:	
Religion, % of pop.		cable	13.9
Christian	78.6	satellite	12.7
Non-religious	19.0	Telephone lines per 100 pop.	41.9
Muslim	2.1	Mobile telephone subscribers	
Jewish	0.1	per 100 pop.	108.4
Other	0.1	Broadband subs per 100 pop.	24.4
Hindu	<0.1	Internet hosts per 1,000 pop.	90.5

a Gross.

SWEDEN

Area	449,964 sq km	Capital	Stockholm
Arable as % of total land	6.4	Currency	Swedish krona (Skr)

People

Population	9.5m	Life expectancy: men	79.7 yrs
Pop. per sq km	21.0	women	83.8 yrs
Average annual growth		Adult literacy	...
in pop. 2010–15	0.7%	Fertility rate (per woman)	1.9
Pop. under 15	16.9%	Urban population	85.8%
Pop. over 60	25.5%		per 1,000 pop.
No. of men per 100 women	99.2	Crude birth rate	11.9
Human Development Index	89.8	Crude death rate	9.6

The economy

GDP	Skr3,550bn	GDP per head	$55,040
GDP	$524bn	GDP per head in purchasing	
Av. ann. growth in real		power parity (USA=100)	82.8
GDP 2007–12	0.9%	Economic freedom index	73.1

Origins of GDP

Components of GDP

	% of total		% of total
Agriculture	2	Private consumption	48
Industry, of which:	25	Public consumption	27
manufacturing	16	Investment	19
Services	73	Exports	49
		Imports	-43

Structure of employment

	% of total		% of labour force
Agriculture	2.0	Unemployed 2012	8.0
Industry	19.5	Av. ann. rate 2000–12	6.8
Services	77.9		

Energy

	m TOE		
Total output	32.5	Net energy imports as %	
Total consumption	49.0	of energy use	34
Consumption per head			
kg oil equivalent	5,190		

Inflation and finance

Consumer price		av. ann. increase 2008–13	
inflation 2013	0.0%	Narrow money (M1)	4.4%
Av. ann. inflation 2008–13	0.9%	Broad money	1.8%
Repurchase rate, Dec. 2013	1.00%	H'hold saving rate, 2013	12.2%

Exchange rates

	end 2013		2013
Skr per $	6.42	Effective rates	2005 = 100
Skr per SDR	9.89	– nominal	106.60
Skr per €	8.85	– real	99.20

Trade

Principal exports		Principal imports	
	$bn fob		*$bn cif*
Machinery & transport equip.	64.1	Machinery & transport equip.	57.3
Chemicals & related products	18.8	Mineral fuels & lubricants	26.3
Mineral fuels & lubricants	17.2	Chemicals & related products	18.5
Raw materials	11.6	Foods, drink & tobacco	14.3
Total incl. others	**172.7**	Total incl. others	**164.1**

Main export destinations		Main origins of imports	
	% of total		*% of total*
Germany	9.8	Germany	17.3
Norway	9.8	Denmark	8.4
Denmark	6.4	Norway	8.3
Finland	6.4	Netherlands	6.9
EU27	56.9	EU27	67.3

Balance of payments, reserves and aid, $bn

Visible exports fob	185.2	Overall balance	0.5
Visible imports fob	-164.7	Change in reserves	2.0
Trade balance	20.5	Level of reserves	
Invisibles inflows	120.0	end Dec.	52.2
Invisibles outflows	-99.6	No. months of import cover	2.4
Net transfers	-9.5	Official gold holdings, m oz	4.0
Current account balance	31.4	Aid given	5.24
– as % of GDP	6.0	– as % of GDP	1.00
Capital balance	-11.8		

Health and education

Health spending, % of GDP	9.6	Education spending, % of GDP	7.0
Doctors per 1,000 pop.	3.8	Enrolment, %: primary	101
Hospital beds per 1,000 pop.	2.7	secondary	97
Improved-water source access,		tertiary	74
% of pop.	100		

Society

No. of households	4.6m	Cost of living, Dec. 2013	
Av. no. per household	2.1	New York = 100	101
Marriages per 1,000 pop.	5.3	Cars per 1,000 pop.	469
Divorces per 1,000 pop.	2.5	Colour TV households, % with:	
Religion, % of pop.		cable	57.5
Christian	67.2	satellite	20.1
Non-religious	27.0	Telephone lines per 100 pop.	43.8
Muslim	4.6	Mobile telephone subscribers	
Other	0.8	per 100 pop.	124.6
Hindu	0.2	Broadband subs per 100 pop.	32.3
Jewish	0.1	Internet hosts per 1,000 pop.	651.1

SWITZERLAND

Area	41,293 sq km	Capital	Berne
Arable as % of total land	10.1	Currency	Swiss franc (SFr)

People

Population	7.7m	Life expectancy: men		80.1 yrs
Pop. per sq km	188.0		women	84.9 yrs
Average annual growth		Adult literacy		...
in pop. 2010–15	1.0%	Fertility rate (per woman)		1.5
Pop. under 15	14.8%	Urban population		74.0%
Pop. over 60	23.4%			per 1,000 pop.
No. of men per 100 women	96.7	Crude birth rate		10.3
Human Development Index	91.7	Crude death rate		8.2

The economy

GDP	SFr592bn	GDP per head	$78,930
GDP	$631bn	GDP per head in purchasing	
Av. ann. growth in real		power parity (USA=100)	102.8
GDP 2007–12	1.2%	Economic freedom index	81.6

Origins of GDP		Components of GDP	
	% of total		% of total
Agriculture	1	Private consumption	57
Industry, of which:	27	Public consumption	11
manufacturing	19	Investment	21
Services	73	Exports	52
		Imports	-42

Structure of employment

	% of total		% of labour force
Agriculture	3.5	Unemployed 2012	4.2
Industry	20.3	Av. ann. rate 2000–12	3.7
Services	72.5		

Energy

	m TOE		
Total output	12.3	Net energy imports as %	
Total consumption	25.4	of energy use	51
Consumption per head			
kg oil equivalent	3,207		

Inflation and finance

Consumer price		av. ann. increase 2008–13	
inflation 2013	-0.2%	Narrow money (M1)	12.0%
Av. ann. inflation 2008–13	-0.1%	Broad money	8.2%
Money market rate, Dec. 2013	0.01%	H'hold saving rate, 2013	13.3%

Exchange rates

	end 2013		2013
SFr per $	0.89	Effective rates	2005 = 100
SFr per SDR	1.37	– nominal	128.90
SFr per €	1.23	– real	113.20

Trade

Principal exports		Principal imports	
	$bn fob		*$bn cif*
Chemicals	84.3	Chemicals	42.0
Precision instruments, watches & jewellery	47.0	Machinery, equipment & electronics	31.3
Machinery, equipment & electronics	35.5	Precision instruments, watches & jewellery	20.3
Metals & metal manufactures	12.7	Motor vehicles	18.2
Total incl. others	**214.0**	**Total incl. others**	**188.7**

Main export destinations		Main origins of imports	
	% of total		*% of total*
Germany	20.8	Germany	31.1
United States	11.7	Italy	10.7
France	7.5	France	8.8
Italy	7.5	China	5.8
EU27	55.9	EU27	74.7

Balance of payments, reserves and aid, $bn

Visible exports fob	332.1	Overall balance	184.5
Visible imports fob	-296.1	Change in reserves	200.5
Trade balance	36.0	Level of reserves	
Invisibles inflows	187.8	end Dec.	531.1
Invisibles outflows	-157.1	No. months of import cover	14.1
Net transfers	-12.7	Official gold holdings, m oz	33.4
Current account balance	53.9	Aid given	3.05
– as % of GDP	8.5	– as % of GDP	0.48
Capital balance	84.2		

Health and education

Health spending, % of GDP	11.3	Education spending, % of GDP	5.2
Doctors per 1,000 pop.	3.9	Enrolment, %: primary	103
Hospital beds per 1,000 pop.	5.0	secondary	96
Improved-water source access,		tertiary	54
% of pop.	100		

Society

No. of households	3.6m	Cost of living, Dec. 2013	
Av. no. per household	2.2	New York = 100	118
Marriages per 1,000 pop.	5.3	Cars per 1,000 pop.	536
Divorces per 1,000 pop.	2.2	Colour TV households, % with:	
Religion, % of pop.		cable	82.4
Christian	81.3	satellite	16.0
Non-religious	11.9	Telephone lines per 100 pop.	56.5
Muslim	5.5	Mobile telephone subscribers	
Other	0.6	per 100 pop.	130.2
Hindu	0.4	Broadband subs per 100 pop.	39.9
Jewish	0.3	Internet hosts per 1,000 pop.	700.8

TAIWAN

Area	36,179 sq km	Capital	Taipei
Arable as % of total land	...	Currency	Taiwan dollar (T$)

People

Population	23.2m	Life expectancy:[a] men		76.7 yrs
Pop. per sq km	644.0		women	83.2 yrs
Average annual growth		Adult literacy		...
in pop. 2010–15	0.3%	Fertility rate (per woman)		1.1
Pop. under 15	14.3%	Urban population		78.0%
Pop. over 60	17.0%			per 1,000 pop.
No. of men per 100 women	101	Crude birth rate		9.0
Human Development Index	...	Crude death rate[a]		7.0

The economy

GDP	T$14,077bn	GDP per head	$20,390
GDP	$475bn	GDP per head in purchasing	
Av. ann. growth in real		power parity (USA=100)	74.3
GDP 2007–12	2.9%	Economic freedom index	73.9

Origins of GDP		Components of GDP	
	% of total		% of total
Agriculture	2	Private consumption	60
Industry, of which:	30	Public consumption	12
manufacturing	24	Investment	19
Services	68	Exports	73
		Imports	-64

Structure of employment

	% of total		% of labour force
Agriculture	...	Unemployed 2012	5.9
Industry	...	Av. ann. rate 2000–12	4.7
Services	...		

Energy

	m TOE		
Total output	...	Net energy imports as %	
Total consumption	...	of energy use	...
Consumption per head,			
kg oil equivalent	...		

Inflation and finance

		av. ann. increase 2008–13	
Consumer price			
inflation 2013	0.8%	Narrow money (M1)	10.6%
Av. ann. inflation 2008–13	0.8%	Broad money	5.1%
Money market rate, Dec. 2013	0.6%		

Exchange rates

	end 2013		2013
T$ per $	29.86	Effective rates	2005 = 100
T$ per SDR	46.03	– nominal	...
T$ per €	41.25	– real	...

Trade

Principal exports		Principal imports	
	$bn fob		*$bn cif*
Electronic products	83.4	Machinery & transport equip.	89.5
Basic metals	28.1	Mineral fuels & lubricants	68.9
Precision instruments,		Electrical machinery & equip.	45.4
clocks & watches	23.4	Chemicals & related products	35.9
Mineral products	22.1		
Total incl. others	**301.2**	Total incl. others	**270.5**

Main export destinations		Main origins of imports	
	% of total		*% of total*
China	28.4	Japan	17.6
Hong Kong	13.3	China	15.2
United States	11.6	United States	8.8
Singapore	7.0	South Korea	5.6

Balance of payments, reserves and debt, $bn

Visible exports fob	299.8	Change in reserves	17.6
Visible imports fob	−269.0	Level of reserves	
Trade balance	30.7	end Dec.	403.9
Invisibles inflows	74.9	No. months of import cover	15.0
Invisibles outflows	−53.5	Official gold holdings, m oz	0.0
Net transfers	15.3	Foreign debt	130.8
Current account balance	49.6	– as % of GDP	27.5
– as % of GDP	10.4	– as % of total exports	34.8
Capital balance	−68.5	Debt service ratio	5.3
Overall balance	−21.4	Aid given	0.30
		– as % of GDP	0.06

Health and education

Health spending, % of GDP	...	Education spending, % of GDP	...
Doctors per 1,000 pop.	...	Enrolment, %: primary	...
Hospital beds per 1,000 pop.	...	secondary	...
Improved-water source access,		tertiary	...
% of pop.	...		

Society

No. of households	7.6m	Cost of living, Dec. 2013	
Av. no. per household	3.1	New York = 100	82
Marriages per 1,000 pop.	5.4	Cars per 1,000 pop.	263
Divorces per 1,000 pop.	2.5	Colour TV households, % with:	
Religion, % of pop.		cable	84.6
Other	60.5	satellite	0.4
Buddhist	21.3	Telephone lines per 100 pop.	68.7
Non-religious	12.7	Mobile telephone subscribers	
Christian	5.5	per 100 pop.	126.5
Hindu	<0.1	Broadband subs per 100 pop.	23.9
Jewish	<0.1	Internet hosts per 1,000 pop.	282.0

a 2012 estimates.

THAILAND

Area	513,115 sq km	Capital	Bangkok
Arable as % of total land	30.8	Currency	Baht (Bt)

People

Population	69.9m	Life expectancy: men		71.0 yrs
Pop. per sq km	136.0	women		77.7 yrs
Average annual growth		Adult literacy		...
in pop. 2010–15	0.3%	Fertility rate (per woman)		1.4
Pop. under 15	18.2%	Urban population		35.6%
Pop. over 60	14.5%			per 1,000 pop.
No. of men per 100 women	96.7	Crude birth rate		10.4
Human Development Index	72.2	Crude death rate		7.7

The economy

GDP	Bt11,375bn	GDP per head	$5,480
GDP	$366bn	GDP per head in purchasing	
Av. ann. growth in real		power parity (USA=100)	18.7
GDP 2007–12	2.8%	Economic freedom index	63.3

Origins of GDP		**Components of GDP**	
	% of total		% of total
Agriculture	12	Private consumption	56
Industry, of which:	44	Public consumption	14
manufacturing	34	Investment	30
Services	44	Exports	75
		Imports	-74

Structure of employment

	% of total		% of labour force
Agriculture	39.6	Unemployed 2012	0.7
Industry	20.9	Av. ann. rate 2000–12	1.4
Services	39.4		

Energy

	m TOE		
Total output	68.7	Net energy imports as %	
Total consumption	119.1	of energy use	42
Consumption per head			
kg oil equivalent	1,790		

Inflation and finance

Consumer price		av. ann. increase 2008–13	
inflation 2013	2.2%	Narrow money (M1)	9.8%
Av. ann. inflation 2008–13	2.3%	Broad money	10.0%
Money market rate, Dec. 2013	2.20%		

Exchange rates

	end 2013		2013
Bt per $	32.81	Effective rates	2005 = 100
Bt per SDR	50.53	– nominal	...
Bt per €	45.25	– real	...

Trade

Principal exports	$bn fob	Principal imports	$bn cif
Machinery, equip. & supplies	92.2	Machinery, equip. & supplies	91.2
Food	28.7	Fuel & lubricants	48.1
Manufactured goods	28.7	Manufactured goods	40.7
Chemicals	23.1	Chemicals	24.1
Total incl. others	227.9	Total incl. others	251.5

Main export destinations	% of total	Main origins of imports	% of total
China	11.7	Japan	19.8
Japan	10.2	China	14.8
United States	10.0	United States	6.3
Hong Kong	5.7	United Arab Emirates	5.1

Balance of payments, reserves and debt, $bn

Visible exports fob	225.8	Change in reserves	6.6
Visible imports fob	-219.8	Level of reserves	
Trade balance	6.0	end Dec.	181.4
Invisibles inflows	57.4	No. months of import cover	7.3
Invisibles outflows	-77.1	Official gold holdings, m oz	4.9
Net transfers	12.2	Foreign debt	134.2
Current account balance	-1.4	– as % of GDP	38.2
– as % of GDP	-0.4	– as % of total exports	46.6
Capital balance	13.9	Debt service ratio	4.0
Overall balance	5.2	Aid given	0.02
		– as % of GDP	0.00

Health and education

Health spending, % of GDP	3.9	Education spending, % of GDP	5.8
Doctors per 1,000 pop.	0.3	Enrolment, %: primary	97
Hospital beds per 1,000 pop.	2.1	secondary	87
Improved-water source access,		tertiary	51
% of pop.	96		

Society

No. of households	21.3m	Cost of living, Dec. 2013	
Av. no. per household	3.2	New York = 100	81
Marriages per 1,000 pop.	4.7	Cars per 1,000 pop.	...
Divorces per 1,000 pop.	1.1	Colour TV households, % with:	
Religion, % of pop.		cable	9.9
Buddhist	93.2	satellite	4.9
Muslim	5.5	Telephone lines per 100 pop.	9.5
Christian	0.9	Mobile telephone subscribers	
Non-religious	0.3	per 100 pop.	127.3
Hindu	0.1	Broadband subs per 100 pop.	8.2
Jewish	<0.1	Internet hosts per 1,000 pop.	52.9

TURKEY

Area	779,452 sq km	Capital	Ankara
Arable as % of total land	26.7	Currency	Turkish Lira (YTL)

People

Population	74.5m	Life expectancy: men	71.7 yrs
Pop. per sq km	94.0	women	78.5 yrs
Average annual growth		Adult literacy	94.1%
in pop. 2010–15	1.2%	Fertility rate (per woman)	2.1
Pop. under 15	25.7%	Urban population	75.1%
Pop. over 60	10.8%		per 1,000 pop.
No. of men per 100 women	99.5	Crude birth rate	16.9
Human Development Index	75.9	Crude death rate	5.7

The economy

GDP	YTL1,417bn	GDP per head	$10,670
GDP	$789bn	GDP per head in purchasing	
Av. ann. growth in real		power parity (USA=100)	35.8
GDP 2007–12	3.1%	Economic freedom index	64.9

Origins of GDP		**Components of GDP**	
	% of total		% of total
Agriculture	9	Private consumption	70
Industry, of which:	27	Public consumption	15
manufacturing	18	Investment	20
Services	64	Exports	26
		Imports	-32

Structure of employment

	% of total		% of labour force
Agriculture	23.6	Unemployed 2012	9.2
Industry	26.0	Av. ann. rate 2000–12	10.3
Services	50.4		

Energy

	m TOE		
Total output	32.1	Net energy imports as %	
Total consumption	112.5	of energy use	71
Consumption per head			
kg oil equivalent	1,539		

Inflation and finance

Consumer price		av. ann. increase 2008–13	
inflation 2013	7.5%	Narrow money (M1)	21.8%
Av. ann. inflation 2008–13	7.5%	Broad money	15.4%
Money market rate, Dec. 2013	8.6%		

Exchange rates

	end 2013		2013
YTL per $	2.14	Effective rates	2005 = 100
YTL per SDR	3.29	– nominal	...
YTL per €	2.95	– real	...

Trade

Principal exports		Principal imports	
	$bn fob		$bn cif
Agricultural products	26.2	Fuels	33.8
Textiles & clothing	16.1	Chemicals	29.6
Iron & steel	13.7	Mechanical equipment	24.8
Transport equipment	13.1	Transport equipment	18.9
Total incl. others	**152.5**	Total incl. others	**236.5**

Main export destinations		Main origins of imports	
	% of total		% of total
Germany	8.6	Russia	11.3
Iraq	7.1	China	9.0
Iran	6.5	Germany	9.0
United Kingdom	5.7	United States	6.0
EU27	39.0	EU27	37.1

Balance of payments, reserves and debt, $bn

Visible exports fob	163.3	Change in reserves	31.2
Visible imports fob	-228.6	Level of reserves	
Trade balance	-65.2	end Dec.	119.1
Invisibles inflows	48.4	No. months of import cover	5.5
Invisibles outflows	-33.1	Official gold holdings, m oz	11.6
Net transfers	1.4	Foreign debt	337.5
Current account balance	-48.5	– as % of GDP	43.1
– as % of GDP	-6.1	– as % of total exports	158.6
Capital balance	70.3	Debt service ratio	26.0
Overall balance	22.8	Aid given	2.53
		– as % of GDP	0.32

Health and education

Health spending, % of GDP	6.3	Education spending, % of GDP	...
Doctors per 1,000 pop.	1.7	Enrolment, %: primary	102
Hospital beds per 1,000 pop.	2.5	secondary	89
Improved-water source access,		tertiary	61
% of pop.	97		

Society

No. of households	19.3m	Cost of living, Dec. 2013	
Av. no. per household	3.9	New York = 100	84
Marriages per 1,000 pop.	8.0	Cars per 1,000 pop.	...
Divorces per 1,000 pop.	1.6	Colour TV households, % with:	
Religion, % of pop.		cable	7.0
Muslim	98.0	satellite	51.0
Non-religious	1.2	Telephone lines per 100 pop.	18.7
Christian	0.4	Mobile telephone subscribers	
Other	0.3	per 100 pop.	91.5
Hindu	<0.1	Broadband subs per 100 pop.	10.6
Jewish	<0.1	Internet hosts per 1,000 pop.	97.0

UKRAINE

Area	603,700 sq km	Capital	Kiev
Arable as % of total land	56.1	Currency	Hryvnya (UAH)

People

Population	44.9m	Life expectancy: men	62.8 yrs
Pop. per sq km	75.0	women	74.3 yrs
Average annual growth		Adult literacy	99.7%
in pop. 2010–15	-0.6%	Fertility rate (per woman)	1.5
Pop. under 15	14.5%	Urban population	69.7%
Pop. over 60	21.3%		per 1,000 pop.
No. of men per 100 women	85.2	Crude birth rate	10.8
Human Development Index	73.4	Crude death rate	16.8

The economy

GDP	UAH1,409bn	GDP per head	$3,870
GDP	$176bn	GDP per head in purchasing	
Av. ann. growth in real		power parity (USA=100)	14.1
GDP 2007–12	-0.9%	Economic freedom index	49.3

Origins of GDP		Components of GDP	
	% of total		% of total
Agriculture	9	Private consumption	71
Industry, of which:	30	Public consumption	19
manufacturing	15	Investment	18
Services	61	Exports	51
		Imports	-59

Structure of employment

	% of total		% of labour force
Agriculture	17.2	Unemployed 2012	7.7
Industry	20.7	Av. ann. rate 2000–12	8.4
Services	62.1		

Energy

	m TOE		
Total output	85.5	Net energy imports as %	
Total consumption	126.4	of energy use	32
Consumption per head			
kg oil equivalent	2,766		

Inflation and finance

Consumer price		av. ann. increase 2008–13	
inflation 2013	-0.3%	Narrow money (M1)	11.3%
Av. ann. inflation 2008–13	6.5%	Broad money	12.0%
Money market rate, Dec. 2013	11.67%		

Exchange rates

	end 2013		2013
UAH per $	7.99	Effective rates	2005 = 100
UAH per SDR	13.31	– nominal	67.40
UAH per €	11.02	– real	97.90

Trade

Principal exports		Principal imports	
	$bn fob		*$bn cif*
Manufactures	42.0	Manufactures	47.4
Food	17.9	Fuels	26.2
Ores & metals	4.8	Food	7.6
Fuels	3.4	Ores & metals	2.5
Agricultural raw materials	0.7	Agricultural raw materials	0.8
Total	**68.8**	Total	**84.7**

Main export destinations		Main origins of imports	
	% of total		*% of total*
Russia	25.7	Russia	30.6
Turkey	5.4	China	8.8
Egypt	4.2	Germany	7.6
Italy	3.6	Belarus	5.6
EU27	24.9	EU27	31.0

Balance of payments, reserves and debt, $bn

Visible exports fob	64.4	Change in reserves	-7.2
Visible imports fob	-86.3	Level of reserves	
Trade balance	-21.8	end Dec.	24.5
Invisibles inflows	29.2	No. months of import cover	2.7
Invisibles outflows	-24.6	Official gold holdings, m oz	1.1
Net transfers	3.0	Foreign debt	135.1
Current account balance	-14.3	– as % of GDP	77.9
– as % of GDP	-8.1	– as % of total exports	132.4
Capital balance	8.8	Debt service ratio	35.4
Overall balance	-4.2		

Health and education

Health spending, % of GDP	7.6	Education spending, % of GDP	6.2
Doctors per 1,000 pop.	3.5	Enrolment, %: primary	106
Hospital beds per 1,000 pop.	9.0	secondary	98
Improved-water source access,		tertiary	80
% of pop.	98		

Society

No. of households	19.9m	Cost of living, Dec. 2013	
Av. no. per household	2.3	New York = 100	72
Marriages per 1,000 pop.	6.1	Cars per 1,000 pop.	...
Divorces per 1,000 pop.	1.1	Colour TV households, % with:	
Religion, % of pop.		cable	23.2
Christian	83.8	satellite	15.5
Non-religious	14.7	Telephone lines per 100 pop.	29.8
Muslim	1.2	Mobile telephone subscribers	
Jewish	0.1	per 100 pop.	130.3
Other	0.1	Broadband subs per 100 pop.	8.0
Hindu	<0.1	Internet hosts per 1,000 pop.	62.0

UNITED ARAB EMIRATES

Area	83,600 sq km	Capital	Abu Dhabi
Arable as % of total land	0.6	Currency	Dirham (AED)

People

Population	8.1m	Life expectancy: men		76.1 yrs
Pop. per sq km	94.0		women	78.1 yrs
Average annual growth		Adult literacy		...
in pop. 2010–15	2.5%	Fertility rate (per woman)		1.8
Pop. under 15	15.3%	Urban population		85.5%
Pop. over 60	1.0%			per 1,000 pop.
No. of men per 100 women	228.3	Crude birth rate		14.8
Human Development Index	82.7	Crude death rate		1.0

The economy

GDP	AED1,410bn	GDP per head	$41,690
GDP	$384bn	GDP per head in purchasing	
Av. ann. growth in real		power parity (USA=100)	80.0
GDP 2007–12	1.6%	Economic freedom index	71.4

Origins of GDP		**Components of GDP**	
	% of total		% of total
Agriculture	1	Private consumption	9
Industry, of which:	60	Public consumption	22
manufacturing	9	Investment	49
Services	39	Exports	41
		Imports	...

Structure of employment

	% of total		% of labour force
Agriculture	3.8	Unemployed 2012	3.8
Industry	23.1	Av. ann. rate 2000–12	3.3
Services	73.1		

Energy

			m TOE
Total output	190.1	Net energy imports as %	
Total consumption	66.1	of energy use	-188
Consumption per head			
kg oil equivalent	7,407		

Inflation and finance

Consumer price		av. ann. increase 2008–13	
inflation 2013	1.1%	Narrow money (M1)	12.8%
Av. ann. inflation 2008–13	1.0%	Broad money	9.4%
Interbank rate, Q4 2013	0.8%		

Exchange rates

	end 2013		2013
AED per $	3.67	Effective rates	2005 = 100
AED per SDR	5.66	– nominal	100.00
AED per €	5.06	– real	105.40

Trade

Principal exports		Principal imports	
	$bn fob		*$bn cif*
Re-exports	135.7	Precious stones & metals	52.2
Crude oil	94.0	Machinery & electrical equip.	36.5
Gas	14.5	Vehicles & other transport	
		equipment	23.0
		Base metals & related products	16.7
Total incl. others	**350.1**	Total incl. others	**261.0**

Main export destinations		Main origins of imports	
	% of total		*% of total*
Japan	15.4	India	16.9
India	13.4	China	13.7
Iran	10.7	United States	10.4
Thailand	5.5	Germany	5.1

Balance of payments, reserves and debt, $bn

Visible exports fob	350.1	Overall balance	3.2
Visible imports fob	-221.9	Change in reserves	9.8
Trade balance	128.2	Level of reserves	
Invisibles inflows	36.2	end Dec.	47.0
Invisibles outflows	-84.8	No. months of import cover	1.8
Net transfers	-13.1	Official gold holdings, m oz	0.0
Current account balance	66.6	Aid given	1.07
– as % of GDP	17.3	– as % of GDP	0.28
Capital balance	-11.3		

Health and education

Health spending, % of GDP	2.8	Education spending, % of GDP	...
Doctors per 1,000 pop.	1.9	Enrolment, %: primary	108
Hospital beds per 1,000 pop.	1.1	secondary	...
Improved-water source access,		tertiary	...
% of pop.	100		

Society

No. of households	1.7m	Cost of living, Dec. 2013	
Av. no. per household	5.0	New York = 100	74
Marriages per 1,000 pop.	1.8	Cars per 1,000 pop.	266
Divorces per 1,000 pop.	0.5	Colour TV households, % with:	
Religion, % of pop.		cable	1.0
Muslim	76.9	satellite	98.4
Christian	12.6	Telephone lines per 100 pop.	21.4
Hindu	6.6	Mobile telephone subscribers	
Other	2.8	per 100 pop.	149.6
Non-religious	1.1	Broadband subs per 100 pop.	10.3
Jewish	<0.1	Internet hosts per 1,000 pop.	45.6

UNITED KINGDOM

Area	242,534 sq km	Capital	London
Arable as % of total land	25.1	Currency	Pound (£)

People

Population	62.8m	Life expectancy: men		78.5 yrs
Pop. per sq km	256.0	women		82.4 yrs
Average annual growth		Adult literacy		...
in pop. 2010–15	0.6%	Fertility rate (per woman)		1.9
Pop. under 15	17.6%	Urban population		80.1%
Pop. over 60	23.2%			per 1,000 pop.
No. of men per 100 women	96.8	Crude birth rate		12.2
Human Development Index	89.2	Crude death rate		9.4

The economy

GDP	£1,567bn	GDP per head	$38,920
GDP	$2,476bn	GDP per head in purchasing	
Av. ann. growth in real		power parity (USA=100)	69.0
GDP 2007–12	-0.6%	Economic freedom index	74.9

Origins of GDP		Components of GDP	
	% of total		% of total
Agriculture	1	Private consumption	66
Industry, of which:	21	Public consumption	22
manufacturing	10	Investment	15
Services	79	Exports	32
		Imports	-34

Structure of employment

	% of total		% of labour force
Agriculture	1.2	Unemployed 2012	7.9
Industry	18.9	Av. ann. rate 2000–12	6.0
Services	78.9		

Energy

	m TOE		
Total output	129.5	Net energy imports as %	
Total consumption	188.1	of energy use	31
Consumption per head			
kg oil equivalent	2,997		

Inflation and finance

		av. ann. increase 2008–13	
Consumer price			
inflation 2013	2.6%	Narrow money (M1)	...
Av. ann. inflation 2008–13	3.1%	Broad money	0.4%
Money market rate, Dec. 2013	0.45%	H'hold saving rate[a], 2013	5.1%

Exchange rates

	end 2013		2013
£ per $	0.60	Effective rates	2005 = 100
£ per SDR	1.07	– nominal	82.60
£ per €	0.83	– real	91.80

Trade

Principal exports		Principal imports	
	$bn fob		$bn cif
Machinery & transport equip.	161.4	Machinery & transport equip.	208.0
Chemicals & related products	82.4	Mineral fuels & lubricants	94.6
Mineral fuels & lubricants	66.1	Chemicals & related products	79.0
Food, drink & tobacco	28.1	Food, drink & tobacco	57.9
Total incl. others	**474.6**	Total incl. others	**646.3**

Main export destinations		Main origins of imports	
	% of total		% of total
Germany	10.3	Germany	12.8
United States	9.5	China	8.1
Netherlands	8.0	Netherlands	7.6
France	6.8	France	5.5
EU27	50.2	EU27	47.9

Balance of payments, reserves and aid, $bn

Visible exports fob	474.6	Overall balance	11.6
Visible imports fob	-646.3	Change in reserves	10.6
Trade balance	-171.7	Level of reserves	
Invisibles inflows	548.8	end Dec.	105.1
Invisibles outflows	-435.9	No. months of import cover	1.2
Net transfers	-35.5	Official gold holdings, m oz	10.0
Current account balance	-94.3	Aid given	13.89
– as % of GDP	-3.8	– as % of GDP	0.56
Capital balance	120.9		

Health and education

Health spending, % of GDP	9.4	Education spending, % of GDP	6.2
Doctors per 1,000 pop.	2.8	Enrolment, %: primary	107
Hospital beds per 1,000 pop.	2.9	secondary	97
Improved-water source access,		tertiary	61
% of pop.	100		

Society

No. of households	27.9m	Cost of living, Dec. 2013	
Av. no. per household	2.3	New York = 100	108
Marriages per 1,000 pop.	4.5	Cars per 1,000 pop.	500
Divorces per 1,000 pop.	2.1	Colour TV households, % with:	
Religion, % of pop.		cable	14.4
Christian	71.1	satellite	41.7
Non-religious	21.3	Telephone lines per 100 pop.	52.9
Muslim	4.4	Mobile telephone subscribers	
Other	1.4	per 100 pop.	135.3
Hindu	1.3	Broadband subs per 100 pop.	34.0
Jewish	0.5	Internet hosts per 1,000 pop.	137.5

a Gross.

UNITED STATES

Area	9,372,610 sq km	Capital	Washington DC
Arable as % of total land	17.5	Currency	US dollar ($)

People

Population	315.8m	Life expectancy: men		76.4 yrs
Pop. per sq km	32.0		women	81.2 yrs
Average annual growth		Adult literacy		...
in pop. 2010–15	0.8%	Fertility rate (per woman)		2
Pop. under 15	19.5%	Urban population		83.3%
Pop. over 60	19.7%			per 1,000 pop.
No. of men per 100 women	97.4	Crude birth rate		13.2
Human Development Index	91.4	Crude death rate		8.3

The economy

GDP	$16,245bn	GDP per head	$51,750
Av. ann. growth in real		GDP per head in purchasing	
GDP 2007–12	0.8%	power parity (USA=100)	100
		Economic freedom index	75.5

Origins of GDP — **Components of GDP**

	% of total		% of total
Agriculture	1	Private consumption	69
Industry, of which:	20	Public consumption	16
manufacturing	13	Investment	19
Services	79	Exports	14
		Imports	-17

Structure of employment

	% of total		% of labour force
Agriculture	1.6	Unemployed 2012	8.1
Industry	16.7	Av. ann. rate 2000–12	6.4
Services	81.2		

Energy

	m TOE		
Total output	1,784.8	Net energy imports as %	
Total consumption	2,191.2	of energy use	19
Consumption per head			
kg oil equivalent	7,032		

Inflation and finance

		av. ann. increase 2008–13	
Consumer price			
inflation 2013	1.5%	Narrow money (M1)	10.6%
Av. ann. inflation 2008–13	1.6%	Broad money	3.6%
Fed funds rate, Dec. 2013	0.09%	H'hold saving rate, 2013	4.5%

Exchange rates

	end 2013		2013
$ per SDR	1.54	Effective rates	2005 = 100
$ per €	1.38	– nominal	92.00
		– real	90.90

Trade

Principal exports		Principal imports	
	$bn fob		$bn fob
Capital goods, excl. vehicles	527.4	Industrial supplies	730.4
Industrial supplies	501.1	Capital goods, excl. vehicles	548.6
Consumer goods, excl. vehicles	181.7	Consumer goods, excl. vehicles	516.3
Vehicles & products	146.1	Vehicles & products	297.8
Total incl. others	**1,545.7**	**Total incl. others**	**2,275.3**

Main export destinations		Main origins of imports	
	% of total		% of total
Canada	18.9	China	19.5
Mexico	14.0	Canada	14.4
China	7.2	Mexico	12.3
Japan	4.5	Japan	6.2
EU27	17.2	EU27	16.7

Balance of payments, reserves and aid, $bn

Visible exports fob	1,562	Overall balance	4.5
Visible imports fob	-2,303	Change in reserves	35.3
Trade balance	-741	Level of reserves	
Invisibles inflows	1,434	end Dec.	572.6
Invisibles outflows	-1,004	No. months of import cover	2.1
Net transfers	-130	Official gold holdings, m oz	261.5
Current account balance	-440	Aid given	30.69
– as % of GDP	-2.7	– as % of GDP	0.19
Capital balance	451		

Health and education

Health spending, % of GDP	17.9	Education spending, % of GDP	5.4
Doctors per 1,000 pop.	2.5	Enrolment, %: primary	98
Hospital beds per 1,000 pop.	2.9	secondary	94
Improved-water source access,		tertiary	95
% of pop.	99		

Society

No. of households	121.1m	Cost of living, Dec. 2013	
Av. no. per household	2.6	New York = 100	100
Marriages per 1,000 pop.	6.8	Cars per 1,000 pop.	410
Divorces per 1,000 pop.	2.8	Colour TV households, % with:	
Religion, % of pop.		cable	56.6
Christian	78.3	satellite	29.5
Non-religious	16.4	Telephone lines per 100 pop.	44.4
Other	2.0	Mobile telephone subscribers	
Jewish	1.8	per 100 pop.	95.5
Muslim	0.9	Broadband subs per 100 pop.	28.4
Hindu	0.6	Internet hosts per 1,000 pop.[b]	1,876.3

a Including utilities.
b Includes all hosts ending ".com", ".net" and ".org" which exaggerates the numbers.

VENEZUELA

Area	912,050 sq km	Capital	Caracas
Arable as % of total land	2.9	Currency	Bolivar (Bs)

People

Population	29.9m	Life expectancy:	men	71.7 yrs
Pop. per sq km	32.0		women	77.6 yrs
Average annual growth		Adult literacy		95.5%
in pop. 2010–15	1.5%	Fertility rate (per woman)		2.4
Pop. under 15	28.5%	Urban population		94.3%
Pop. over 60	9.4%			per 1,000 pop.
No. of men per 100 women	100.7	Crude birth rate		19.9
Human Development Index	76.4	Crude death rate		5.3

The economy

GDP	Bs1,635bn	GDP per head	$12,730
GDP	$381bn	GDP per head in purchasing	
Av. ann. growth in real		power parity (USA=100)	25.6
GDP 2007–12	2.0%	Economic freedom index	36.3

Origins of GDP		Components of GDP	
	% of total		% of total
Agriculture	6	Private consumption	59
Industry, of which:	52	Public consumption	12
manufacturing	14	Investment	27
Services	42	Exports	26
		Imports	-24

Structure of employment

	% of total		% of labour force
Agriculture	7.7	Unemployed 2012	7.8
Industry	21.2	Av. ann. rate 2000–12	10.9
Services	70.7		

Energy

	m TOE		
Total output	200.8	Net energy imports as %	
Total consumption	70.2	of energy use	-186
Consumption per head			
kg oil equivalent	2,380		

Inflation and finance

			av. ann. increase 2008–13
Consumer price			
inflation 2013[a]	40.7%	Narrow money (M1)	44.1%
Av. ann. inflation 2008–13[a]	28.5%	Broad money	41.6%
Money market rate, Oct. 2013	1.28%		

Exchange rates

	end 2013		2013
Bs per $	6.28	Effective rates	2005 = 100
Bs per SDR	9.68	– nominal	32.20
Bs per €	8.66	– real	168.30

Trade

Principal exports	$bn fob	Principal imports	$bn cif
Oil	93.8	Intermediate goods	29.5
Non-oil	3.5	Capital goods	13.7
		Consumer goods	8.9
Total	**97.3**	Total	**52.0**

Main export destinations	% of total	Main origins of imports	% of total
United States	36.7	United States	37.3
China	13.5	China	19.8
India	11.3	Brazil	10.7
Netherlands Antilles	7.3	Colombia	5.7

Balance of payments, reserves and debt, $bn

Visible exports fob	97.3	Change in reserves	1.5
Visible imports fob	-59.3	Level of reserves	
Trade balance	38.0	end Dec.	29.4
Invisibles inflows	4.2	No. months of import cover	3.9
Invisibles outflows	-30.2	Official gold holdings, m oz	11.8
Net transfers	-1.0	Foreign debt	72.1
Current account balance	11.0	– as % of GDP	18.9
– as % of GDP	2.9	– as % of total exports	70.9
Capital balance	-8.7	Debt service ratio	5.6
Overall balance	-0.8		

Health and education

Health spending, % of GDP	4.6	Education spending, % of GDP	6.9
Doctors per 1,000 pop.	...	Enrolment, %: primary	102
Hospital beds per 1,000 pop.	0.9	secondary	85
Improved-water source access, % of pop.	...	tertiary	78

Society

No. of households	7.4m	Cost of living, Dec. 2013	
Av. no. per household	4.0	New York = 100	118
Marriages per 1,000 pop.	3.5	Cars per 1,000 pop.	...
Divorces per 1,000 pop.	0.8	Colour TV households, % with:	
Religion, % of pop.		cable	29.3
Christian	89.3	satellite	5.7
Non-religious	10.0	Telephone lines per 100 pop.	25.5
Muslim	0.3	Mobile telephone subscribers	
Other	0.3	per 100 pop.	101.9
Hindu	<0.1	Broadband subs per 100 pop.	6.7
Jewish	<0.1	Internet hosts per 1,000 pop.	43.3

a Estimate.

VIETNAM

Area	331,114 sq km	Capital	Hanoi
Arable as % of total land	21.0	Currency	Dong (D)

People

Population	89.7m	Life expectancy: men	71.2 yrs
Pop. per sq km	268.0	women	80.4 yrs
Average annual growth		Adult literacy	93.4%
in pop. 2010–15	1.0%	Fertility rate (per woman)	1.8
Pop. under 15	22.7%	Urban population	33.6%
Pop. over 60	9.6%		per 1,000 pop.
No. of men per 100 women	97.7	Crude birth rate	15.6
Human Development Index	63.8	Crude death rate	5.7

The economy

GDP	D3,245trn	GDP per head	$1,760
GDP	$156bn	GDP per head in purchasing	
Av. ann. growth in real		power parity (USA=100)	7.3
GDP 2007–12	5.8%	Economic freedom index	50.8

Origins of GDP		Components of GDP	
	% of total		% of total
Agriculture	20	Private consumption	63
Industry, of which:	39	Public consumption	6
manufacturing	17	Investment	27
Services	42	Exports	80
		Imports	-77

Structure of employment

	% of total		% of labour force
Agriculture	47.4	Unemployed 2012	2.0
Industry	21.1	Av. ann. rate 2000–12	2.3
Services	31.5		

Energy

	m TOE		
Total output	66.6	Net energy imports as %	
Total consumption	61.2	of energy use	-9
Consumption per head			
kg oil equivalent	697		

Inflation and finance

Consumer price		av. ann. increase 2008–13	
inflation 2013	6.6%	Narrow money (M1)	14.4%
Av. ann. inflation 2008–13	10.0%	Broad money	21.2%
Treasury bill rate, Oct. 2013	6.24%		

Exchange rates

	end 2013		2013
D per $	21,105.00	Effective rates	2005 = 100
D per SDR	32,502.13	– nominal	...
D per €	29,030.26	– real	...

Trade

Principal exports		Principal imports	
	$bn fob		*$bn cif*
Textiles & garments	15.2	Machinery & equipment	15.7
Crude oil	8.3	Petroleum products	8.9
Footwear	7.3	Textiles	6.9
Fisheries products	6.2	Steel	5.9
Total incl. others	**115.4**	Total incl. others	**114.2**

Main export destinations		Main origins of imports	
	% of total		*% of total*
United States	17.8	China	25.8
Japan	11.8	South Korea	13.9
China	11.2	Japan	10.4
South Korea	5.0	Singapore	6.0
Germany	3.7	Thailand	5.2

Balance of payments, reserves and debt, $bn

Visible exports fob	114.6	Change in reserves	12.0
Visible imports fob	-104.7	Level of reserves	
Trade balance	9.9	end Dec.	25.6
Invisibles inflows	9.9	No. months of import cover	2.5
Invisibles outflows	-18.9	Official gold holdings, m oz	...
Net transfers	8.2	Foreign debt	59.1
Current account balance	9.1	– as % of GDP	44.1
– as % of GDP	5.8	– as % of total exports	44.3
Capital balance	8.3	Debt service ratio	4.1
Overall balance	11.9		

Health and education

Health spending, % of GDP	6.6	Education spending, % of GDP	6.3
Doctors per 1,000 pop.	1.2	Enrolment, %: primary	105
Hospital beds per 1,000 pop.	2.0	secondary	...
Improved-water source access,		tertiary	25
% of pop.	95		

Society

No. of households	24.7m	Cost of living, Dec. 2013	
Av. no. per household	3.6	New York = 100	74
Marriages per 1,000 pop.	5.3	Cars per 1,000 pop.	21
Divorces per 1,000 pop.	0.2	Colour TV households, % with:	
Religion, % of pop.		cable	17.8
Other	45.6	satellite	19.5
Non-religious	29.6	Telephone lines per 100 pop.	11.2
Buddhist	16.4	Mobile telephone subscribers	
Christian	8.2	per 100 pop.	147.7
Muslim	0.2	Broadband subs per 100 pop.	4.9
Jewish	<0.1	Internet hosts per 1,000 pop.	17.6

ZIMBABWE

Area	390,759 sq km	Capital	Harare
Arable as % of total land	10.6	Currency	Zimbabwe dollar (Z$)

People

Population	13.0m	Life expectancy: men	58.8 yrs
Pop. per sq km	33.0	women	60.8 yrs
Average annual growth		Adult literacy	83.6%
in pop. 2010–15	2.8%	Fertility rate (per woman)	3.5
Pop. under 15	39.5%	Urban population	40.6%
Pop. over 60	5.7%		per 1,000 pop.
No. of men per 100 women	97.2	Crude birth rate	31.3
Human Development Index	49.2	Crude death rate	9.0

The economy

GDP	$9.8bn	GDP per head	$710
Av. ann. growth in real		GDP per head in purchasing	
GDP 2007–12	2.0%	power parity (USA=100)	1.5
		Economic freedom index	35.5

Origins of GDP		Components of GDP	
	% of total		% of total
Agriculture	14	Private consumption	80
Industry, of which:	35	Public consumption	27
manufacturing	17	Investment	25
Services	51	Exports	44
		Imports	-76

Structure of employment

	% of total		% of labour force
Agriculture	...	Unemployed 2012	4.0
Industry	...	Av. ann. rate 2000–12	4.6
Services	...		

Energy

	m TOE		
Total output	8.6	Net energy imports as %	
Total consumption	9.3	of energy use	8
Consumption per head			
kg oil equivalent	697		

Inflation[a] and finance

		av. ann. increase 2008–13	
Consumer price			
inflation 2013	1.6%	Narrow money (M1)	...
Av. ann. inflation 2008–13	3.6%	Broad money	...
Treasury bill rate, Aug. 2013	58.0%		

Exchange rates

	end 2013		2013
Z$ per $	...	Effective rates	2005 = 100
Z$ per SDR	...	– nominal	...
Z$ per €	...	– real	...

Trade

Principal exports[a]	$bn fob	Principal imports[a]	$bn cif
Gold	1.0	Machinery & transportation	
Platinum	0.6	equipment	0.5
Tobacco	0.5	Fuels & energy	0.4
Ferro-alloys	0.3	Manufactures	0.3
		Chemicals	0.2
Total incl. others	**3.3**	Total incl. others	**4.8**

Main export destinations	% of total	Main origins of imports	% of total
China	16.0	South Africa	48.7
South Africa	11.5	China	9.4
Congo-Kinshasa	9.2	Zambia	9.4
Botswana	8.2	Botswana	3.2
Italy	3.5	India	2.9

Balance of payments, reserves and debt, $bn

Visible exports fob	4.1	Change in reserves	-0.1
Visible imports fob	-6.7	Level of reserves	
Trade balance	-2.7	end Dec.	0.6
Invisibles, net	-0.7	No. months of import cover	1.0
Net transfers	1.1	Official gold holdings, m oz	0.0
Current account balance	-2.3	Foreign debt	7.7
– as % of GDP	-23.1	– as % of GDP	75.5
Capital balance	1.3	– as % of total exports	202.9
Overall balance	0.1	Debt service ratio	16.8

Health and education

Health spending, % of GDP	...	Education spending, % of GDP	2.5
Doctors per 1,000 pop.	0.1	Enrolment, %: primary	...
Hospital beds per 1,000 pop.	1.7	secondary	...
Improved-water source access,		tertiary	6
% of pop.	80		

Society

No. of households	3.1m	Cost of living, Dec. 2013	
Av. no. per household	4.5	New York = 100	...
Marriages per 1,000 pop.	...	Cars per 1,000 pop.	...
Divorces per 1,000 pop.	...	Colour TV households, % with:	
Religion, % of pop.		cable	...
Christian	87.0	satellite	...
Non-religious	7.9	Telephone lines per 100 pop.	2.2
Other	4.2	Mobile telephone subscribers	
Muslim	0.9	per 100 pop.	91.9
Hindu	<0.1	Broadband subs per 100 pop.	0.5
Jewish	<0.1	Internet hosts per 1,000 pop.	4.3

a Estimates.

EURO AREA[a]

Area	2,578,704 sq km	Capital	–
Arable as % of total land	24.2	Currency	Euro (€)

People

Population	332.1m	Life expectancy: men	80.3 yrs
Pop. per sq km	126.0	women	86.0 yrs
Average annual growth		Adult literacy	...
in pop. 2010–15	0.4%	Fertility rate (per woman)	1.6
Pop. under 15	15.2%	Urban population	76.4%
Pop. over 60	25.1%		per 1,000 pop.
No. of men per 100 women	96.1	Crude birth rate	10.2
Human Development Index	88.3	Crude death rate	10.0

The economy

GDP	€9,504bn	GDP per head	$36,650
GDP	$12,213bn	GDP per head in purchasing	
Av. ann. growth in real		power parity (USA=100)	71.4
GDP 2007–12	...	Economic freedom index	67.2

Origins of GDP		**Components of GDP**	
	% of total		% of total
Agriculture	2	Private consumption	58
Industry, of which:	25	Public consumption	22
manufacturing	16	Investment	18
Services	73	Exports	45
		Imports	-42

Structure of employment

	% of total		% of labour force
Agriculture	4	Unemployed 2012	11.3
Industry	25	Av. ann. rate 2000–12	8.9
Services	71		

Energy

	m TOE		
Total output	467.0	Net energy imports as %	
Total consumption	1,162.5	of energy use	60
Consumption per head			
kg oil equivalent	3,480		

Inflation and finance

Consumer price		av. ann. increase 2008–13	
inflation 2013	1.3%	Narrow money (M1)	6.0%
Av. ann. inflation 2008–13	1.7%	Broad money	0.8%
Interbank rate, Dec. 2013	0.17%	H'hold saving rate, 2013	7.8%

Exchange rates

	end 2013		2013
€ per $	0.73	Effective rates	2005 = 100
€ per SDR	1.12	– nominal	106.09
		– real	97.61

Trade[b]

Principal exports

	$bn fob
Machinery & transport equip.	873.9
Other manufactured goods	472.4
Chemicals & related products	341.7
Mineral fuels & lubricants	156.3
Food, drink & tobacco	123.1
Total incl. others	**2,089.3**

Principal imports

	$bn cif
Mineral fuels & lubricants	676.3
Machinery & transport equip.	559.2
Other manufactured goods	479.8
Chemicals & related products	201.7
Food, drink & tobacco	115.0
Total incl. others	**2,222.4**

Main export destinations

	% of total
United States	17.3
China	8.5
Switzerland	7.9
Russia	7.3
Turkey	4.5
Japan	3.3

Main origins of imports

	% of total
China	16.2
Russia	11.9
United States	11.5
Switzerland	5.9
Norway	5.6
Japan	3.6

Balance of payments, reserves and aid, $bn

Visible exports fob	2,467	Overall balance	-1.3
Visible imports fob	-2,351	Change in reserves	59.5
Trade balance	117	Level of reserves	
Invisibles inflows	1,542	end Dec.	907.2
Invisibles outflows	-1,349	No. months of import cover	2.9
Net transfers	-139	Official gold holdings, m oz	346.7
Current account balance	171	Aid given	42.35
– as % of GDP	1.4	– as % of GDP	0.35
Capital balance	-206		

Health and education

Health spending, % of GDP	10.7	Education spending, % of GDP	5.1
Doctors per 1,000 pop.	3.4	Enrolment, %: primary	102
Hospital beds per 1,000 pop.	5.1	secondary	107
Improved-water source access,		tertiary	60.5
% of pop.	100		

Society

No. of households	163.6	Colour TV households, % with:	
Av. no. per household	2.0	cable	41.0
Marriages per 1,000 pop.	4.1	satellite	25.4
Divorces per 1,000 pop.	2	Telephone lines per 100 pop.	27.9
Cost of living, Dec. 2012		Mobile telephone subscribers	
New York = 100	...	per 100 pop.	113.2
Cars per 1,000 pop.	516	Broadband subs per 100 pop.	27.3
		Internet hosts per 1,000 pop.	390.7

a Data generally refer to the 17 EU members that have adopted the euro: Austria, Belgium, Cyprus, Estonia, Finland, France, Germany, Greece, Ireland, Italy, Luxembourg, Malta, Netherlands, Portugal, Slovakia, Slovenia and Spain.

b EU27, excluding intra-trade.

WORLD

Area	148,698,382 sq km	Capital	...
Arable as % of total land	10.8	Currency	...

People

Population	7,052.1m	Life expectancy: men	67.8 yrs
Pop. per sq km	51.2	women	72.3 yrs
Average annual growth		Adult literacy	...
in pop. 2010–15	1.2%	Fertility rate (per woman)	2.5
Pop. under 15	26.2%	Urban population	53.9%
Pop. over 60	11.7%		per 1,000 pop.
No. of men per 100 women	101.7	Crude birth rate	19.5
Human Development Index	70.2	Crude death rate	8.1

The economy

GDP	$72.7trn	GDP per head	$10,320
Av. ann. growth in real		GDP per head in purchasing	
GDP 2007–12	4.6%	power parity (USA=100)	26.7
		Economic freedom index	57.5

Origins of GDP		**Components of GDP**	
	% of total		% of total
Agriculture	3	Private consumption	60
Industry, of which:	27	Public consumption	18
manufacturing	15	Investment	22
Services	70	Exports	30
		Imports	-30

Structure of employment[a]

	% of total		% of labour force
Agriculture	31	Unemployed 2012	5.9
Industry	24	Av. ann. rate 2000–12	6.5
Services	45		

Energy

	m TOE		
Total output	13,157.5	Net energy imports as %	
Total consumption	12,715.8	of energy use	-3
Consumption per head			
kg oil equivalent	1,890		

Inflation and finance

Consumer price		av. ann. increase 2008–13	
inflation 2013	3.6%	Narrow money (M1)[a]	8.9%
Av. ann. inflation 2008–13	3.7%	Broad money[a]	5.2%
LIBOR $ rate, 3-month, Dec. 2013	0.24%	H'hold saving rate[a], 2013	5.8%

Trade

World exports

	$bn fob		$bn fob
Manufactures	12,544	Ores & minerals	922
Fuels	2,583	Agricultural raw materials	369
Food	1,660	Total incl. others	**18,447**

Main export destinations

	% of total
United States	12.6
China	9.9
Germany	6.2
Japan	4.8
France	3.6
United Kingdom	3.6

Main origins of imports

	% of total
China	11.5
United States	8.7
Germany	7.4
Japan	4.5
Netherlands	3.6
France	3.1

Balance of payments, reserves and aid, $bn

Visible exports fob	18,054	Overall balance	0
Visible imports fob	-17,615	Change in reserves	904
Trade balance	439	Level of reserves	
Invisibles inflows	7,841	end Dec.	13,095
Invisibles outflows	-7,830	No. months of import cover	6.2
Net transfers	-51	Official gold holdings, m oz	1,019
Current account balance	399	Aid given	175.66
– as % of GDP	0.6	– as % of GDP	0.29
Capital balance	-201		

Health and education

Health spending, % of GDP	10.2	Education spending, % of GDP	4.9
Doctors per 1,000 pop.	1.5	Enrolment, %: primary	107
Hospital beds per 1,000 pop.	...	secondary	71
Improved-water source access, % of pop.	89	tertiary	30

Society

No. of households	...	Cost of living, Dec. 2012	
Av. no. per household	...	New York = 100	...
Marriages per 1,000 pop.	...	Cars per 1,000 pop.	123
Divorces per 1,000 pop.	...	Colour TV households, % with:	
Religion, % of pop.		cable	...
Christian	31.5	satellite	...
Muslim	23.2	Telephone lines per 100 pop.	20
Non-religious	16.3	Mobile telephone subscribers	
Hindu	15.0	per 100 pop.	101
Other	13.8	Broadband subs per 100 pop.	19.8
Jewish	0.2	Internet hosts per 1,000 pop.	132.9

a OECD countries.

Glossary

Balance of payments The record of a country's transactions with the rest of the world. The **current account** of the balance of payments consists of: visible trade (goods); "invisible" trade (services and income); private transfer payments (eg, remittances from those working abroad); official transfers (eg, payments to international organisations, famine relief). Visible imports and exports are normally compiled on rather different definitions to those used in the trade statistics (shown in principal imports and exports) and therefore the statistics do not match. The **capital account** consists of long- and short-term transactions relating to a country's assets and liabilities (eg, loans and borrowings). The **current and capital accounts**, plus an errors and omissions item, make up the **overall balance. Changes in reserves** include gold at market prices and are shown without the practice often followed in balance of payments presentations of reversing the sign.

Big Mac index A light-hearted way of looking at exchange rates. If the dollar price of a burger at McDonald's in any country is higher than the price in the United States, converting at market exchange rates, then that country's currency could be thought to be over-valued against the dollar and vice versa.

Body-mass index A measure for assessing obesity – weight in kilograms divided by height in metres squared. An index of 30 or more is regarded as an indicator of obesity; 25 to 29.9 as over-weight. Guidelines vary for men and for women and may be adjusted for age.

CFA Communauté Financière Africaine. Its members, most of the francophone African nations, share a common currency, the CFA franc, pegged to the euro.

Cif/fob Measures of the value of merchandise trade. Imports include the cost of "carriage, insurance and freight" (cif) from the exporting country to the importing. The value of exports does not include these elements and is recorded "free on board" (fob). Balance of payments statistics are generally adjusted so that both exports and imports are shown fob; the cif elements are included in invisibles.

Crude birth rate The number of live births in a year per 1,000 population. The crude rate will automatically be relatively high if a large proportion of the population is of childbearing age.

Crude death rate The number of deaths in a year per 1,000 population. Also affected by the population's age structure.

Debt, foreign Financial obligations owed by a country to the rest of the world and repayable in foreign currency. The **debt service ratio** is debt service (principal repayments plus interest payments) expressed as a percentage of the country's earnings from exports of goods and services.

Debt, household All liabilities that require payment of interest or principal in the future.

Economic Freedom Index The ranking includes data on labour and business freedom as well as trade policy, taxation, monetary policy, the banking system, foreign-investment rules, property rights, government spending, regulation policy, the level of corruption and the extent of wage and price controls.

Effective exchange rate The nominal index measures a currency's depreciation (figures below 100) or appreciation (figures over 100) from a base date against a trade-weighted basket of the currencies of the country's main trading partners. The real effective exchange rate reflects adjustments for relative movements in prices or costs.

EU European Union. Members are: Austria, Belgium, Bulgaria, Cyprus, Czech Republic, Denmark, Estonia, Finland, France, Germany, Greece, Hungary, Ireland, Italy, Latvia, Lithuania, Luxembourg, Malta, Netherlands, Poland, Portugal, Romania, Slovakia, Slovenia, Spain, Sweden and the United Kingdom. Croatia joined on July 1 2013.

Euro area The 18 euro area members of the EU are Austria, Belgium, Cyprus, Estonia, Finland, France, Germany, Greece, Ireland, Italy, Luxembourg, Malta, Netherlands, Portugal, Slovakia, Slovenia and Spain. Latvia joined on January 1 2014. Their common currency is the euro.

Fertility rate The average number of children born to a woman who completes her childbearing years.

G7 Group of seven countries: United States, Japan, Germany, United Kingdom, France, Italy and Canada.

GDP Gross domestic product. The sum of all output produced by economic activity within a country. GNP (gross national product) and GNI (gross national income) include net income from abroad eg, rent, profits.

Household saving rate Household savings as % of disposable household income.

Import cover The number of months of imports covered by reserves ie, reserves ÷ $\frac{1}{12}$ annual imports (visibles and invisibles).

Inflation The annual rate at which prices are increasing. The most common measure and the one shown here is the increase in the consumer price index.

Internet hosts Websites and other computers that sit permanently on the internet.

Life expectancy The average length of time a baby born today can expect to live.

Literacy is defined by UNESCO as the ability to read and write a simple sentence, but definitions can vary from country to country.

Median age Divides the age distribution into two halves. Half of the population is above and half below the median age.

Money supply A measure of the "money" available to buy goods and services. Various definitions exist. The measures shown here are based on definitions used by the IMF and may differ from measures used nationally. Narrow money (M1) consists of cash in circulation and demand deposits (bank deposits that can be withdrawn on demand). "Quasi-money" (time, savings and foreign currency deposits) is added to this to create broad money.

OECD Organisation for Economic Co-operation and Development. The "rich countries" club was established in 1961 to promote economic growth and the expansion of world trade. It is based in Paris and now has 34 members.

Official reserves The stock of gold and foreign currency held by a country to finance any calls that may be made for the settlement of foreign debt.

Opec Organisation of Petroleum Exporting Countries. Set up in 1960 and based in Vienna, Opec is mainly concerned with oil pricing and production issues. Members are: Algeria, Angola, Ecuador, Iran, Iraq, Kuwait, Libya, Nigeria, Qatar, Saudi Arabia, United Arab Emirates and Venezuela.

PPP Purchasing power parity. PPP statistics adjust for cost of living differences by replacing normal exchange rates with rates designed to equalise the prices of a standard "basket"of goods and services. These are used to obtain PPP estimates of GDP per head. PPP estimates are shown on an index, taking the United States as 100.

Real terms Figures adjusted to exclude the effect of inflation.

SDR Special drawing right. The reserve currency, introduced by the IMF in 1970, was intended to replace gold and national currencies in settling international transactions. The IMF uses SDRs for book-keeping purposes and issues them to member countries. Their value is based on a basket of the US dollar (with a weight of 41.9%), the euro (37.4%), the Japanese yen (9.4%) and the pound sterling (11.3%).

List of countries

Wherever data is available, the world rankings consider 183 countries: all those which had (in 2012) or have recently had a population of at least 1m or a GDP of at least $3bn. Here is a list of them.

	Population	GDP	GDP per head	Area '000 sq	Median age
	m, 2012	$bn, 2012	$PPP, 2012	km	yrs, 2012
Afghanistan	33.4	20.5	1,560	652	16.5
Albania	3.2	12.6	9,400	29	32.9
Algeria	36.5	205.8	8,450	2,382	26.9
Andorra	0.085	3.2	37,200[ab]	5	41.8
Angola	20.2	114.1	6,010	1,247	16.3
Argentina	41.1	475.5	17,920[b]	2,780	31.1
Armenia	3.1	10.0	6,540	30	32.7
Australia	22.9	1,532.4	43,820	7,741	37.2
Austria	8.4	394.7	44,120	84	42.7
Azerbaijan	9.4	66.6	10,130	87	29.7
Bahamas	0.4	8.1	31,120	14	31.8
Bahrain	1.4	30.4	28,920	0.8	30.1
Bangladesh	152.4	116.4	1,850	144	25.1
Barbados	0.3	4.2	26,490	0.4	36.9
Belarus	9.5	63.3	15,330	208	39.3
Belgium	10.8	483.3	40,570	31	41.6
Benin	9.4	7.6	1,560	115	18.4
Bermuda	0.069	5.5	86,000[ab]	0.1	42.6
Bolivia	10.2	27.0	5,200	1,099	22.4
Bosnia & Herz.	3.7	17.5	9,390	51	39.5
Botswana	2.1	14.5	16,110	582	22.5
Brazil	198.4	2,252.7	11,720	8,515	30.3
Brunei	0.4	17.0	52,480	6	30.5
Bulgaria	7.4	51.0	16,040	111	43.0
Burkina Faso	17.5	10.7	1,480	274	17.1
Burundi	8.7	2.5	550	28	17.6
Cambodia	14.5	14.0	2,450	181	24.4
Cameroon	20.5	25.3	2,300	475	18.3
Canada	34.7	1,779.6	41,300	9,985	40.1
Central African Rep.	4.6	2.2	1,080	623	19.7
Chad	11.8	12.9	2,140	1,284	15.8
Channel Islands	0.160	8.9	51,970[ab]	0.2	42.0
Chile	17.4	269.9	21,470	756	33.1
China	1,353.6	8,227.1	9,080	9,600	35.4
Colombia	47.6	369.6	10,440	1,142	27.7
Congo-Brazzaville	4.2	13.7	4,350	342	18.8
Congo-Kinshasa	69.6	17.2	420	2,345	17.4
Costa Rica	4.8	45.1	12,730	51	29.7
Côte d'Ivoire	20.6	24.7	2,010	322	19.0
Croatia	4.4	59.2	20,960	57	42.6
Cuba	11.2	68.2a	10,200[ab]	110	40.1
Cyprus	1.1	22.8	30,770	9	35.2

	Population	GDP	GDP per head	Area '000 sq	Median age
	m, 2012	$bn, 2012	$PPP, 2012	km	yrs, 2012
Czech Republic	10.6	196.4	27,520	79	40.3
Denmark	5.6	315.2	42,780	43	41.1
Dominican Rep.	10.2	59.0	10,040	49	25.8
Ecuador	14.9	84.0	9,640	256	26.1
Egypt	84.0	262.8	6,610	1,001	25.2
El Salvador	6.3	23.9	6,990	21	24.1
Equatorial Guinea	0.7	17.7	29,740	28	20.6
Eritrea	5.6	3.1	560	118	18.4
Estonia	1.3	22.4	24,450	45	40.9
Ethiopia	86.5	41.6	1,110	1,104	18.2
Fiji	0.9	3.9	4,880	18	27.1
Finland	5.4	247.5	39,200	338	42.3
France	63.5	2,612.9[c]	36,790	549	40.6
French Guiana	0.250	5.0[a]	18,360[a]	90	24.9
French Polynesia	0.275	7.2	22,000[ab]	4	30.9
Gabon	1.6	18.4	15,770	268	20.7
Gambia, The	1.8	0.9	1,900	11	17.0
Georgia	4.3	15.7	5,830	70	37.6
Germany	82.0	3,428.1	42,700	357	45.5
Ghana	25.5	40.7	2,010	239	20.6
Greece	11.4	249.1	26,040	132	42.8
Guadeloupe	0.406	12.1[a]	26,710[a]	2	37.7
Guam	0.16	4.6[ab]	28,700[ab]	0.5	29.8
Guatemala	15.1	50.2	5,020	109	19.4
Guinea	10.5	5.6	1,050	246	18.6
Guinea-Bissau	1.6	0.8	1,100	36	19.1
Haiti	10.3	7.8	1,210	28	22.2
Honduras	7.9	18.4	4,170	112	21.9
Hong Kong	7.1	263.3	51,100	1	42.4
Hungary	9.9	124.6	22,640	93	40.6
Iceland	0.3	13.6	39,100	103	35.5
India	1,258.4	1,858.7	3,870	3,287	26.4
Indonesia	244.8	878.0	4,880	1,905	27.8
Iran	75.6	552.4	12,280	1,745	28.5
Iraq	33.7	215.8	7,440	435	19.7
Ireland	4.6	210.8	43,830	70	35.3
Israel	7.7	257.6	31,350	22	30.1
Italy	61.0	2,014.7	34,930	301	44.3
Jamaica	2.8	14.8	8,920	11	27.7
Japan	126.4	5,961.1	35,620	378	45.9
Jordan	6.5	31.0	6,040	89	23.4
Kazakhstan	16.4	203.5	13,670	2,725	29.4
Kenya	42.7	40.7	1,740	580	18.8
Kosovo	1.8	6.4	7,500[b]	11	27.4
Kuwait	2.9	183.2	46,390	18	29.2
Kyrgyzstan	5.4	6.5	2,360	200	24.6
Laos	6.4	9.4	2,880	237	21.4

	Population	GDP	GDP per head	Area '000 sq	Median age
	m, 2012	$bn, 2012	$PPP, 2012	km	yrs, 2012
Latvia	2.2	28.4	21,810	64	41.5
Lebanon	4.3	42.9	14,370	10	29.8
Lesotho	2.2	2.4	1,930	30	20.7
Liberia	4.2	1.7	640	111	18.5
Libya	6.5	62.4[a]	12,690[b]	1,760	26.6
Liechtenstein	0.04	4.8[a]	89,400[ab]	0.2	42.1
Lithuania	3.3	42.3	24,360	65	39.3
Luxembourg	0.5	55.2	89,510	3	39.0
Macau	0.6	43.6	86,340	0.03	37.4
Macedonia	2.1	9.6	11,830	26	37.1
Madagascar	21.9	10.0	960	587	18.4
Malawi	15.9	4.3	750	118	17.2
Malaysia	29.3	305.0	16,920	331	27.4
Mali	16.3	10.4	1,200	1,240	16.3
Malta	0.4	8.7	28,960	0.3	40.9
Martinique	0.4	11.8[a]	26,710[a]	1	41.7
Mauritania	3.6	4.2	2,560	1,031	19.8
Mauritius	1.3	10.5	14,900	2	34.6
Mexico	116.1	1,178.1	16,430	1,964	27.0
Moldova	3.5	7.3	3,370	34	35.8
Monaco	0.03	6.1[a]	65,500[ab]	0.002	50.5
Mongolia	2.8	10.3	5,370	1,564	26.8
Montenegro	0.6	4.4	14,360	14	37.1
Morocco	32.6	96.0	5,220	447	27.0
Mozambique	24.5	14.2	1,010	799	17.3
Myanmar	48.7	55.8[b]	1,630[b]	677	29.0
Namibia	2.4	13.1	7,440	824	21.2
Nepal	31.0	19.0	1,460	147	22.4
Netherlands	16.7	770.6	43,340	42	41.8
New Caledonia	0.3	9.8	37,700[ab]	19	32.8
New Zealand	4.5	171.3	32,930	268	37.0
Nicaragua	6.0	10.5	4,010	130	23.1
Niger	16.6	6.8	770	1,267	15.0
Nigeria	166.6	262.6	2,620	924	17.8
North Korea	24.6	14.4	1,800[ab]	121	33.6
Norway	5.0	500.0	66,140	324	39.0
Oman	2.9	78.1	26,220	310	26.3
Pakistan	180.0	225.1	2,740	796	22.5
Panama	3.6	36.3	16,350	75	27.9
Papua New Guinea	7.2	15.7	2,850	463	20.9
Paraguay	6.7	25.5	6,040	407	23.9
Peru	29.7	203.8	10,770	1,285	26.5
Philippines	96.5	250.2	4,340	300	23.0
Poland	38.3	489.8	22,780	313	38.8
Portugal	10.7	212.3	25,960	92	42.2
Puerto Rico	3.7	101.5	16,300[ab]	9	35.7
Qatar	1.9	192.4	91,190	12	31.7

	Population	GDP	GDP per head	Area	Median age
	m, 2012	$bn, 2012	$PPP, 2012	'000 sq km	yrs, 2012
Réunion	0.9	22.4[a]	23,930[a]	3	30.7
Romania	21.4	169.4	18,060	238	39.4
Russia	142.7	2,014.8	23,590	17,098	38.3
Rwanda	11.3	7.1	1,330	26	18.2
Saudi Arabia	28.7	711.0	31,210	2,150	27.5
Senegal	13.1	14.0	1,910	197	18.1
Serbia	9.8	37.5	11,800	88	38.7
Sierra Leone	6.1	3.8	1,340	72	19.1
Singapore	5.3	274.7	60,800	0.7	38.1
Slovakia	5.5	91.1	25,840	49	38.2
Slovenia	2.0	45.3	28,480	20	42.4
Somalia	9.8	1.3	600[ab]	638	16.3
South Africa	50.7	384.3	11,020	1,219	26.0
South Korea	48.6	1,129.6	30,010	100	39.4
South Sudan	10.7	10.2	1,120[b]	644	18.6
Spain	46.8	1,323.0	32,130	506	41.4
Sri Lanka	21.2	59.4	6,150	66	31.4
Sudan	35.0	58.8	2,160	1,879	19.2
Suriname	0.5	5.0	8,720	164	28.5
Swaziland	1.2	3.7	5,160	17	20.1
Sweden	9.5	523.9	42,870	450	41.0
Switzerland	7.7	631.2	53,190	41	42.0
Syria	21.1	60.0	5,000[a]	185	22.4
Taiwan	23.2	475.3	38,460	36	38.7
Tajikistan	7.1	7.6	2,190	143	21.7
Tanzania	47.7	28.2	1,580	947	17.5
Thailand	69.9	366.0	9,660	513	36.9
Timor-Leste	1.2	1.3	1,660	15	16.6
Togo	6.3	3.8	1,030	57	18.9
Trinidad & Tobago	1.4	23.3	26,550	5	33.3
Tunisia	10.7	45.7	9,640	164	30.3
Turkey	74.5	789.3	18,550	784	29.4
Turkmenistan	5.2	35.2	10,410	488	25.6
Uganda	35.6	20.0	1,330	242	15.8
Ukraine	44.9	176.3	7,300	604	39.7
United Arab Emirates	8.1	383.8	41,400	84	30.0
United Kingdom	62.8	2,475.8	35,720	244	40.2
United States	315.8	16,244.6	51,750	9,832	37.4
Uruguay	3.4	49.9	15,780	176	34.4
Uzbekistan	28.1	51.1	3,530	447	25.3
Venezuela	29.9	381.3	13,270	912	27.0
Vietnam	89.7	155.8	3,790	331	29.8
Virgin Islands (US)	0.1	1.6[ab]	14,500[ab]	0.4	40.2
West Bank & Gaza	4.3	8.0[ab]	2,900[ab]	6	19.1
Yemen	25.6	35.6	2,450	528	19.1
Zambia	13.9	20.6	1,680	753	16.6
Zimbabwe	13.0	9.8	760[b]	391	19.5

	Population	GDP	GDP per head	Area	Median age
	m, 2012	$bn, 2012	$PPP, 2012	'000 sq km	yrs, 2012
Euro area (17)	332.1	12,213.3	36,970	2,629	42.8
World	7,052.1	72,682.0	12,210	136,162	29.2

a Latest available year.
b Estimate.
c Including French Guiana, Guadeloupe, Martinique and Réunion.

Sources

AFM Research
Airports Council International, *Worldwide Airport Traffic Report*
Art Newspaper, The

Bloomberg
BP, *Statistical Review of World Energy*
Business Software Alliance

CAF, *The World Giving Index*
CBRE, *Global Prime Office Occupancy Costs*
Central banks
Central Intelligence Agency, *The World Factbook*
Clarkson Research, *World Fleet Monitor*
Corporate Resources Group, *Quality of Living Report*

Demographia: World Urban Areas

The Economist
www.economist.com
Economist Intelligence Unit, *Cost of Living Survey; Country Forecasts; Country Reports; Global Outlook – Business Environment Rankings*
ERC Statistics International
Euromonitor, *International Marketing Data and Statistics; European Marketing Data and Statistics*
Eurostat, *Statistics in Focus*

Facebook
Finance ministries
Food and Agriculture Organisation

Global Democracy Ranking
Global Entrepreneurship Monitor

The Heritage Foundation, *Index of Economic Freedom*

IFPI
IMD, *World Competitiveness Yearbook*
IMF, *International Financial Statistics; World Economic Outlook*
International Centre for Prison Studies
International Cocoa Organisation, *Quarterly Bulletin of Cocoa Statistics*
International Coffee Organisation
International Cotton Advisory Committee, *March Bulletin*
International Diabetes Federation, *Diabetes Atlas*
International Grains Council
International Institute for Strategic Studies, *Military Balance*
International Labour Organisation
International Rubber Study Group, *Rubber Statistical Bulletin*
International Sugar Organisation, *Statistical Bulletin*
International Telecommunication Union, *ITU Indicators*
International Union of Railways
Internet Systems Consortium
Inter-Parliamentary Union

Johnson Matthey

McDonald's

National statistics offices
Nobel Foundation

OECD, *Development Assistance Committee Report; Economic Outlook; Environmental Data; Government at a Glance; OECD.Stat; Revenue Statistics*